The Emergence of the Laity in the Early Church

Alexandre Faivre

Translated by
David Smith

Paulist Press
New York  *Mahwah*

Book design by Kathleen Doyle.

Map by Frank Sabatté, C.S.P.

Copyright © Les Editions du Centurion, 1984. Originally published as LES LAICS AUX ORIGINES DE L'EGLISE, Paris. English translation copyright © 1990 by The Missionary Society of St. Paul the Apostle in the State of New York.

Library of Congress Cataloging-in-Publication Data

Faivre, Alexandre.
    [Laïcs aux origines de l'Eglise. English]
    The emergence of the laity in the early church/Alexandre Faivre;
    translated by David Smith.
       p. cm.
    Translation of: Les laïcs aux origines de l'Eglise.
    Includes bibliographical references.
    ISBN 0-8091-3123-4
    1. Laity—History. 2. Church history—Primitive and early church,
ca. 30-600. I. Title.
BR195.L27F3513   1990
262'.15'09015—dc20   89-27804
                            CIP

Published by Paulist Press
997 Macarthur Boulevard
Mahwah, New Jersey 07430

Printed and bound in the
United States of America

CONTENTS

iii

PART I
THE FIRST AND SECOND
CENTURIES

THE BIRTH OF A LAITY

CHAPTER 1

The Wonderful Time When There Was Neither Clergy Nor Laity

Attracted by the light of the church's origins, lay people may be dazzled by certain truths. But if a moth comes too close to the light that draws it so irresistibly and flies in circles around it, its wings may be singed. How disappointing and even cruel that light is! The Christian who goes back to the origins soon discovers that there is no question of "lay" in the New Testament. There is no trace of the term! There is not even a trace of any reality that could be transposed and put in parallel with our contemporary phenomenon of the "laity." On the contrary, most of the elements that we use to help us to define the laity today as a specific category are quite absent from the New Testament, at least when the laity is not being explicitly contested.

Christ the High Priest and Jesus' Anticlericalism

Christ put himself above everything in the Jewish society of his own time that might have introduced an element of categorization or inequality dividing those who had been called by God. He set aside all prejudices and risked giving deep scandal when he ate with publicans, mixed with Samaritans, conversed with women leading a bad life. He put his own life at risk when he dared to raise his voice against the religious authorities. We are bound, then, to ask: With such an attitude, how could Jesus ever have been led to institute for the future different classes of Christians? And can we possibly regard him, in relation to his own period, as anticlerical? Is he not more than or different from that?

"If Jesus were on earth, he would not be a priest at all, since there are priests who offer gifts according to the law."[1] We read this statement in the epistle to the Hebrews—the same letter that tells us elsewhere that Christ is the great high priest in heaven. In fact, Jesus, who "was descended from Judah, the tribe in connection with which Moses said nothing about priests,"[2] placed himself outside the dichotomy between priest and layman. He certainly preached in the synagogues[3] and ate at the homes of certain pious laymen who were Pharisees,[4] but this did not prevent him from speaking out against those same Pharisees and legalists who claimed to possess total knowledge.[5] He taught in the temple, but he also performed an act of violence in the same temple when he drove the merchants out of it.[6] And when the leaders of priestly and lay power—the high priests and the elders of the people—joined forces to ask him "By what authority are you doing these things?" he refused to answer them and made them examine their own consciences.[7]

"Beware of the scribes, who like to go about in long robes and to have salutations in the marketplaces and the best seats in the synagogues and the places of honor at feasts."[8] Should we regard this warning by Jesus as an "anticlerical" instruction? Whether this is the case or not, we should not forget that the scribes, who were well educated, did not come from priestly families, but were often laymen from the lower classes. The man who became a scribe had the opportunity to leave the class into which he had been born. The best known example is undoubtedly Hillel, who became one of Israel's most famous masters, although he began as a beggar. It is also important to note that the scribes were not always hostile to Jesus. According to both Matthew and Mark, some were ready to be converted.[9] Jesus was also not either for or against the laity or the clergy of his own time, just as he was not for one or other social class. He was critical of all attitudes and rejected all forms of human power that claimed to be absolute, whether they were based on wealth or whether they were cultic or simply intellectual in origin. "They were astonished at his teaching, for he taught them as one who had authority and not as the scribes."[10]

The Ideal Community
Having All Goods in Common

There was a very positive insistence on the absence of class and sharing within the communities during the apostolic period. In the descriptions of Christian groups given in Acts, the communion between the different members is emphasized: "The company of those who believed were of one heart and soul, and no one said that any of the things which he possessed was his own, but they had everything in common."[11] A need to make this text more precise is reflected in certain manuscripts: "The company of those who believed were of one heart and soul and there was among them no distinction (separation, setting apart)."

This insistence on the unity of the Christian community can be found in the case of the first converts: "They devoted themselves to the apostles' teaching and fellowship, to the breaking of bread and the prayers"[12] and "all who believed were together and had all things in common and they sold their possessions and goods and distributed them to all, as any had need."[13] There is nothing to indicate that spiritual divisions were ever allowed to find their way into this ideal community, in which such care was taken to remove all the material divisions that might have led to the introduction of profane wealth. All believers lived as equals.

We are told in Acts that it was at Antioch that the disciples were first given the name "Christian."[14] This word does not seem to have been widely used to begin with by Christians themselves, who described themselves as "disciples"[15] or simply as "believers."[16] What must strike and even shock modern man most of all, however, is the early Christians' habit of calling themselves "saints" without any trace of nuance or of degree in this "holiness." There are countless examples of the use of this term both in Acts and in the letters of Paul. The community of Jerusalem was not the only one to be entirely "holy"—there were also saints in Rome,[17] Corinth and the whole of Achaia.[18] This "holiness" affected the whole community and was passed on to children, even if only one of the parents was a Christian.[19] There were no lay people in these churches, all the members of which were called to be saints. All the members were "fellow citizens of the saints"[20] and that fellow citizenship went beyond the frontiers of the ancient city, in other words, the local community. Writing to the Christians of Corinth, Paul addresses "those sanctified in Christ Jesus, called to be saints together with all those who in every place call on the name of our Lord Jesus Christ, both their Lord and ours."[21]

A Chosen People—A Clerical People?

One Lord, one election, one holiness! Among the heirs (kleronomoi) of the promise made to Abraham, "there is neither Jew nor

Greek, there is neither slave nor free, there is neither male nor female."[22] The original meaning of the Greek word *kleros* was the instrument used to draw lots. Then, by extension, it came to mean the lot or share resulting from drawing lots, whether that lot was material—a share in an inheritance or domain or a plot of ground enabling a colony to be established—or whether it was constituted by a law or a social responsibility. Matthias, for example, received the *kleros* or lot of the twelfth missing apostle and took Judas' place. But, quite apart from the "lots" or specific responsibilities, there was a lot that was common to all Christ's disciples.

In his epistle to the Colossians, Paul speaks of the "*kleros* of the saints"[23] and in Acts he uses the expression "inheritance" (*kleronomia*) among (all) those who are sanctified.[24] Christians have also been born again through Christ "to an inheritance which is imperishable, undefiled and unfading."[25] Paul tells the Galatians: "If you are Christ's, then you are Abraham's offspring, heirs (*kleronomoi*) according to the promise."[26]

Among Christians, the dignity of being "elected" or chosen is the best share that can befall one. In Christ, Christians have been "set apart" (*kleronomai*) or "named in advance."[27] Paul was clearly aware of the obligation imposed on "God's chosen ones, holy and beloved"[28] by the fact of their election to behave well.[29] But he claimed that this election preceded the creation of the world.[30]

It is not a question here of making a distinction between being called and being chosen, or of knowing finally who will inherit the eternal kingdom of God. What is under consideration is the lively sense that Christians have of being both co-heirs of Christ and of constituting a lot set apart from the time that they were marked with a seal by the Spirit of the promise. It is in fact a question not only of a theology of grace, but also of a sense of belonging to a group and of the outline of a frontier. And what justifies this belonging to this particular lot is neither a function of government or direction, nor a more advanced level of holiness or any special merit, but membership of the people. By whom is the *kleros* constituted in the first epistle of Peter? Not by the elders appointed to oversee the flock, but by the flock itself.[31]

The Christian as King,
Priest and Prophet

In the New Testament, then, the term kleros is applied not simply to the ministers, but to the whole of the believing people. What, however, are we to understand by the word that was traditionally used in Judaism and the pagan world to denote priests—*hiereus*? Here the facts are even clearer. This word is never applied to ministers. It is only used either for Christ himself or for the whole of the believing people.[32]

The most explicit text in this case can be found in the first epistle of Peter: "You (believers) are a chosen race, a royal priesthood, a holy nation, God's own people." These believers have the task of building up a spiritual house for "a holy priesthood, to offer spiritual sacrifices acceptable to God through Jesus Christ."[33] Christians, who are "fellow citizens with the saints," are God's house and a "holy temple," a "dwelling place of God in the Spirit."[34]

Paul exhorts Christians to give God "spiritual worship."[35] For them, Christ has inaugurated a new path through the veil.[36] This means that those who have been baptized in Christ are called to follow him in penetrating into the holy of holies of the temple in order to give to God the spiritual worship which is the true cult.

The priestly function—the true priesthood—is peculiar to Christ, who has enabled all Christians to share in it. In the Christian communities of the first century, there was no independent priestly function that was exercised by a special caste or minister. The laity as such was not recognized in the New Testament, which speaks only of people, a holy people, a chosen people, a people set apart, a kleros entirely responsible for carrying out a royal priesthood and calling on each one of its members to give to God true worship in spirit.

One searches the New Testament in vain for a theology of the laity. Neither laymen nor priests can be found in it, at least in the sense in which we understand those words today. The inheritance was a joint inheritance, shared equally between all the heirs. The people experience their vocation as believers collectively. The lot which God had promised since the time of Abraham and distributed in Christ was not divided unequally. The elders, those presbyters who could not be called priests, were not in control of that lot as though they were masters. They had to take great care to be models that would make it possible for the members of the kleros to identify themselves as chosen people.

The Complementarity of the Charisms

A priesthood common to all, one single call to holiness and one election—these did not mean that there was no diversity of spiritual gifts. The word of wisdom and the word of knowledge, faith, the gift of healing and that of tongues and the interpretation of tongues[37]— all these gifts are so many possible ways that the baptized people had of expressing their election. All these different factors existed and were accepted in the community, but they all had one aim—the common good and the gathering together of all the people.

Alongside those who had been given one or other of these gifts, was there also a category of simple believers who just remained passive? Reading what Paul has to say about those who practiced the gift of tongues, it is possible to believe that this was the case. The apostle says: "If you bless with the spirit, how can anyone in the position of an outsider (=an uninitiated person, *idiotes*) say the 'amen' to your thanksgiving when he does not know what you are saying?"[38]

It is fairly clear that this scene has to be situated within the framework of the Christian assembly.[39] The fact that these uninitiated persons occupied a special place in the Christian assembly may indicate that this was a general and officially recognized condition. Unlike the text of 2 Corinthians 11:6, in which Paul sees himself as uninitiated (*idiotes*) with regard to eloquence, although not with regard to knowledge, the idiotai of 1 Corinthians 14 would seem to be described as uninitiated in a general way.

Who, then, are these idiotai who occupy a special place and are content simply to say "amen"? Are they sympathizers who had not yet been converted? Are they catechumens? Or are they simply believers without any special charism and should they therefore be regarded as distant ancestors of lay people insofar as the lay people can be defined as those who have no specific function in worship?[40] This is quite possible. Has Paul not warned us, after all, that all do not perform miracles and do not have the gift of healing and that all do not speak in tongues and do not interpret?[41]

According to Paul, all these gifts are given with the building up of the community in mind, and it is with regard to their usefulness within the community that they are hierarchically ordered. There is no question of a hierarchy of power or of holiness. What is involved is a hierarchy of service. When, for example, there is no one to interpret, those who speak in tongues can speak to each other or converse inwardly with God, but their gift is not important for the community. In regarding certain gifts as superior to others and in giving first place to the apostles, second place to prophets and third place to teachers and following these by other gifts—miracles, healing, helping and administrating and finally various kinds of tongues,[42] what Paul has in mind is the service that they perform in building up the community. It is also because the only possible hierarchy is a hierarchy of service that he gives the first place, before all these gifts, to the gift of charity.[43]

Here too, then, we find the Christian paradox. The spiritual gift that is the least well defined and the most general and that gives to the person who possesses it no particular place or function and no status or special recognition within the assembly—that is the gift that is placed above all other gifts. Those who are provided with certain particular gifts, Paul emphasizes, should not overestimate themselves because of this. As he says elsewhere, both the person who prophesies and the one who serves, both the one who teaches and the one who exhorts, and both the person who contributes and the one presides or does acts of mercy should avoid proud self-satisfaction, because they are all "individually members one of another."[44]

This necessary complementarity of the gifts, this co-responsibility of grace, is also stated in principle in the first epistle of Peter, although the author does not have recourse to the traditional analogy of the members of the one body. In his words, "as each has received a gift, employ it for one another, as good stewards of God's varied grace."[45]

The Variety of Functions

The apostles, the twelve, the seven, prophets, teachers, evangelists, shepherds, presbyters, deacons, *episkopoi*—the list is endless. There is an astonishing variety of titles in the New Testament. But does the title always define the holder's function? We find in the first epistle to Timothy, for example, the statement: "If anyone aspires to the office of bishop (*episkopos*) . . ."[46] But later in the same letter, we also find the words: "Let the elders (=*presbuteroi*, presbyters) who preside well . . . especially those who labor in preaching and teaching," which shows that the presbyters could also have various functions. Who are those in the epistle to the Romans who prophesy, those who serve, those who teach, those who exhort, those who contribute, those who preside and those who do acts of mercy?[47] Why does Paul not name them—surely only because their function is more important than their title? In the same way, in the first epistle to the Thessalonians, who are those who "labor" among Christians and are "over" them in the Lord and "admonish" them?[48]

Turning to the pastoral epistles, which present us with a more advanced stage in the organization of the church, what do we learn about Timothy? We learn that he is Paul's "true child in the faith,"[49] that he must be a "good minister (diakonos) of Christ" and a faithful disciple of the "good doctrine,"[50] that he possesses a spiritual gift that has been conferred on him by a prophetic intervention accompanied by the imposition of hands by the members of the college of presbyters,[51] that he has certain tasks of government[52] and teaching[53] to carry out, and finally that he has work to do in preaching the gospel and in perfecting his ministry (*diakonia*).[54]

Was he an apostle because of his spiritual gift, a presbyter because of the imposition of hands that he received, an episkopos because of his function of overseeing or a teacher (*didaskalos*) because of his function of teaching? The author of the epistles does not give him any of these titles. So, surely that means that the work carried out and the service given count far more than any title. Certainly Timothy was not Everyman. Nor was he any ordinary Christian. But he was above all a brother to his fellow Christians and a fellow worker of God.[55]

We may conclude, then, that the work to be done takes first place. If the idea gradually gained ground that certain members of the community had to be particularly "above reproach" (the *episkopos* in 1 Tim 3:2) or serious and worthy (deacons in 1 Tim 3:8), this was not so much because the title implied membership of an elite caste, but rather because the carrying out of "good work"[56] made certain demands of the person doing it.

The Work of Women
in the Primitive Community

It is above all the women in the New Testament—and this may be a sign for the future—who show most clearly that it is possible to separate the function, the status and the title from each other.

Any search for examples of women's ministries in the New Testament must begin with the section in the first epistle of Timothy devoted to widows. In fact, in the case of widows, this was first and foremost a status justified by a state of necessity. A "real widow" was above all a woman who had no family to help her.[57] Widows also had to be "without reproach," but we do not know whether this demand was justified by their status or simply by the Christian ideal. The function of the "real widow" did not call for great originality, since she had simply to devote her nights and days to prayer.

Other kinds of work that the widow should perform are also mentioned in the epistle. She should produce a testimony of her good actions. She should have "brought up children, shown hospitality, washed the feet of the saints, relieved the afflicted" and practiced every form of good work.[58] It is important to emphasize, however, that all these works are precisely those that the widow should have carried out before being recognized, at the time when she was an ordinary Christian. The "real widow" would continue to perform all these good works once she was recognized, but they were not in any way confined to her by virtue of her special status any more than prayer was her prerogative. It was the task of every Christian to pray. In the case of widows, then, the special nature of the title did not imply the special nature of the function.

Numerous other functions that were necessary for the life of the community were also carried out by women without this implying any title or a special status distinguishing them from other, ordinary Christian women. There is the case of Tabitha or Dorcas, a woman at Joppa, a woman who was "full of good works and acts of charity" and who made tunics and cloaks and distributed them.[59] Another example is Mary, the mother of John Mark, who let her house in Jerusalem be used for meetings of the Christian assembly.[60] Then there is "a woman named Lydia, from the city of Thyatira, a seller of purple goods," who urged Paul and his companions to stay in her house.[61] But, in the New Testament, there are cases of women like Tryphaena who went further than material services and seem to have shared in the work of evangelization.[62] One of them, Prisca or Priscilla, shared with her husband the title of Paul's "fellow worker in Christ Jesus."[63] She accompanied Paul on his mission[64] and was, with her husband, responsible for completing the instruction of Apollos.[65]

The services performed by women were sufficiently important for them to be regarded as true ministries, even though they had no precise title or status. These women ministers did not constitute a clergy or a caste, but continued simply to be part of the people. The first letter to Timothy, alluding to women ministers comparable to *diakonoi*, does not give them any particular title, but only recommends that "the women likewise must be serious, no slanderers, but temperate and faithful in all things."[66]

The women in this case were probably those who, like Phoebe, the patroness of Christians and of Paul, were able to claim a title as ministers or as *diakonos*.[67] But although the ministry occasionally gave rise to a special honor and consideration, it was possible for all ordinary Christians to become ministers, and nothing implies that it was necessary to be set apart. Whereas deacons who carried out their function well "gained a good standing for themselves,"[68] this was, it would seem, not so in the case of women.

In the case of the functions carried out by men, we can certainly say that, even according to the pastoral epistles, the service performed was more important than the honorary title. But as far as the functions fulfilled by women were concerned, we have simply to recognize that they existed in fact, but that the women who performed them had no corresponding title or rank. In this case, the situation described in the pastorals is to some extent analogous to that brought about by the revision of the church's canon law, namely that women can perform numerous functions, very similar to those performed by men, but they have no access to the corresponding institutional ministries. They are legally permitted to give readings or distribute communion, for example, but they cannot be instituted as readers or as acolytes.[69]

But to return to the first epistle to Timothy, since we can add to what we have already said. It is true not only that women do not seem to have had access to certain titles, but also that they were forbidden to perform certain functions. They had, for example, to remain silent and they were not allowed to teach or to have authority over men.[70] It is worth noting that this statement introduces a new element that contradicts what we know about such women as Prisca or Try-

A Christian woman who placed her inheritance at the disposal of the community
Rome, Commodilla Catacomb

phaena. This precept is certainly in accordance with the statement made in 1 Corinthians 14:34 that women should remain silent in the church assembly, but it is in contradiction to Paul's testimony in the same letter about women who prophesy[71] and to what we know about the four daughters of Philip who prophesied.[72]

It cannot be disputed that what we have here is the beginning of segregation among Christians.

Ideal and Reality
in the Primitive Christian Communities

There was still no distinction between clergy and laity at the time of the pastorals, but Christianity had moved a long way from the idyllic state outlined in the Acts of the Apostles. It was no longer a total and general rule to have all goods in common—even if this had ever been the case in the beginning.

This partly explains the instructions regarding the help given to widows. There were at this time undoubtedly distinctions and separations between Christians. The church had ceased to be a community in which all the members proclaimed themselves to be saints, and had become a community which checked whether the character of certain members was "beyond reproach," giving rise to the supposition that there were degrees in this state. Within these communities in which all the people were regarded as chosen, and set apart, especially designated and elected by God's good pleasure, certain members were beginning to acquire an "honorable rank" for themselves. In a people in which everyone was a priest and called to give God spiritual worship, there was clearly a growing tendency to present as something bound by a status that spiritual worship made night and day in the widow's prayer. The clergy had not yet appeared, but specific functions, titles and statuses had.

Frontiers were already being drawn between the brothers in the life of the Christian community. There were already groups of people who had been reduced to playing a passive role. Either because they had not yet received the Spirit or because they did not take part in manifesting the pouring out of the Spirit, the idiotai or less gifted occupied a place apart in the assembly. The women had to remain silent. They were not allowed to teach or to have functions with authority. Are these not clear precursory signs of the establishment of a group of Christians who are defined primarily by their negativity and their submission?

CHAPTER 2

The Appearance of the Laity

As we have seen, we can look in vain for the term "lay" in the New Testament. The laity is an unknown species in the texts of the gospel. Paradoxically, there is a *kleros* to be found in those texts, although, as we have seen, this word does not point to a caste or to a separate section of the community, but is used to describe the whole of the Christian people.

The word *laikos* was, it would seem, also unknown to the authors of the Septuagint, the Greek version of the Old Testament. It can, however, be found in certain profane texts from the third century B.C. onward, when it was apparently used to designate the local population as opposed to the administration.[1]

We have to wait until the end of the first century before the term makes its appearance in a religious and specifically Christian context. This date may strike us as being very late, if we regard the laity as a very early phenomenon in Christianity and are tempted to trace it back to the origins of the life of faith. It is in fact relatively early if it is remembered, for example, that, at the time when Clement of Rome was speaking for the first time of "lay," some of the New Testament texts had still not been written. But this is a sterile debate and we should rather consider the implications of the event and ask the question: Does this new word in the Christian vocabulary point to a new attitude? Does it correspond to a precise reality? What were the circumstances that prevailed when the term *laikos* first appeared in the first epistle of Clement of Rome to the Corinthians?

We who have so many keys to the future can see this first appearance of the word as a remarkable fact or as a precursory sign, bearing within itself certain factors that would influence the future. But did this precursory sign really occur at the right time? What impact did it really have on people living at that time? Was the situation in the church sufficiently developed for true lay people to

15

be created? I shall try to answer these questions by situating the text of Clement's letter within its historical perspective.

A Text Born of Polemics

Clement's epistle to the Corinthians is a circumstantial document, a polemical text or, more precisely, a text destined to restore peace within and, if possible, to resolve a situation of conflict. The facts as they emerge from the epistle itself are as follows: There was discord within the church of Corinth. The reason for this restlessness seems to have been the institutional order. The presbyters, who had performed their functions in an honorable manner that was quite beyond reproach, had been or were in the process of being deprived of those functions. The affair had given rise to scandal and Clement was offering his advice. Many Christians had been discouraged by these partisan quarrels and non-believers had been given opportunities for blasphemy. There was an urgent need to preach concord and a return to order. In his letter, Clement even advises those who had caused the discord to give themselves up and to go into voluntary exile, so that Christ's flock might live in peace with their appointed presbyters.[2]

But before suggesting this, the author sets himself the task of describing the order that should be brought about. This task gives him an opportunity to draw an idyllic portrait of the right order and the harmony that prevailed in the primitive community at Corinth. He does not include in this portrait the friction caused by those supporting Paul and the partisans of Apollos.[3] He then provides as an example for Christians an outline of the cosmic order harmoniously governed by the creator's plans and concludes with a demonstration of the kind of discipline that is necessary in the community. It is in this context that he employs first the image of soldiers under the authority of commanders, then that of the mutual subordination of members of the same body, and finally the example provided by the levitical hierarchy. The word *laikos*, lay, appears twice in the same sentence in this last context, and this is the only time that it appears in the text.

Clement does not employ the word in the rest of his letter. On the contrary, he uses various terms to describe Christians: "those of the brotherhood," "brothers," "the elect," "those called and made holy," "the multitude," "a holy portion," "the share of the Father's election," and so on. The phrase that occurs most frequently, however, in Clement's letter to describe the members of the Christian community is "Christ's flock." That flock is distinguished by its leaders, the appointed presbyters or the proud men who want to raise themselves above the flock. Although Christians are, in Clement's opinion, the elect or a holy portion, this does not prevent him from making a constant distinction between the flock and those who are in charge of it, while reserving for himself the right to remind those who would like to be included among the rulers that it is "better to be found in lowliness among the elect of Christ's flock than to receive excessive honors and to be excluded from his hope."[4]

The Place of the Laity in Worship

Clement's constantly repeated wish is that everyone should remain in his place. "Each in his own rank" is a phrase that occurs twice in his letter. On both occasions, he is offering Christians models of behavior.[5] In the first case, that model is a military one and he concludes with the words: "Not all of them are commanders-in-chief or leaders of a thousand, a hundred or fifty men and so on, but each in his own rank executes the orders of the king and the rulers." In the second case, after having described the Old Testament cultic hierarchy, Clement uses the same formula again to exhort Christians: "In the same way, may each of our brothers, each one keeping to his own rank, please God by acting with a right conscience, with dignity and without infringing the rules prescribed for his function."

This parallel use of the same expression clearly proves that the thrust of all these descriptions is above all respect for order and that both the image of the army in the first case and that of Israel's liturgy in the second are no more than examples. They are analogies offered to stimulate reflection on the part of the Christian community. We should not see in either purely and simply a description of the organization of the Christian church.

Is there an exact counterpart in Christian worship to the layman in the liturgy of the Old Testament? Not according to the text of the epistle. Clement simply says: "The high priest has had assigned to him the functions (*leitourgiai*) that are peculiar to him. Priests have had their own special place marked out for them. Levites have had their particular ministries (*diakoniai*) imposed on them and the lay-man (*anthropos laikos*) is bound by precepts that are peculiar to lay people."[6]

The high priest, priests and levites, then, can all avail them-selves of something special that has been assigned to them—a func-tion, a place or a ministry. The layman, on the other hand, is "bound by lay precepts." The text would therefore seem to make a distinc-tion on the one hand between the three degrees of the hierarchy, each of which has something special that characterizes them all, and on the other the layman, who appears to belong to a category of his own, the only attribute of which is submission. The differences of attribution that exist between the levitical hierarchy and the laity do not, however, mean that members of the hierarchy can exert power over the laity. They have not chosen their place and their function, any more than lay people have. It should, moreover, be noted that the verbs in the text are in the past tense: the high priest *has had* special functions assigned to him, priests *have had* their place marked out and levites *have had* their ministries imposed on them. The members of the levitical hierarchy, then, like the laity, experience the fate that is ascribed to them by the sovereign will and good pleasure of the Master.

The main thrust of the text, then, is that each person should stay "in his own rank" and please God. It may well be the case that, within the context of the cult of the Old Testament, the layman seems at this time to have had no function and no ministry, but this should not lead us necessarily to conclude that there were laymen in the Christian community with only a passive part to play. The very opposite is true. The author of the epistle to the Corinthians employs the word "we" in the communal sense and is therefore clearly ad-dressing all his brothers, in this way letting it be understood that each one has to exercise a function (*leitourgia*). In the Christian community, these functions are like the members of the same body —they are different, but complementary. For the author, this com-plementarity implies that each member of the community is not required to do simply anything anywhere and in any way, especially within the context of worship. This necessary harmony also does not in any sense imply that a particular category of Christian should be excluded from any *leitourgia*. But, in the light of these conditions, what is the purpose of the Old Testament image and what may its special impact have been?

The Old Testament Models

The conflict within the community of Corinth was so radical that forceful arguments were required to resolve it. The analogy of Old Testament cult provided powerful images and accounts. Clement continues to use this analogy in the following chapter of his letter, stating that those who do not act in conformity with the will of the Master deserve the death penalty. Here he must surely be thinking of the story of the revolt and the subsequent punishment of Korah, Dathan and Abiram.[7] According to this popular account, two hundred and fifty of the children of Israel, led by Korah, Dathan and Abiram, challenged the authority of Moses and Aaron in the name of the holy character of the whole community. They worked to obtain priestly functions for themselves and did not hesitate to take censers and make an offering to Yahweh. This offering was regarded as an "irregular" fire and those who were in revolt were swallowed up in the ground and "went down alive into Sheol," while the two hundred and fifty men offering incense were consumed by the fire of Yahweh.

Those to whom Clement was writing could not have remained unaware of the story of Korah, Dathan and Abiram, since he had already spoken about their jealousy at the beginning of his letter.[8] Then, later in the letter, in Chapter 43, he tells the story of Aaron's rod[9] and this account follows immediately after the story in the book of Numbers of the revolt of Korah, Dathan and Abiram. Then, toward the end of the epistle, in Chapter 51, he returns to the same theme, speaking of the terrible punishment of those who revolted against Moses—their "going down alive into the grave." In this context, then, the analogy of Old Testament worship is very forceful and gives the epistle the character of absolute constraint with regard to the rules laid down for the function to be carried out by each member of the Christian community.

Toward a Negative Definition of the Laity

Is it possible, in such a context and with all the repressive images conveyed by the Old Testament analogy, to find any definition of the layman other than the Christian "who is forbidden to . . ." or "who can or may not . . ." or "who is destined to passive obedience"?

Certainly the epistle of Clement to the Corinthians contains to all intents and purposes this very negative connotation of the term "layman." He is the last to be named in the list of those who play a part in worship. Unlike the three levitical orders, each of which has something special and of their own, the lay category is much more vague. It seems to consist exclusively of submission and is expressed in passive terms. The layman Clement states, is "bound by lay precepts."

We have, however, also seen that the part that each one plays is attributed to him by the will of God and that all of them, from the high priest to the layman, are also passive and submissive in the presence of God's will. It is also worth stressing in this context that the revolt of Korah, Dathan and Abiram was, as a popular uprising, a revolt on the part of levites with regard to Aaron's priesthood. The prohibition against going beyond the role attributed to them is therefore not intended to be applied in particular to laymen. It applies to all those who do not stay in their own rank.

Finally, it is important to note the most important aspect of all. This is not that Clement mentions the layman at the bottom of the hierarchy, but rather that he does not forget to mention him. In Chapter 40:2–3, he outlines the plan of his argument: The Master "has commanded that the offerings and the liturgical functions should take place not in a haphazard and disorderly way, but at predetermined times and moments. Where and by whom they should be carried out he has himself determined by his sovereign will. . . ."

Clement then goes on to reply, in 40:4, to the question: "By whom should the offerings be made and the liturgical functions be carried out?" and, in 41:2, he tells us where they should take place. The fact that he is anxious to mention the layman among those who make offerings and perform liturgical functions, when the Old Testament context does not lend itself at all well to this because in it no function, place or special ministry is attributed to the layman, shows clearly that, for Clement, each Christian has a *leitourgia* or a function in the liturgical offering. He is not able to subscribe to a theology that aims to make offerings and liturgical functions a monopoly of certain Christians to the detriment of the whole of the people of God. Does he not, after all, state, in the sentence that immediately follows our text on the laity, that each Christian has a *leitourgia* (function) to fulfill? His words are worth repeating: "In the same way, may each of our brothers, each one keeping to his own rank, please God by acting with a right conscience, with dignity and without infringing the rules prescribed for his function."[10]

The Scruples of a Latin Translator

The layman is a strange being, subject to mutation, born the prisoner of an analogy, conditioned by a climate of conflict and formed in a cultic environment. There is nothing to indicate that this mutating being should be called upon to become a species. It is hardly possible at this stage to distinguish the basic characteristics of the race that he will engender. But why is he called a "layman"?

Clement's text is the first in which the term "lay" is used in the religious sense. Why does he employ this term in -*ikos* (*la-ikos*), which fundamentally expresses the idea of a category? It may be because he regarded it as the best way of translating a semitic term, but it may also be simply because he had a certain propensity to use adjectives in -*ikos*. It is not possible to claim that these adjectives are very numerous in the whole of the epistle, but what can be said is that they are never (with the exception of *pneumatikos*, spiritual) borrowed from the New Testament. In one case, that of the word *pantokratorikos*,[11] used in the sense of "almighty," Clement does not hesitate to form a neologism in -*ikos* that does not occur anywhere else either in religious or in profane literature.

Whatever Clement's reasons may have been for adopting the term *laikos*, it is even more important for us to consider how it was received subsequently. Fortunately, we have the testimony of a Latin translator working in the second half of the second century A.D. to help us here. It would seem that this translator was rather shocked by the author's application of the adjective *laikos* to a human being. Whatever the case may be, he translates the term *laikos* differently, according to whether it refers to a man or whether it is used as an abstract concept. So Clement's words: "The layman is bound by lay precepts" becomes in Latin: *Plebeius homo laicis praeceptis datus est.*

In Clement's first use of the Greek word *laikos*, then, the "layman" becomes in translation "the plebeian man"—in other words, the man who forms part of the *plebs*, the vulgar or popular section of the people, and was not one of the *patricii* or privileged class. The Latin translator's scruples disappear in the case of the author's second use of the word, however, and he simply transfers the Greek term (*laikos*) into Latin and speaks of "lay precepts." It is undoubtedly because the word "lay" seemed to the translator to be an adjective with a negative connotation that could only be used to describe things that he refused to apply it to a man and preferred in the latter case to employ the adjective "plebeian," however lacking in honor this may have been.

Whether in Greek or in Latin, it was a long time before the term "lay" entered into current usage in religious language. Almost a century passed before it appeared a second time in Christian literature. The first to use it after Clement of Rome were Clement of Alexandria, who was writing for Greek readers, and Tertullian, the early Latin father. It is obvious, then, that the innovation introduced by Clement of Rome at the end of the first century A.D. passed unnoticed and that, however much we are concerned nowadays with this first "layman," his contemporaries were quite indifferent to him.

The Layman without a Face

The "layman" who is mentioned by Clement of Rome is in fact not a Christian, but a Jew. Or, to be more precise, he is a hybrid and synthetic being. This "layman" is presented to us as fulfilling a specific function within the framework of Jewish cultic practice. This is totally artificial and only corresponds to the image of the simple baptized person who takes part in reality in Christian worship by bringing to it the spiritual offering of a life regulated according to the Christian ideal. There is therefore a distortion of the Old Testament image by the Christian reality and the layman is therefore placed in an ambiguous position.

The category of "layman," then, occurs in response to a need to include the totality of the people in the classification of the Old Testament cultic functions and to do this so that order might prevail everywhere. But the term lacks both solidity and original content. All that we can say with some certainty is that the function of the Old Testament layman was different from each of the functions previously listed in Clement's text. The paradox is to be found in the fact that the layman without any clearly defined function had been placed in the Old Testament image in order to recall the reality of the function of his Christian counterpart. To affirm the positive character of the function of the simple Christian, a notion with a negative character was created.

The layman can only really exist and proliferate when he has a "face to face" or an opposite pole on the basis of which he can define himself. This face to face only exists in an embryonic form in the Old Testament cultic model provided in the text of Clement's epistle to the Corinthians. It is important, then, to emphasize that this text does not deal with an antinomic relationship consisting purely of the two poles clerical and lay. On the contrary, what we have here is a relationship of difference and complementarity between the layman and the high priest, the priests and the levites. In the reality of Christianity at the end of the first century A.D., there was no theological face to face for the layman. As we have seen, the notion of kleros is applied in the first epistle of Peter to the whole of the people and, for Clement too, all Christians are chosen and form a "holy portion."

With the exception of Ignatius of Antioch, who applies the notion of kleros to the martyr, we have to wait until the beginning of the third century before encountering the term kleros used to describe a limited group within the Christian community. It was only then that certain Christian ministers became clergy. It was also at that time that the term "layman" came to be employed again. This was not purely by chance. By analogy with the Old Testament layman, the Christian layman—insofar as there was any desire to admit his existence at all—could only be defined negatively.

Finally, it would certainly not be wrong to ask whether, in the primitive church, the layman is not simply the result of a literary blunder. Would it not be true to say that Clement was far too anxious to insist on the parallel between the Old Testament institutions and the organization of the Christian community? The aim of the Old Testament analogy was surely to provide a model of the order that prevailed in the sphere of cult, despite the great variety of individual attributes. If, however, ministers in the Christian communities participated in the spiritual priesthood no more and no less than and in the same way as ordinary believers, this was not the case in the organization of cult under the old covenant. But Clement, in an attempt to make a term for term comparison between them, no doubt felt obliged to go beyond the levites in his description of cultic activity in the Old Testament and include non-ministers in it.

The result of this is the appearance in history of a layman whose only attribute was to obey precepts and, by a mirror effect, of the subsequent tendency to make the Christian layman bear the consequences of this particular attribute. At the time that Clement was writing, the Christian layman was still no more than a mirage or a literary fiction. For approximately a hundred years, the originality of Christ's disciples and the unity of the race of Christians took precedence over the diversity of attributes among members of the church, even though Christianity became, as it spread everywhere, a genus rather than a species, and as the number of the baptized increased, a distinction came to be made among them between subspecies.

CHAPTER 3

The Period of Christ's Disciples

From the second century onward, the Christian communities were big enough for institutional leaders and a certain specialization or "professionalization" in the most essential functions to appear in any consistent group. It was already obvious in the first century that, as they grew, those communities would inevitably become subject to the general rule, according to which the expansion of the group was paralleled by an increase in the number of lukewarm or weak members. In the second century, then, the contrast between the different ways of being a Christian became more pronounced and the gulf between the specialized ministers and those Christians who had no function became deeper. How was this situation seen by Christian authors at the time? How was the unity of Christianity, as opposed to the different ways of being a Christian, expressed? And how did ordinary Christians experience their identity?

The idea of the "layman," as expressed by Clement of Rome at the end of the first century, can hardly be fitted into Christian thinking of the period. For the whole of the second century, Christians were more preoccupied with the task of defining their relationship with Christ than with defining the relationships that existed among themselves. The type of questions that took precedence at a time when conversions were frequent and when the first great heresies were already beginning to appear, together with the struggle against them, were: How could one and why should one be a disciple of Christ? This concerned the Christian authors of the second century to such an extent that they spent no time evolving a theology of the laity. The term "lay" does not appear anywhere in the writings either of Justin Martyr (ca. 150 A.D.) or of Irenaeus (ca. 180). Both the apologist Justin and the theologian Irenaeus, however, were firmly convinced of the eminent dignity of all Christians.

Justin, a Philosopher in Search of a Master

"Justin, the son of Priscos, the son of Baccheios, from Flavia Neapolis in Syria of Palestine."[1] This is how the man who may be regarded as the most important of the second century apologists described his identity in addressing the emperor in defense of the name of Christians. Although he was fiery in his defense of that name—a name that some pagans used to insult those who believed in Christ—Justin was not born into a Christian family. He only discovered Christianity after a long intellectual and moral search. In his own words, "while I was still a disciple of Plato, I heard the accusations made against Christians, but, seeing them intrepid in the face of death and of all that men fear, I understood that it was not possible for them to have lived in vice and the love of pleasure."[2]

At the beginning of his *First Apology,* he introduces himself without stating his origins or his position in society, but in the *Second Apology,* he proudly declares: "I am a Christian. I glory in it and I admit that all that I want is to be recognized as such."[3] This pride and dignity resulted in his dying as a martyr about 165 A.D.

"Christian," it would seem, was the term that Justin preferred to use to describe his brothers and sisters, the members of the community to which he belonged, although he was aware that, for many people, the name referred to an irreligious heresy[4] and that Christians were cursed by the Jews and persecuted by the nations.[5] This did not lead him, however, to employ another term. On the contrary, he chose rather to focus attention on what was essential. A distinction had to be made between different kinds of Christian: "A name is neither good nor bad. It is necessary to judge the actions that are associated with it."[6] In the light of this, Justin preferred to call certain people by the name of their leader and to speak, for example, of Marcionites, Basilidians, Saturnilians or Valentinians,[7] insisting that he and all true Christians had nothing in common with those who only confessed the "name" of Jesus.

On the other hand, it is also important to recognize that, apart from these cases, Justin was anxious to preserve the universal nature of the name "Christian." He does not hesitate to apply this title to those who truly believe in Christ. "They are united to him in one soul, one synagogue and one church,"[8] he says and makes the Jew Trypho call those members of the nations who recognize Jesus as Lord, Christ and God "Christians."[9]

He is well aware that this universalism includes many divergences, but he makes a distinction between divergence and heresy. He does not, however, try to conceal the fact that even Christians whose doctrine is "pure and pious" may think differently from a man who regards his doctrine as "integrally orthodox."[10] Groups of men whose doctrine is not, in his opinion, in any way perfect can certainly co-exist within the Christian framework, without harming the mutual tolerance of Christians. In the same way as he feels no need to find a special name for Christians who are not "integrally orthodox" in doctrine, so too he experiences no need to distinguish between clergy and laity.

It should be noted that Justin does not employ pietistic vocabulary, according to which Christians were called not only "chosen" but also "saints" and "perfect." He sees them rather as "brothers" or as "illuminated" and defines the Christian above all as a "disciple."[11] He regards himself as included among those Christians who are disciples "of the pure and true teaching of Jesus."[12] He also seems to have been convinced that it is impossible to do philosophy without having been someone's disciple.

At the beginning of his *Dialogue with Trypho,* he spends a long time describing his own search for a true philosophy. If we are to believe what he says, he seems to have entrusted himself to every possible master in turn—Stoics, Peripatetics and Pythagoreans, for example—until he became finally convinced by a Platonist. Then, after this, a mysterious old man persuaded him to move from Platonism to Christianity.

But this story in the *Dialogue* seems too well constructed and beautiful to be true and it is possible to contest its authenticity. What cannot be denied, however, is that, in the search for truth, Justin insists above all on the need to meet a master, whose disciple he can become. He cannot conceive of a philosophy or a religion in any other terms than those of a school,[13] founders and initiators.[14]

Although, at the beginning, his approach seems to be very intellectual, Justin, who clearly wants to build a bridge between Christianity and philosophy, does not in the long run try to convince his readers by purely rational argument. As a result of his conversion by the old man, he was himself quite certain that Christianity could provide more than merely intellectual argument. Speaking about the prophets, for example, the old man had told him: "They did not speak in the form of an argument. They went beyond all argument and bore faithful witness to the truth. Events both in the present and in the past force us to believe what they said. The wonders that they performed make them worthy of our faith."[15]

Justin also says of Christ: "On the basis of his works and the power that accompanied them, we can all understand that he is the new law, the new covenant and the expectation of those who in all the nations are looking forward to the good things of God."[16] That is why those who are "illuminated" or instructed in the name of Christ are able to give up the way of error.[17] It is also why those who believe in the truth of the teachings and in Christian doctrine can promise to live in accordance with that truth and those teachings.[18] Christians are made disciples not only by intellectual conviction, but also by every aspect of their lives. They have received God's grace[19] and Justin is anxious to show that they believe in doctrines that are "filled with the divine Spirit and are overflowing with power and flourishing with grace."[20]

Priest or Layman—A False Problem

"Justin . . . the layman."[21] The Christian philosopher has often been introduced in this way, because it is difficult to find any better place for him in the early Christian community. But, as we have seen, the term "layman" is never used by Justin himself. He never applies it either to himself or to others. For him, "the people (demos) and the ekklesia represent a plurality of men, but, because they are only one, they are called by one name."[22] Applying this principle more strictly to the church, Justin finds several excellent ways of expressing and justifying this unity. He says, for example: "It is to those who believe in him, to those who are united to him in one soul, one synagogue and one church, that the word of God speaks as to his daughter, the church, which is constituted by his name and shares in his name (because we all call ourselves Christians)."[23]

The name "Christian" was enough for Justin. It called for no particular function and no special distinction, responsibility or ministry. Justin, the master who wore the philosopher's cloak and wrote in the hope that the emperor would read what he had written, regarded even his own skill as an apologist as worthless. Whatever may have distinguished him from other Christians—this was something that he tried to share with others. "A grace has been given to me by God, who alone has enabled me to understand his scriptures. I invite everyone to share in that grace, freely and liberally, so that I shall not be condemned on that score at the judgment that the Author of all things, God, must make by my Lord Jesus Christ."[24] Surely it is hardly possible to state more clearly than this that all individual grace is destined to be shared among the whole of the people of God!

The gratuitous nature of Christian teaching is a strict principle. It is based on the initial gratuity of God's gift. What has been gratuitously received cannot later be sold or bargained for,[25] nor can it be kept exclusively by one person or claimed by one particular individual. The consequence of this principle of gratuity in the concrete is the popular spread of Christianity, evidence of the fact that Christian doctrine is accessible to all classes of people. Justin's pupil, Tatian, expresses this idea very clearly: "Among us, it is not only the rich who cultivate philosophy. The poor also gratuitously enjoy the teaching. The presents of this world cannot, after all, make up for what comes from God. We therefore welcome all those who want to listen, whether they are old women or young children. All ages are equally honored. We only keep all impurity at a distance."[26]

Christianity, then, is seen as open and welcoming to people of all conditions, and this prevents it from becoming too intellectualized. It has certainly to be presented as a doctrine, and those who adhere to this doctrine are presented as disciples of a teaching, but Athenagoras, who was Tatian's contemporary, openly admits that many of those disciples are uneducated people, workers and old women and would be unable to express the doctrine in which they believe in the form of a learned discourse.[27] But is that so very important? These lowly and humble disciples preach by their works and make new disciples by their example!

Justin never lays claim in his writings to any institutional recognition or to any ministry in an attempt to justify his authority. He feels no need to do this. He regards the service that he offers to his fellow human beings as a duty and a necessity. In his view, it would be unthinkable for any Christian not to accept that the individual grace that he has received from God is destined to be offered to and shared among the whole of humankind. It seems to him to be worthless to provide an account of his own individual mission, because, for him, the whole church must be missionary.

Was this man, who was so anxious to achieve a reconciliation between pagan philosophy and the good news, to give Christianity a

"Among us, it is not only the rich who cultivate philosophy"

basis in pagan culture and to proclaim the gospel to the whole of humanity, a lay member of Catholic Action without knowing it? This is, of course, an anachronistic comparison, but it is not just a question of terminology. Justin was not simply unaware of the name "layman"—he also did not even know of the existence of the reality that we would now call a "laity."

For Justin, there was no division between Christians, no antinomy between clergy and laity and not even a difference between the priest and the Christian. According to him, "it is in memory of the suffering that he endured for men, whose souls are purified from all perversity, that Jesus Christ our Lord has commanded us to make this bread of thanksgiving so that we may at the same time give thanks to God for having created for man the world with all that it contains, for having set us free from the evil state in which we were and for having finally destroyed the principalities and powers through the one who suffered according to his will."[28]

In this passage and others, Justin speaks of "us." Surely this is not an "us" of majesty or distinction invested with any special function! He is speaking of "us, the nations"[29] or, as he says in Chapter 116 of his *Dialogue*, of "the true archpriestly race" of God, of those who, through the name of Jesus, have believed in the God who has made all things. "God himself bears witness to this," he states in the same context, "when he says that 'in all places among the nations pure and acceptable sacrifices are offered,' and God does not receive sacrifices from anyone except his priests."[30]

Justin's real originality is to be found in the radical nature of this affirmation that all Christians are priests. In the writings of this master, the idea of priesthood is always applied exclusively to Christians as a whole and never to one particular type of minister. Neither in the *Dialogue* nor in the two *Apologies* is there any reference to a ministerial priesthood superimposed on or added to the universal priesthood of all Christians. At first sight, this affirmation may shock modern readers and make them ask at once: How, then, was the eucharist celebrated? Justin himself provides us with the answer to this question.

The Celebration of the Eucharist

There are two descriptions of the eucharist in the *First Apology*, The first is an outline of the eucharist celebrated in a baptismal context[31] and the second is an account of the Sunday eucharist.[32] Two types of function emerge from Justin's outline of the baptismal eucharist. The first function is that of the "one presiding over the assembly of the brothers" and the second is the function of "the ministers whom we call deacons."

In the case of the Sunday eucharist, Justin allows us to presuppose that "the who who reads" is present. The eucharist that he describes is in fact one that took place on Sunday morning in the course of the liturgy of the word. It is important to emphasize this, as this was not always the case. In a letter to Trajan,[33] written about 112–113 A.D., Pliny the Younger explains that Christians had two kinds of assembly. One took place at dawn and consisted of praise, while the other was an evening meeting and took place during a meal. The second, then, was the eucharist in the strict sense. This means that the single meeting during which both the liturgy of the word and the eucharist were celebrated could only result in an increase in the importance of the one presiding over it.

It is therefore all the more remarkable that Justin does not give any special title to the "one presiding over the assembly of the brothers." He simply uses the present participle, literally "the (one) presiding," to record his function. We also have the evidence of the first epistle to Timothy and the *Shepherd of Hermas*,[34] according to which the functions of presiding are attributed to presbyters. Justin, on the other hand, does not speak in this context either of presbyters or of *episkopoi*. Why not?

Some scholars have suggested that, because he was writing his *Apology* for readers who were outside Christianity and strangers to it, he did not want to encumber his text with ideas that might have seemed to them to be too technical. This is not a very convincing argument, above all because Justin takes the trouble to state, in his description of the ministers who give "to each of those who are present a portion of the consecrated bread, wine and water," that they are "the ministers whom we call deacons." So, if the author of the *Apology* did not feel any need to define the title of "the (one) presiding" more precisely, this must surely be at least because the minister's title seemed to him to be of secondary importance in relation to the ministry that he carried out.

Three different types of person, then, can be distinguished in the celebration of the eucharist as described by Justin: the one presiding, the one who reads (or the ones who read) and the ministers called deacons. Several questions arise at once. Is the first, the president, simply included among the deacons? Should the word "deacon" be regarded as a general term pointing without differentiation to all Christian ministers? And finally, is the president a deacon-*episkopos*, in other words, a "servant-overseer"?

It is not easy to find an answer to these questions. We can certainly say that, in the works that have come down to us, Justin does not use the words "presbyters" or "*episkopoi*" for Christian ministers. The functions of "the (one) presiding," however, may well have had a certain charismatic aspect, but they do seem to have been sufficiently important not to have been left entirely to chance or entrusted simply to any Christian of good will. What we have in the case of the president is undoubtedly a stable function and, even if he was not necessarily a lifelong president, he had to be chosen from a relatively limited and predetermined group.

Certain powers were implied in the president's function. He had to admonish and exhort the people after the reading. He had to improvise the eucharistic prayer "to the best of his ability"—this was the charismatic aspect of his function. He had to preside over the "distribution of the eucharisted elements." And, finally, he had to collect the gifts and help "all those who are in need." The last function was by no means the least important, since it presupposed management ability, a real knowledge of the goods and property belonging to different members of the community and sufficient authority to be able to resolve the conflicts that might result from the redistribution of those goods. It could give the one presiding a position similar to that of the Roman *patronus* and make those who received help his "customers." This function consisting of the management of goods and property was, as we shall see, to play an important part later in the constitution of the Christian clergy.[35]

In conclusion, it is possible to say that, in the "assembly of the brothers" gathered together to celebrate the eucharist, there was no title which gave some Christians precedence over others, no theology that introduced any distinction or categorization between the Christians present and no reservation in the participation of the whole assembly in the priestly role of Jesus Christ as the one high priest according to the order of Melchisedek. There was, however, one role that predominated, that of the "one presiding," and there was similarly a group of Christians who could feel that they were particularly dependent on that president—those who received help.

Belonging to the People of God Through Baptism

Even the most humble and the poorest Christians were washed and redeemed by baptism and were no longer "children of necessity and ignorance" but "children of election and knowledge."[36] These baptized disciples, who believed in the truth of the teachings and the doctrines of the Christians, had, according to Justin, reached the state of being "illuminated." The apologist outlines this state in his *First Apology*: "We are called atheists. Yes, we certainly confess that we are atheists in respect of these supposed gods! But we believe in the most true God, the Father of righteousness, of wisdom and of the other virtues, the God who is without any admixture of evil. Together with him, we worship and adore in spirit and truth the Son who came from him and who has given us these teachings and the host of other good angels who accompany him and are like him as well as the prophetic Spirit. That is the doctrine which we have learned and which we hand on liberally to anyone who wants to be instructed."[37]

Later in his *First Apology* (Chapter 61), the author describes how those who believe are baptized in the name of God the Father and master of the universe, of the Son, who was crucified under Pontius Pilate, and of the Holy Spirit, who has predicted through the prophets the whole history of Jesus. In his *Dialogue,* he tells us that this baptismal bath or water of life is the "bath of repentance and of knowledge of God"[38] and that baptism is a "spiritual circumcision."[39] The nations may therefore rejoice with the people of God.[40] Christians can be regarded as the true Israel.[41] They are the race of Jacob, born of faith and the spirit.[42] Christ is "the head of another race, the race that has been regenerated by him, by water, faith and the wood that contained the mystery of the cross."[43] This people, the *ekklesia,* in which all men are only one,[44] is "constituted by the name of Christ and shares in his name."[45] It was for this church and for the synagogue that Christ came "granting equal dignity to all those who keep his commandments."[46]

All of Christ's disciples, Justin insists, have this "equal dignity." There is in Christianity neither clergy nor laity—only "children of election and knowledge." It is clear, then, that he presents us with an idea of the Christian that is in a sense gnostic. In other words, for him, the Christian is above all a disciple, someone who has agreed to be instructed and believes in the teachings that have been offered to him and puts them into practice. His "gnosticism," however, is entirely without pride. Baptism is the bath of knowledge, but it is also the bath of repentance. The candidate for baptism has to be washed free of his sins before he can be illuminated. The Christian's knowledge is not intended to remain esoteric. Every Christian must make it his duty graciously to hand on the teaching that he has received to all those who agree to become disciples in their turn.

According to Justin, then, Christians are a specific race of people in the world, destined to increase and spread.[47] In his apocalyptic view, it is the presence of this race of Christians that delays the final judgment of the world. The author of the epistle to Diognetus claims, in more Platonic terms, that Christians are the soul of the world and uphold it.[48] Those who have been constituted as the church by the name of Christ, who are gathered together under the common name of Christian and who have equal dignity and are illuminated, then, become in their turn a light for the world and the source of a gift for their fellowmen by the growth of their people. In Justin's own words, if God "has not yet passed his judgment or if he still does not pass judgment, this is because he knows that there are every day some who, instructed in the name of his Christ, leave the way of error and receive his gifts, each one according to what he is worthy to receive, illuminated in the name of that Christ. One receives the spirit of understanding, another that of counsel, one that of power, another that of healing, one the spirit of prophecy, another the spirit of teaching and yet another that of the fear of God."[49]

Irenaeus of Lyons:
Better Than a Priest—A Spiritual Disciple

If Justin's works are compared with those of Irenaeus of Lyons, one is bound to conclude that the latter seems to speak a little less of Christians and much more of the church. In the writings of Irenaeus, Christians are generally contrasted with the Jews.[50] He is certainly aware of belonging to the "us" of Christians[51] and he associates this collective identity with the confession of faith in one and the same God the Father and creator. This title does not, however, seem to be enough to account for his faith. His writings are strongly marked by the fact that heretics also lay claim to Christ. He says, for example: "The brother is exposed to his brother's trap, just as the church suffers in the same way on behalf of those of its own race."[52]

But, although he uses the word "brother,"[53] just as he uses the word "Christian," he frequently tends to employ them with reference to the past. He seems in fact to have a special preference for the term "disciple," or, rather, "true disciple." In this way, he is able to distinguish between all those who lay claim to Christ. We may therefore say that, like Justin, Irenaeus also believes that the true disciples—those who have received, in the name of Jesus Christ, the grace of the Son of God—work for the good of other men and sometimes lead them to embrace the faith and to enter the church.

In the church, these true disciples make use of the charisms that they have received for the greatest good of the Gentiles, thus distributing gratuitously what they have received gratuitously.[54] Provided with many graces in the name of Jesus Christ, they are, as Justin described them, both missionaries and disinterested. Whether they are disciples of the Lord or disciples of the apostles, they are truly spiritual and confess one and the same God. They also interpret the Old and the New Testaments in the light of that unity[55] and, helped by the Spirit, they judge all men in the light of that interpretation.

Characterized by the graces that they have received and by their missionary and disinterested spirit, these disciples, who were called Christian for the first time at Antioch, are also priests. In Symmachus' Greek translation of the Old Testament, Ahimelech says to David, in the episode when the latter eats the showbread: "I have no lay bread at hand, but there is only consecrated bread."[56] Irenaeus refers to this episode in connection with the passage in the gospel containing an allusion to it[57] and does not use the term "lay." What he says in fact is: "Priest—David was a priest in God's eyes, although he was persecuted by Saul, since every righteous king has priestly rank. Priest—all the Lord's disciples are also priests, those who have as their inheritance here neither a field nor a home, but who devote themselves unceasingly to serving the altar and God."[58] Irenaeus is quite categorical here, insisting explicitly: "As I have shown in the previous book, the levites and the priests are all the Lord's disciples, who also infringe the sabbath laws in the temple and are not held guilty."[59]

Is there, according to Irenaeus, a specific sacrificial function fulfilled by particular persons alongside this universal priesthood of all believers? There is no evidence of this in his writings. When he speaks of the Christian oblation, offering or sacrifice, he does not put special ministers on the stage.[60] Those who offer are simply "the disciples,"[61] "we"[62] or the church,[63] and sometimes he just uses the passive form of the verb.[64] He never mentions at any time a particular subject who might claim for himself alone the act of offering.

Despite the very high status that he gives to the notion of the spiritual disciple, Irenaeus seems to reject the idea of distinguishing between Christians. He does not recognize the terms "clergy" and "laity" and gives all the disciples priestly rank. He was clearly quite opposed to the Valentinians' practice of making a distinction between the "simple," the "common people" and the "perfect."[65] It is paradoxical and worth noting that the Valentinians should have given a specific name to the "crowd" of simple people without knowledge whom they addressed in their speeches and writing. That name is not what we would have expected, that is, "lay" ("belonging to the people"), but "ecclesiastic."[66]

Good and Bad Presbyters

It would seem, then, that Irenaeus refused to classify Christians in different categories. But did he not have an indirect way of making a rather more subtle distinction? Are there no degrees in his idea of perfect, true, spiritual disciples? Is there not, in his view, a "typical" disciple?

What cannot be denied is that he was influenced in his thinking by those whom he was attacking and that he had a exalted idea of perfect, spiritual man. On the other hand, he also presents us with an image of the "presbyter, the disciple of the apostles," as a perfect type of disciple,[67] but that type cannot be regarded as exclusive. Irenaeus also presents us, for example, with John as the "Lord's disciple," but this does not prevent him in any way from extending that idea to include all the disciples. The presbyters are not the only spiritual disciples, and the dignity of presbyter, which is so emphasized in Irenaeus' work by the ideas of succession and charism of truth, can also be relativized. If we need to be convinced of this, we have only to look at the recommendation that he was given when he left for Rome.

"Do we in fact recognize the rank that justice can confer on someone if we had above all to recommend him as a presbyter of this church, since that is, after all, his situation?"[68] It was in these terms that the martyrs of Lyons presented Irenaeus, about 177 A.D., to the church of Rome, where they were sending a letter. Two facts emerge from this statement. The first is that Irenaeus was a presbyter of the community of Lyons. The second is that this title, given to him by men, does not always necessarily correspond to the rank that justice may confer on a person. It is possible to think that this statement can be explained by the context. In other words, the community responsible for writing the letter had recently suffered so much from persecutions that the ranks and honors lavished on men by human justice—even when those men were Christians—might seem to be very meager in comparison with the rank acquired by martyrs in the presence of God's justice.

The rank of presbyter, then, is nothing without the charisms and the behavior that should accompany it. Irenaeus speaks, for example, of "those who are regarded by many as presbyters, but who are really slaves of their passions and who do not reveal the fear of God in their hearts, but who offend others, are filled with pride because of their leading position and do evil things in secret, saying 'No one will see us.' "[69] Such "presbyters" will, Irenaeus insists, be unmasked and eliminated. Their dignity on earth is nothing in comparison with the state of the true, spiritual disciple. His dignity takes precedence over all "ranks" and is in principle due exclusively to the graces which are received at baptism and which are spread throughout the church. As Irenaeus himself says, "It is where God's charisms are that we have to be instructed in the truth."[70]

But Where Is the Truth To Be Found?

Irenaeus soon shows us the way in the continuation of the above text: "It is where God's charisms are that we have to be instructed in the truth. In other words, the truth is with those in whom the succession in the church from the apostles, unassailable integrity of behavior and the incorruptible purity of the word are to be found. These men preserve our faith in the one God who has created all things. They make our love for the Son of God, who has achieved such great 'economies' for us, grow and they provide for us a very certain explanation of the scriptures."[71]

"These men" mentioned by Irenaeus are without any doubt good presbyters. So every Christian who reads the scriptures correctly and every man who loves God will, according to Irenaeus, "move forward to the point where he will see God and hear his word"[72] and thus become a "perfect disciple"—but only on condition that he reads those scriptures in accordance with the interpretation of the good presbyters!

It is clear, then, that the idea of "spiritual disciple" transcends all the categories that may exist among Christians. Each individual is called to become a spiritual disciple, a perfect man. But he will never reach that ideal state so long as he goes in the opposite direction to that of the good presbyters, who are the types and the guides of perfect disciples. In the concrete, those presbyters constitute the sociological landmark of Irenaeus' spiritual Christianity. The charisms are the privilege of all Christian disciples, but the "charism of truth" is to be found above all in the reality of the presbyter. In the writings of Irenaeus, that reality is neither clerical nor lay. For those who want to become spiritual disciples, one thing is necessary: to listen to the presbyters who are in the church.[73]

A Provisional Conclusion:
How Should the Silence of the Texts Be Interpreted?

From the first New Testament texts until Irenaeus' treatise *Against Heresies*, that is, from 40 to 180 A.D., the word "lay" only occurred once. Even then, it was used in an Old Testament image and was not directly applied to Christians. This means that there was more than a century and a half of Christianity without "laity," despite the existence of an Old Testament typology and the availability of the terminology.

It would therefore be useless to ask what part was played by a laity in early Christianity. In the first Christian communities, all believers formed the lot chosen by God, all were called to be saints, all were elected and all were equal in dignity. This ideal of unity in holiness and election was made an ethnic reality by the disappearance of the barrier between Jews and the nations. It became a reality at the social level when both slaves and free men and men and women were called. At the economic level it was achieved by the desire to have all things in common. Finally, when each believer took part in worship in spirit and in truth, a form of worship in which the only priest was Jesus Christ, and when each baptized Christian had a liturgical function to perform, that unity in holiness and election was achieved liturgically.

The difference in function was not one existing between those who were active and those who were not active in the liturgy. It was to be found in the way in which each believer's liturgical function was regulated. In Christianity, each Christian was active liturgically in his own way, and there was, for this reason, no real laity. It would be an anachronism to think that the services performed by the simple faithful outside the framework of worship were "lay ministries." Justin may well not have been an episkopos, a deacon or a presbyter, nor was he a "layman," and when he took part in the Christian liturgical offering, he may not have been presiding, but he carried out a liturgical function that was not essentially different from that of the "one presiding."

In the first two centuries of its life, the church had this remarkable characteristic: its unity was too theocentric—or rather too Christocentric—to accommodate itself to a theology emphasizing a human centralism. Because they are gratuitous gifts of God, the charisms of the church do not belong to any man in particular, but are destined always to be shared and distributed among all those who may be called and illuminated in their turn. In just the same way, the church's functions are not the property of any human institution which may centralize them in order later to delegate them. For this reason, it is impossible to find a dependence in the early church of lay people on a clergy. There were only Christians and disciples claiming Christ as their master.

But who, then, are those who know Christ? Where are the true disciples? The gnostics were ironical in their treatment of the members of the great church, calling them "non-initiated," "ecclesiastics" or "psychics." Irenaeus, on the other hand, believed that each one of the believers in the church was called to be a spiritual disciple, because the church gave all believers directly the Spirit and the truth. To distinguish the true church from the "heretical assemblies," believers were, he thought, invited to be at one with the good presbyters, who were responsible for a correct interpretation of the scriptures, and in whom the succession from the apostles and the charism of truth were to be found. Because of this, these presbyters became "masters" for Christ's disciples. They were soon to become clergy.

PART II
THE THIRD CENTURY

THE PEOPLE OF GOD
SPLIT IN TWO

CHAPTER 4

Lay People, Disciples
and Spiritual Masters

When the Spiritual Took Precedence Over the Institutional

The beginning of the third century was a turning point in the history of the believing people. The term "lay"—a word that we have barely encountered in the first century in the epistle of Clement of Rome—suddenly came into use again. At the same time, the idea of "clergy" was formed and became used more extensively. The early third century was also a period of great masters—such men as Tertullian, Clement of Alexandria and Origen, who together have left us an immense number of treatises, the fruit of their impressive work as teachers and authors. These men were not, however, simply intellectuals. They were also spiritual writers. In the Christian communities of their own time, the membership of which was growing rapidly, these men found that they had to reconcile the necessary institutionalization of Christianity with its spiritual dimension. They succeeded in doing this, each of them in his own way. At the end of his life, Tertullian even decided finally in favor of the charismatic by joining the Montanist movement of the new form of prophecy. Clement of Alexandria, on the other hand, seems to have remained relatively at home in the church in which he lived, while Origen stayed in the church only at the price of many journeys and difficulties.

A fourth great master, Irenaeus, had calmly postulated the equivalent relationship presbyter = truth = church = spiritual disciple in general terms, while at the same time making sure that it was possible to distinguish between the good and the bad presbyter by following the indirect way of the tradition of the apostles. But was the thing so easy to admit when the man confronting you was not a presbyter who was only anxious to transmit a correct interpretation of scripture, but a monarchical bishop steeped in authority and obliged to respond to new situations in the church by referring to the apostolic age? When certain thinkers encountered the solutions suggested, they could only reject Irenaeus' equivalent relationship presbyter = church = truth.

It shocked Tertullian deeply that those who had committed adultery and fornication were admitted to penitence, and he violently apostrophized Callistus, the bishop of Rome, in the following passage: "You say that the church has the power to remit sins. . . . I take note of your declaration and ask you what right you have to usurp the power of the church. . . . Let us acknowledge that Peter received the power to remit sins. . . . That power also belongs to the spiritual men whom Peter represents, that is, to the apostles or the prophets. For the church has been constituted above all by the Spirit. . . . So the church remits sins, but it is the church-Spirit acting through the organ of spiritual men and not what you mean by the church, that is, all the bishops."[1]

Without going to such extremes as Tertullian and without challenging the bishops as categorically as he, both Clement of Alexandria and Origen felt the need to assess and to define the place of the clergy, which was increasing in numbers and importance in the spiritual world as they understood it. For it is true that, as the number of Christians was increasing at this time, so too was the number of leaders who were needed for the various communities. At the same time, however, the real spiritual values of Christianity were being lost. Origen was very conscious of this: "In truth, if we judge things according to the reality and not according to the number, and if we judge things according to attitudes and not according to the assembled crowds, we shall see that we are now no longer believers. Ah, it is a long time since the wonderful time of fervor and of the martyrs! Then there were few believers, but they were true believers, following the narrow way leading to life. Now they are numerous, but, as there are not many who are chosen, few are worthy to be chosen and to be blessed."[2]

In that church, which, in their opinion, was troubled by a degree of laxity, Clement and Origen refused to accept a lower ideal. They continued to give precedence to the spiritual over the institutional and to make a distinction within the church between Christian and Christian and presbyter and presbyter. The higher they raised their ideal of the spiritual priesthood, the more circumspect they became with regard to the hierarchy that was increasing in numbers and importance. "Anyone can carry out solemn liturgical functions in the presence of the people, but few men are sufficiently holy in their way of life, well instructed in doctrine and formed in wisdom to be entirely capable of revealing the truth of things and of teaching the knowledge of faith."[3] In other words, spiritual qualities took precedence over liturgical functions and the titles that accompanied them. In spite of everything, this necessary emphasis did not stand in the way either of the development of a clergy or of the appearance of a Christian laity.

TERTULLIAN, AN UNCOMPROMISING LAYMAN

We know very little about the life of Tertullian. He was born in Carthage about 160 A.D. and reveals very few facts in his writings about the precise circumstances of his conversion to Christianity. When did he die? For that date, we have to be satisfied with conjectures based on his literary works, and all that we can say is that it was between 197 and about 200 A.D. It is generally believed that only death could reduce this impulsive writer to silence!

According to Jerome, Tertullian was a priest,[4] but he does not indicate the sources on which he drew for this information, and his testimony is quite isolated. J. Quasten believes that Jerome was right, but admits that "Tertullian never alludes to his clerical state, but it would be hardly possible to explain his special position and the importance of his teaching function if he had remained a layman."[5] In Tertullian's time, the need to be "ordained" in order to exercise a teaching function is undoubtedly one of the false pieces of evidence that Jerome was unable to avoid using. Tertullian himself never refers in any of his works to "his" clerical state, but what emerges from all his writings—and particularly from those completed before his break with the great church—is a very firm attitude regarding the dignity and the rights of lay people.[6] He was a violent polemicist and a man of sharp and passionate convictions. His views with regard to lay people can be more readily explained if he had himself been a layman and had held them as views directly relating to his own personal position. What is almost certain, however, is that, after breaking with the church, he was in complete solidarity with lay people and used the word "we."[7]

The Laity from Which the Hierarchy Comes

Tertullian's silence about his own precise situation is all the more intriguing, in that his works are among the first Christian writings in which we are given a structure of the church as organized in two groups—clergy and laity. He identifies the laity with the *plebs* or ordinary people, who are distinguished from the "priestly" or "ecclesiastical order"[8] of bishops, presbyters and deacons[9] and, in a very general way, from the clergy,[10] who are regarded as "leaders" (*duces*) and pastors.[11]

Does this mean that laymen are Christians of a lower order who can follow a less exalted ideal? Tertullian the Montanist would answer this question quite unambiguously. It is from the laity that the church's hierarchy comes. They therefore have to be individually as pure as the members of the clergy. They have to obey the same laws as the leaders so that they can be recruited into the clergy. In answer to a claim that "the apostle allowed a second marriage inasmuch as it is only the members of the clergy whom he binds with the yoke of monogamy," Tertullian wrote: "How is it possible for Paul to want the whole of the church's hierarchy to consist of persons who have been married only once if that rule is not first observed by the laymen from whom the church's hierarchy comes? If all Christians are not constrained to marry only once, where shall we look for monogamists to enter the clergy? Shall we have to institute a separate order of persons married only once, from which the clergy is to be recruited?"[12]

In the perspective revealed here by Tertullian, the church's hierarchy is a direct product of the laity. The constitution of a special "order" preparing for entry into the clergy was for him quite unthinkable, because such an order would form a barrier between the clergy and the laity. Lay people claimed a priestly dignity equal to that of priests. Because they had the same dignity as priests, they also had identical duties. The hierarchy appeared only as an expression of the dignity and the duties of the whole Christian people. "We would be mad to think that what priests are not permitted to do, lay people are. Although we are lay, are we not priests? It is written: He has made us a kingdom of priests for God his Father."[13] The difference between the "order" and the people is the fact of a decision taken by the church and that decision is sanctified by the assembled "order."[14] Lay people are priests according to the will of

God. The distinction between the "order" (*ordo*) and the "people" (*plebs*) has its origin in a decision made by the church and its sanctification by the assembled "ecclesiastical order" and, in practice, probably by the bishop assisted by the presbyterium.

But what does this decision (*auctoritas*) on the part of the church mean? Did Tertullian only intend to stress the ecclesiastical —and not the divine—origin of the distinction between *ordo* and *plebs*? This is the usual interpretation of this text.[15] But Tertullian may perhaps have wanted to go further by reminding his readers that this distinction only existed by the consent of the whole church—including the *plebs*—and not by a simple decision made by the hierarchical authorities. In fact, in the following sentence, he says quite clearly that the lay people fully constitute the church. "Where there is no bench of the ecclesiastical order," he says, "you, layman, offer and baptize and you are your own priest. In other words, where there are three persons, though they are laymen, there is the church."

Although he was an incorrigible polemicist, then, Tertullian was able to find the means, in a moral exhortation directed above all toward the laity, of shooting an arrow at the members of the ecclesiastical order, by recalling that that order could not exist without a decision in which the *plebs* also had a say. This is clearly a twofold lesson in humility. Not only should the members of the ecclesiastical order remember that lay people are also priests by virtue of the will of God, they should also bear firmly in mind that their existence as members of the ecclesiastical order is due to a decision made by the assembled people. In this sense too, then, the hierarchy comes from the laity.

Ministry for Life and Ministry for a Time

We have just seen how insistently Tertullian proclaimed that lay people are priests. Yet he was also angered by the way in which heretics undertook ordinations. It was, in his opinion, "haphazard, capricious and frivolous." He was astonished how "they entrusted even lay people with priestly functions (*munus*)."[16] Was Tertullian the Catholic here contradicting a Tertullian who let his Montanist sympathies become visible in his *Exhortation to Chastity*?

It is only an apparent contradiction. He is complaining above all of the arbitrary way in which the heretics behave. So he deliberately uses the term "function" or *munus,* which in Roman law meant the obligation imposed on the citizen by the order of a magistrate, in contrast to the term "charge" or *honor,* which pointed to a magistrature accepted as the result of an election or at the invitation of other citizens. What Tertullian is disputing here is the arbitrary decision coming from above and lacking the slow and serious approach subject to verification by the community. "In the rebels' camp, attempts are made to win believers by promotion," he says. "So they have one bishop today and tomorrow another. A man who is a deacon today will be a reader tomorrow and a man who is today a priest will tomorrow be a layman. They even entrust lay people with priestly functions."[17]

The point of his statement is undoubtedly to be found in his use of the words "today" and "tomorrow." What he is clearly criticizing above all is the rapid and artificial movement of change that was taking place in the "rebels' camp." Later in the same text, he stresses balance as the mark of a church that listens to the will of God: "Where God is, there is the fear of God which is the beginning of wisdom, and where the fear of God is, there are also a serious approach to life, scrupulous zeal, eagerness to care, sensitive decisions, a mature balance in communion, promotion because of loyal service, religious submission, zeal in divine services, a modest way of acting and a united church, in which everything belongs to God."[18]

Tertullian does not tell us whether we ought to be presbyters, deacons or bishops for life, but he calls for a serious approach to the choice of ministers, a certain constancy in the exercise of ministries and a degree of experience in carrying out certain functions. He admits that, where the need arises, laymen can and must, for the time being, carry out priestly functions and that they are perfectly worthy to carry them out, but he calls for a certain order in the normal everyday carrying out of those functions. It is, however, possible for lay people to intervene at the choice of the ministers in verifying that order.

The Financial Contribution of the Laity

"Approved elders are our presidents and they obtain that honor not at the price of money, but by the evidence of their virtue, since there is no price attached to any of the things of God."[19] In spite of everything, however, lay people have to support the members of the

ecclesiastical orders, or at least they have to give them a fee. We may know that the bishop received a "double fee,"[20] but we do not know how much it was or whether it was enough for those who received it to live on. We also do not know whether the financial contribution for the needs of the community was simply made by the laity or whether the members of the ecclesiastical orders who were sufficiently well off also contributed in this way.

Tertullian tells us that there was a common money chest or fund. He stresses that it was not simply those who were appointed to provide for the needs of the community because they were rich who donated to this fund. Christians were nobody's customers and money could not influence the life of the community or make it change direction. There was no question of preventing the most wealthy members of the community from giving a great deal, but accepting even a considerable donation was always subject to the faithfulness that the giver was showing toward the community of the church.

In connection with this, Tertullian speaks of the way in which the church of Rome returned a gift of 200,000 sesterces (an enormous sum of money in those days) as soon as Marcion's heterodox intrigues became apparent. Each person's contribution to the local church's common fund was intended to form a vital minimum amount enabling the community to remain independent. "Even though we have a kind of common money chest, it is not formed by the collection of "fees" contributed by the elect, as though religion were put up for auction. Each person makes a modest donation on a regular day each month or whenever he chooses and only if he so chooses and only if he is able. For no one is compelled. All contributions are given freely."[21]

This regular contribution was not made without calling for the tithe, but it was a freely given contribution and, although it was given by the whole of the laity, the clergy do not seem to have been excluded. It was, after all, not intended simply to provide "fees" for the clergy. The money was also used to help all those who were in need. Tertullian mentions, for example, orphans, old servants and "those who have been shipwrecked, condemned to the mines, banished to islands or imprisoned." It was not necessary to belong to an "order" to benefit from the church's help. Tertullian protested vehemently against the admission of a young virgin into the "order of widows" so that she might receive material aid, saying: "If the bishop had been obliged to give her some relief, he could surely have supplied it in another way, without failing to respect the rule."[22]

Had Women a Place Among the Laity?

Widows belonged to an *ordo* and were included among the members of ecclesiastical orders.[23] Sinners who wanted to be reconciled lay down before both them and the presbyters during the assembly. It is, however, doubtful whether Tertullian was thinking of them when he wrote that, as we have seen above, "where there is no bench of the ecclesiastical order," the laity might "offer (the eucharist) and baptize."[24] Widows probably never offered the eucharist and never baptized, even in the absence of members of the male "ecclesiastical order." The "order of widows" was certainly honored and it was assimilated into the clergy by being related on various sides to different categories of those receiving assistance. We can only conclude that widows had an ambiguous status.

What, then, was the status of those women who did not belong to any "ecclesiastical order" and therefore ought logically to be included among the laity? "From now onward, women have a right to all the functions fulfilled by the laity." No, it was not Tertullian who said this! It was said on January 25, 1983 when the new Code of Canon Law was presented.[25] Such a pronouncement would never be made by the Carthaginian jurist who wrote in his treatise *On the Veiling of Virgins*: "A woman may not speak in the church, nor baptize, nor offer, nor claim the right to any function exercised by a man, still less to the priestly ministry."[26]

Tertullian was angered by the impudence of a heretic who dared to teach and was afraid that some women might even go so far as to baptize![27] He never even considered seriously that a woman might claim the right that is dormant in the minds of virtually every layman, namely the right to exercise priestly functions, the right to do what the priest does. "Are we not all priests?" he asks, as we have seen above, in his *Exhortation to Chastity*, without thinking of the consequences that women—as well as men—might be able to draw from this sentence. In fact, even when he speaks about lay people in this very context, Tertullian is only thinking of men and nowhere in any of his treatises does he seem to give the title "lay" to women. In his writings, women cannot claim the same rights as laymen.

"Where there are three persons, though they are laymen, there is the church."

Photo André-Ziolo. Third Century Catacomb of St Calixtres

SHOULD TEACHING BE LEFT TO THE LAITY?

Tertullian not only questioned the institution of the church. He was also, whatever Jerome thought, a layman. But he still had a very strong influence on the church of Carthage. Cyprian certainly recognized the intellectual power of this man who had so castigated the church's bishops. This is clear from the words that he used to address to his secretary when he wanted to consult the works of this hot-headed author: "Hand me the master!"

Tertullian, the learned layman, was certainly not an isolated case at the beginning of the third century. From that time onward, however, the local churches, anxious to preserve unity and centralized around the episcopate, wondered whether it was wise to leave the teaching of faith to independent laymen. The church of Alexandria was particularly notable for its catechetical teaching and it could therefore not remain unaffected by this problem.

Homage to the Unknown Layman:
Pantaenus, the Founder of the Catechetical School of Alexandria

Little is known about Pantaenus, apart from the fact that he was a master of universal renown. In charge of the catechetical school of Alexandria, he taught "orally and in writing the treasures of the divine dogmas." It has not proved possible to identify any of his writings with certainty, but one of his pupils was Clement, who was later called to follow him as the head of the school of Alexandria, and his teaching has certainly survived in Clement's written work. What cannot, however, be determined is how much of that work is the master's and how much is the disciple's. In a famous passage, Clement paid homage to the master whom he discovered at Alexandria: "He was literally a Sicilian bee, plundering the flowers in the fields of the prophets and the apostles and yielding pure knowledge in the souls of those who heard him."[28]

This interpreter of the scriptures was trained in the school of the Stoic philosophers before he became, in or about the year 180, the head of the school of Alexandria. His disciple and successor Clement was probably a presbyter, but we do not know with any certainty what was the status of his master in the church. As in the case of Justin, we believe that the function of *didaskalos* or "catechetical teacher" was sufficient in itself and that this function did not require confirmation by any form of "ordination." If it had been confirmed in this way, this function of *didaskalos* might have been so influential that it would even have eclipsed the title of presbyter. Was Pantaenus ordained or was he a layman? Before this question can be answered, we must ask: What meaning could the term "lay" have had in the church of Alexandria at that time? As we cannot, of course, consult the writings of Pantaenus himself, we have to look at those of Clement.

The Laity According to Clement of Alexandria

Clement uses the term "lay" or "laity" even less often than Tertullian, and he certainly does not contrast it with the word "clergy." In fact the term only appears three times in the whole of his work. It occurs twice as an adjective and once as a noun. We also have to take into account in one of these cases that there is no certainty regarding the text itself, since there are variants in the different manuscripts. In this text, *laikos* appears to be used in a pejorative sense to express what is "common" or even "coarse" and is even compared with a word meaning "licentious."[29]

If this case is excluded, we are left with only two uses of the word *laikos*. One of these also has a pejorative meaning, being compared with *apistia* or unfaithfulness. Clement is speaking of the three parts of the temple—the holy of holies, to which only the high priest is admitted, the holy place, where the priests gathered, and the forecourt or vestibule, where the people were permitted. The holy place, Clement writes, is separated from the forecourt by a "curtain which was a barrier against profane unfaithfulness (*laikos apistias*) and was stretched in front of five columns to exclude those who were on the forecourt."[30] This is also the only case in the whole of Clement's work in which the word *laikos* is used in the context of Old Testament worship.

Clement of Alexandria, however, was familiar with the letter written by his namesake Clement of Rome to the Corinthians and frequently refers to it in his *Stromateis* IV, 16,105,1 to 18,113,3, using it to paint a portrait of the typical gnostic. But although he quotes passages immediately preceding and following the one in which Clement of Rome speaks for the first time of a layman, the head of the school of Alexandria passes over this passage without stopping, as though he attached no importance at all to it.

This reduces us to the third case and the only text in which

Clement of Alexandria employs the term *laikos* as a noun. Here the author is trying to refute encratite theories attacking marriage. To add strength to his argument, he calls on Saint Paul, pointing out that the apostle did not condemn marriage and recalling that he in fact advised young women who were widowed to remarry in order to avoid scandal.[31] Clement continues: "The apostle undoubtedly admits that 'the husband of only one woman,' whether he is a presbyter, a deacon or a layman, if he makes use of marriage without fault, will be saved by begetting children."[32]

What strikes us first and foremost is that Clement is not contrasting the laity and the clergy here, but is associating the layman with presbyters and deacons within the same discipline. It is also worth noting that, in the one text in which Clement is authentically and positively interested in the laity, it would seem to be a lay man, not a woman. This should not surprise us, as we have already seen how Tertullian, when he was speaking of the laity, was also almost always thinking exclusively of men.

But it is surely possible to go a little further in this matter. Is it, for example, not surprising that Clement should think that the lay man must, like the presbyter or the deacon, be a "husband of only one woman"? In the first letter to Timothy, the demand is made of the episkopos and deacons that they should be the "husband of only one woman," but the same is not required of the laity.[33] The epistle to Titus provides us with a possible explanation here, in that it seems to call for candidates for the function of presbyter to be the "husband of only one woman."[34] Should, then, the layman too not be the "husband of only one woman" because he might one day be called to other functions? The fact that the layman is associated in this requirement with presbyters and deacons would lead us to think that what Clement had essentially in mind was the episcopal function that he mentions a little later, saying again in that context that the episkopos must be the "husband of only one woman."[35] In this context, then, lay men should perhaps be defined not as the whole body of Christians without exception, but as men who were likely to be subject one day to the demands of the priesthood.

In Carthage, Tertullian asked: "If all (including laymen) are not confined to contracting only one marriage, where shall we find anyone married only once to enter the clergy? Or shall we have to institute a separate order of people from which the clergy will be recruited?"[36] In Alexandria at the same period, Clement, it would seem, was confronted with a similar problem. We cannot, however, determine whether Clement interpreted the obligation to be the "husband of only one woman" strictly, that is, as a prohibition to contract a second marriage, or whether he regarded it simply as an obligation to faithfulness within a monogamous marriage. It is difficult for us to say whether laymen were all the "non-ordained" male members of the community—in which case all the men had to try to remain "husbands of only one woman"—or whether they really formed that reserve of future possible members of the clergy about whom the ascetic and hot-headed Tertullian did not want to hear.

The Life of the Distinguished Christians of Alexandria

Was a layman, the "husband of only one woman," faultless in his attitude toward marriage and destined to be saved by begetting children, more perfect than the average Christian? Was he an elect member of the community of all the elect baptized Christians? In the prosperous city of Alexandria, wealthy as a result of its trade and rich in culture, it was not always easy to practice in a radical way the Christian ideal. Clement of Alexandria was obviously very conscious of this difficulty when he wrote: "There are now, among the elect, some who are more particularly elect."[37]

This knowledge of human weakness did not prevent the paedagogus from offering to those who heard him an ideal of simplicity and sobriety. Christians should dress in white, not in brightly colored clothes. Women should avoid ornaments, jewels, luxurious or alluring sandals, and wear simple white shoes, except when they were traveling, when they could wear shoes with studs. Men should as far as possible go barefoot. Women should not use makeup, but eat a balanced diet and in this way keep their skin pale and naturally clear. Do not eat too much, Clement urged Christians, and do not lie too long in bed! Throw away your soft couches and cushions full of down, "the wealth of blankets, rugs embroidered with gold and Persian carpets of many colors threaded with gold, long gowns stained with purple dye and costly fur-lined cloaks, those fabrics of sparkling colors loved by the poets and woolen outer garments!"[38] Be satisfied with what is strictly necessary and turn away from what is superfluous! He urged Christians to avoid doing anything that was contrary to the natural order and to exercise moderation in their marriages, always keeping in mind the bringing of children into the world. And you women, do not make up your faces and color your hair, but take part in healthy activities like weaving wool and cooking. Add a little good taste and decency to these counsels and do not snap your fingers to call your servants or kiss passionately in their presence. If you do all this and more, you will be doing what is essential in the moral teaching of the paedagogus—a teacher who, it must be admitted, was very concerned with appearances.

Did Christians in fact follow this ideal of simplicity and ascesis? It is obvious that they did not, and the amount of time and space that Clement spends in condemning certain practices is clear enough evidence that such bad behavior was deeply rooted in the lives of those who heard him. It is clear from his writings that the master of Alexandria was constantly criticizing those who were deeply attached to jewels and precious stones, dyed and embroidered fabrics and luxury goods of every kind. His description of what certain people habitually ate would have pleased a Rabelais: "The belching of those who are weighed down with wine, the grunting of those who are filled to the brim with food, the wheezing of those who are wrapped up in their blankets, the gurgling of those whose bellies are bloated—this is enough to overwhelm the power of the soul to see and to fill the mind with a multitude of false images."[39]

The people whom Clement was describing in these accounts were undoubtedly confusing the opulence of the banquet with the frugality of the Christian agape. For Clement, "the worst fall of all is the one in which the agape, which must not fall, is thrown down from heaven to the level of the sauce."[40]

The ideal that Clement is suggesting is, of course, that the Christian should be satisfied with onions, olives, vegetables, milk and cheese or fruit, that he should eat roasted or boiled meat if necessary, but preferably fish or honey, and that he should drink only moderately.[41] He should get up at dawn, dress simply in white garments and praise God. During the day he should devote himself to a healthy activity, including physical exercise. His home should not contain useless luxuries. At night, after praying and giving thanks to God, he should sleep, but not heavily, and get up and take exercise the following morning, especially when there was less daylight. He should even get up during the night to pray, and he should be chaste and act within the permitted limits in his approach to marriage.

But was it necessary to discourage the rich by telling them to give up all their possessions? Clement did not think so. All that he asked of the prosperous merchants of Alexandria was that they should eradicate their passion for wealth and use their possessions for good purposes.[42] He advised them to accept a spiritual director who would guide them in their responsibilities.[43] That spiritual director could, of course, have been Clement himself. In that case, he, the paedagogus, would undoubtedly have told them: "God himself has created the human race so that we might share in his own possessions, having first shared with all men and placed at their disposal as a common good his own Logos, having made all things for all men. All things, then, are held in common, and the rich must not want to have them more than others. To say 'That is at my disposal —I have a surfeit of it and why should I not enjoy it to the full?' is neither human nor sociable! What is more in conformity with charity is to say: 'That is at my disposal and why should I not share it with those who do not have it?' "[44] Clement may not have called on the rich citizens of Alexandria to put their belongings in common in such a radical way as the early Christians in the Acts of the Apostles, but he at least urged them not to let themselves be engulfed in total selfishness and asked them seriously to practice charity.

Layman on Earth and Priest in Heaven?

The ordinary believers of Alexandria, then, were more or less perfect and they responded more or less perfectly to their vocation as the elect. Were the bishop, the presbyters and the deacons any better? Clement relativized the institutional church and believed that the heavenly hierarchy did not necessarily correspond to the human hierarchy:

> That man is a true presbyter of the church and a true dea-
> con of the will of God who does and teaches the things of
> the Lord. It is not because men are ordained or because a
> man is a presbyter that he is regarded as righteous, but it is
> because he is righteous that he is made a presbyter. . . . The
> orders of bishop, presbyter and deacon in the church here
> below are, I think, imitations of the heavenly glory and of
> that economy that is waiting, according to the word of the
> scriptures, for those who have followed in the footsteps of
> the apostles to live in the perfection of righteousness, in
> conformity with the gospel.[45]

Those who are not bishops, presbyters or deacons should not, however, despair. What is above all important is to be righteous and to be directed toward perfection, in the expectation that one will later attain the true titles and heavenly glory, the titles that are awarded here below being no more than imitations. Those who are perfect in righteousness will be carried off on the clouds to fulfill first the office of deacon and then that of presbyter, until they reach the stature of the perfect man.[46] It is clear, then, that Clement sacralized the hierarchy of the church at the same time as relativizing it, because he regarded it as an imitation of the steps toward heavenly glory, human deacons and presbyters being, in his view, no more than imitations, but, it should be noted, in spite of everything very faithful imitations. It would seem therefore that he regarded the perfect man as a heavenly episkopos.

The man who succeeded Clement as the head of the school of Alexandria was even more critical of the hierarchy here on earth than his predecessor. There is, of course, no doubt that Origen had several reasons for criticizing certain aspects of the episcopate, and we shall return later to the unpleasant dealings that he had with his bishop Demetrius and the difficulties that he experienced in being both a layman and a didaskalos or catechetical teacher. In making a distinction between the title and the merit, he was, of course, only following Clement's way of thinking. He told priests, for example, to look honestly at themselves: "If they are conscious of being great and knowledgeable and very advanced in Christian teaching, then they should recognize that they possess the sovereign pontificate not only in name but also in merit. If not, they should see themselves as lower in rank, even though they may possess the title of the highest rank."[47]

Origen was very cautious in his evaluation of the merits and the real way of carrying out the priestly ministry. He asks, for example: "Who observes and performs the priestly duties? Who, on the other hand, is the one who has the rank and the honors of the priesthood without fulfilling the works and the ministry of the priest? 'He who searches mind and heart' is the one who may know that!"[48] He did not think of merit as depending on a man's rank or his function. In his opinion, the function (*kleros*) took the title and the honor to such a point that it could give rise to envy, but it did not necessarily ensure salvation, "since there are many—even many priests—who will be lost, and many—even many laymen—who will be pronounced blessed."[49] He did not hesitate to say: "There are many members of the clergy who do not live in such a way as to derive benefit from their function (*kleros*)."[50]

He was nonetheless conscious of the high dignity to which members of the clergy were called. He respected the degrees in rank within the hierarchy, and although he knew that there could be a certain gap between outward appearances and the spiritual reality, he refused to place the laity on an equal footing with the clergy. In his view, there was a progression in the demand to be perfect from layman to deacon, presbyter and bishop. This hierarchical scale had to be expressed by progressive stages in the penitential discipline. "Is a catechumen not entitled to more mercy than an ordinary believer? Does a layman not deserve to be pitied if he is compared with a deacon? Does a deacon not have the right to be forgiven more than a presbyter? . . . What value is there in placing the first on the bishop's throne if I cannot carry out the works required of my dignity?"[51]

This scale of values was to be found not only in the duties performed or in a greater or lesser strictness of judgment exercised, but also in the powers possessed by Christians of different rank. A layman could not, for example, cleanse himself of his sins, because the best took onto themselves the faults of those below them and the strongest accepted the defects of the weakest.[52] That at least is the idea that emerges from one of Origen's homilies, in which he states: "If an Israelite, that is to say, a layman, commits a sin, he cannot wipe it out himself. He has to look for a levite. He needs a priest. How shall I express it? He looks for someone better and higher. He needs a high priest if he is to obtain remission of his sins. But if the priest or the high priest commits a sin, he can cleanse himself of it, so long as he has not sinned against God."[53]

There is also, according to Origen, a hierarchical scale in knowledge and perfection progressing from the laity and up to the members of the clergy. Priests had in principle to be perfect in their knowledge of doctrine as well as in their behavior and in virtue.[54] They were permitted to enter the secret forecourt of sound doctrine, whereas levites could acquire knowledge of other doctrines. "There are, after all, others to which the sons of Israel may have access. By the sons of Israel I mean the laity. I do not, however, mean strangers, if they have not already been included within the Church of the Lord."[55]

Although he was treated as inferior, the fact remains that the layman was still, in Origen's opinion, the member of a people. He was still a son of Israel. He belonged to the church of the Lord and was different from strangers who had not been baptized. But what was that church? And was the word "lay" simply and solely synonymous with "baptized"? Were the terms totally interchangeable?

The Faithful Laity of the True Church
Without Spot or Wrinkle

Lay people, then, were, according to Origen, lower than deacons and priests, but superior to strangers and pagans,[56] and they belonged to the church. But what did that church consist of in Origen's view? It would seem that he made a distinction between those who called on the Lord and Christ's true disciples: "Those who call (on the name of Christ) are distinct from the church and the disciples are light for them, just as Christ is light for the church."[57]

Origen is even more explicit in his exegesis of Paul's threefold address "to the church of God established at Corinth, to those who have been made holy in Christ Jesus, called to be saints with all those who, in whatever place it may be, call on the name of Jesus Christ our Lord."[58] "We have shown," he claims, "that the only ones who are worthy of praise are those who can be called church, whereas those who are worthy of blame, but should not be seen as separated from us, and because they are still struggling against sin, are those who call (on the name of the Lord) and are not yet church. Let us therefore hasten to leave the company of those who call (on the name of Christ) and go up to the church without spot or wrinkle."[59]

According to Origen, there should be no remarrying in that church without spot or wrinkle. It should not be forgotten that, in the period in which he was writing, there were second, third or even fourth marriages in the church. Origen was careful to point out in this context that remarriage was an obstacle preventing the person who married again from achieving an ecclesiastical dignity (bishop, presbyter, deacon or widow). He also believed that the person who remarried was probably excluded from the church without spot or wrinkle, but was not definitively condemned. He supported his argument by an exegesis of 1 Corinthians 2: "I recall having said . . . that there is a difference between 'the church' and 'those who call on the name of the Lord.' I believe that the person who has married only once, the virgin and the one who has preserved chastity are of the church of God, whereas, even if his conduct is exemplary and he excels in all virtues, the one who remarries does not belong to that 'church' or to the number of those who are without spot or wrinkle or to anything similar, but is in the second rank and is one of those who calls on the name of the Lord. They are, however, saved in the name of Christ, although they are not crowned by him."[60]

There were therefore baptized Christians who called on the name of the Lord and whom Origen did not regard as being really of the "Church" because they had remarried. How, then, should those who did not achieve an ecclesiastical dignity, but who nonetheless kept themselves pure by not remarrying and therefore belonged to the church without spot or wrinkle, be described? It is hardly possible not to be reminded in this context of the lay people who, according to Clement of Alexandria, had to be the husband of only one woman. Seen in that light, lay people may be regarded as baptized Christians who have married only once and are therefore members of the church without spot or wrinkle and who share in the "assembly of the first-born." They do not perhaps represent the whole of the faithful, but they have to be distinguished from those who "call on the name of the Lord."

Does this image of the layman correspond to the reality or does it only represent an ideal? It is possible that, for a very short time, during the period when Clement was living and teaching in Alexandria, the term "lay" described those who were regarded as the true members of the church—in other words, those who refrained from marrying again. It was probably no longer the same at the time of Origen, however much he may have regretted it.

The main task or ministry that lay people had therefore at the time of Origen was to free the "priests and Levites" from any material concern that might prevent them from giving themselves totally to the service of God.[61] But their religious role did not stop there. They also shared in the synaxis, the church's meeting for worship, on condition that they respected the conventions of prayer, like the bishop, the presbyter or the deacon.[62] In the explanation that he gives of his point of view on this question in his Discourse with Heracleides—an exposition in which he presents this point of view as his own personal one—Origen basically does no more than simply take up Clement of Rome's idea that everyone should participate in the liturgy, "each one keeping to his own rank . . . without infringing the rules prescribed for his function."[63]

Origen or the Stumbling Block
of the Lay Didaskalos

The famous master of Alexandria was not a presbyter. Although he was honored and consulted by Christians everywhere, he learned to his cost that this placed him in a difficult situation when, in 216 or thereabouts, during a journey to Palestine, the bishops of Caesarea and Jerusalem invited him to preach in their churches. Demetrius, the bishop of Alexandria, who was, of course, Origen's own bishop, reacted very quickly to this by protesting and calling Origen back to Alexandria, since he regarded it as wrong for a layman to preach a homily in the presence of bishops. Alexander of Jerusalem and Theoctistus of Caesarea, however, objected to Demetrius' argument.

According to Eusebius, Demetrius "added, in his letter, that laymen had never been known to preach in the presence of bishops and that even now this had never happened, but I do not know how he can say such an obviously wrong thing. For wherever there are men who are able to do good for their brethren, they are asked by their holy bishops to address the people. Examples of this are Evelpis being invited by Neon at Lavanda, Paulinus by Celsus at Iconium and Theodorus by Atticus, another of our blessed brothers, at Synnados. It is probable that the same happens in other places without our knowing it."[64]

There were, then, in Cappadocia at the beginning of the third century, educated laymen teaching not only in special schools, but also being entrusted with the task of preaching homilies. The bishop of Alexandria, who, Eusebius suspected, was probably jealous of Origen, refused to give a privilege that might apparently have been given quite easily in other places to a lay didaskalos belonging to his own church. He also continued to refuse to make Origen a presbyter. Later, however, Origen had to entrust Heraclas with the task of teaching the elements of faith to beginners because of the overwhelming numbers of pupils coming to his catechetical school and devote himself exclusively to the more advanced students. It was then that the bishop of Alexandria decided to admit not Origen himself, but Heraclas to the presbyterate. It is undoubtedly because of this treatment that Origen, deeply wounded by the mean actions of his bishop, finally agreed to be ordained by the bishop of Caesarea.

Heraclas succeeded Demetrius as bishop of Alexandria and was replaced as head of the catechetical school by Dionysus, one of Origen's students, who in turn followed Heraclas as bishop of the see. Origen, then, was the last of the great lay *didaskaloi* or catechetical teachers.

Catechists and Doctors

By teaching only the more advanced students in his school, Origen was able to count on greater understanding and discretion on the part of a more educated public. He was also able to refine his exegesis with greater freedom, to be more fearless and daring in his interpretations and in this way fulfill what he saw as his true function, that of doctor. At the same time, as we have seen, he handed over the task of teaching beginners and catechumens to Heraclas. The work of the catechist was more simple and called for less originality than that of the doctor and for this reason may have seemed less prestigious. Yet the paradox is that the catechist, Heraclas, was ordained by Bishop Demetrius, whereas the doctor, Origen, was condemned to remain as a layman.

There can be no doubt that personal questions played a part in Demetrius' decision, but the fact of his ordination of Heraclas rather than of Origen is, apart from this, quite easy to explain. The catechist's work was with the mass of the people. He determined to a great extent the entry of Christians into the church and played an important part in defining the identity of the church group. He had to remain in close contact with the bishops, who were guardians of the rule of faith and of the unity of the Christian group. We know too that catechists could also be involved in liturgical activities.[65] For all these reasons, the bishops were clearly led to integrate their catechists into the ranks of their clergy. The elitist teaching of a man like Origen, on the other hand, could hardly have been seen as essential for the community at least by a bishop of apparently rather limited vision such as Demetrius.

The earliest texts in which the function of the catechist is mentioned can be found in the *Pseudo-Clementine Literature.* Several apocryphal texts, including the *Letter of Saint Peter to James,* the

The Sarcophagus of Santa Maria Antiqua, the Forum, Rome

Photo by Roger Viollet

Epistle of Clement to James, the *Clementine Homilies* and the so-called *Clementine Recognitions,* are grouped under this heading. The dating of these texts is difficult because there are so many different strata and rereadings. In their final form, they can be situated in the fourth century, but the source material probably originated at the time of Origen, that is, in the first half of the third century, and elements of even earlier material, including the passages referring to the catechist, were undoubtedly reused in this original nucleus.[66]

Clement's letter to James contains a fictitious account of the accession of Clement to the episcopate. It insists on catechists carrying out their function only after they have themselves been catechized and on their being knowledgeable, experienced and clear-thinking men of irreproachable character.[67] According to the letter of Clement to James, the catechist's function was one that was not dependent on what we would later call the clergy. The catechist is presented in this letter as a recruiting officer. The author compares the church to a ship and calls on his readers to see "God as the master of that ship, Christ as the pilot, the bishop as the man on lookout, the presbyters as those in charge of the crew, the deacons as leading the oarsmen, the catechists as the recruiting officers and the rest of the brethren as the passengers."[68]

This independent catechist, however, must have been an embarrassment to the final editor of the letter of Clement, either because he seemed to him to be an anachronism or because he wanted him to disappear so that he could give greater authority to the bishop as the recruiting officer. For whatever reason, the fact remains that, in his use of the metaphor of the church as a ship, the final editor retains the technical terms bishop, presbyter and deacon, but "forgets" the specific term "catechist" and simply alludes in a general way to the "recruiter."[69] Later, the *Pseudo-Clementine Homilies* refer to catechist-presbyters, whom the faithful are to "honor" by giving them material support, just as they have to "honor" their bishop, deacons and widows in the same way.[70] Later still, however, in the *Pseudo-Clementine Recognitions,* there is no trace of the function of "catechist." It seems to have finally disappeared.

When the "independent" function of catechist had apparently become an embarrassment, an attempt seems to have been made to obscure it by giving the bishop total control with regard to faith. At the same time, however, the teaching of catechumens continued to be essential for the survival of Christian communities. Clearly the bishop could not devote the whole of his time to this task, with the result that he tended increasingly to entrust it to his presbyters, especially when the Christian communities began to grow in numbers. It was at this time that the function of simple catechist ceased to exist in practice.

This was not, however, the final transformation of this function. It became more important again as soon as it was entrusted to the presbyters, to such an extent that an attempt was even made to find a more noble title for the task. In the middle of the third century, Cyprian of Carthage was speaking about doctor-presbyters who were helped by doctor-readers.[71] By that time, then, even the term "catechist" had disappeared.

Culture and Priesthood

The official teaching of the catechumens was not the only sphere in which the need for culture was felt in the church. Was the clergy always equal to this task? Origen clearly doubted this when he said: "I acknowledge that it is one thing to carry out the functions of the priesthood and another thing to be well instructed and perfect in everything."[72]

Certainly, after his unpleasant encounters with his bishop, Demetrius, Origen had good reason to be bitter, and this may have made him partial in his judgments. On the other hand, however, he was not alone in speaking about the lack of culture among the clergy. We know that, in a number of cases, the bishop himself may not have been well educated. The *Apostolic Church Order*, which was edited between the middle of the second and the beginning of the fourth century, considers this hypothesis calmly: "The candidate (for the episcopate) should be well instructed and able to explain the scriptures. If he is not well educated, he should be gentle and filled with charity for everyone. If a man gives cause for any kind of criticism, he should not be raised by the people to the episcopate."[73]

In the same *Apostolic Church Order*, we read too that a well-instructed reader who is able to speak clearly and act as an evangelist also has his place in the Christian community. Such a reader would undoubtedly have been able to help a bishop who was not very cultured. He would probably also have done more than simply "read." He would also have interpreted the texts and preached the homily during the liturgy of the word, which may at that time still have been celebrated separately from the eucharistic synaxis. Under those conditions, culture and priesthood might not have been dependent on each other and the reader would have had an "honorable" place in the community. According to the *Apostolic Church Order*, that place was after the presbyters and before the deacons.

Very soon, however, or more slowly, according to the particular place, it became necessary for a close bond to be established between culture and priesthood. As in the case of the catechist, we can gain an insight, by reading the *Pseudo-Clementine Literature*, into the stages of a development that led to the end of a mainly cultural function and the emergence of a cultic hierarchy. The so-called Letter of Saint Peter to James, which is full of Judaeo-Christianity, insists firmly on the qualities that were needed in the case of a man to whom the books would be entrusted. In another text, the "Solemn Commitment," James is presumed to be carrying out these instructions and to be ensuring that those to whom the books were entrusted should commit themselves to be subject to the bishop. He even goes so far as to say:

> Listen to me, my brothers and companions in the service (of God)! If we put these books at the disposal of the first person who comes, and if they are falsified by daring men or if their true meaning is distorted by (false) interpretations— and you know that this has already happened—those who are sincerely looking for the truth will always be reduced to go astray. It is better, then, that we should keep them in our own hands and that we should only communicate them with all the above-mentioned precautions and only to those who want to live piously and to work for the salvation of others.[74]

The function of interpreting, then, was taken over by the bishop. This change can be expressed in rather naive and sectarian terms by saying that it is possible, by reading the "Solemn Commitment" to understand why the cultural functions were gradually absorbed by the cultic ministries. It was because of the fear of heresy and the resulting breakdown of the Christian community in which heresy occurred that it was regarded as necessary to preserve intellectual unity. This unity strengthened the identity and the shape of the assembly in which the eucharist was celebrated.

Laity and Clergy: From Difference to Inequality

At the beginning of the third century, the term "lay" was used to describe men—and not, it would seem, women—who belonged to the church, but were not bishops, presbyters or deacons or who were not, in a more general way, members of the clergy. The layman was quite certainly regarded as inferior to the clergy at that time. He needed them and had a special need of the high priest (the bishop) for the remission of his sins. In principle, he could not reach the same level of perfection as his priests and levites in doctrine and at the same time he was treated less strictly than a deacon or a presbyter if he sinned.

From this period onward, the layman's function was to release the priest and levite from all his material concerns, thus enabling him to devote himself exclusively to the service of the altar, a task that was necessary for everyone's salvation. It is here that we can find the true and concrete foundation for the distinction that came to be made between the laity and the clergy.

In fact, all the Christian teachers writing at the beginning of the third century took pains to relativize the titles and dignities common in the church on earth and to remind their readers that everyone is called to be one of the community of the righteous. Origen, for example, believed that everyone was moving toward a perfection that would end in a heavenly priesthood. Like Clement of Rome, he insisted that the laity shared fully in the eucharistic synaxis. Tertullian, on the other hand, thought that, in the absence of the clergy, laymen were all priests. The distinction between the clergy (or ministers of the altar) and the laity was, in those conditions, of a practical and symbolic and not of an ontological order. The fundamental problem is how to know where the results of this difference between clergy and laity in the practical and symbolic order ceased.

We have seen that Origen drew a number of conclusions from this at the penitential level, giving the priest the power to purify laymen and also to purify himself, so long as he did not sin against God. This question seems more than that of liturgical action to have been at the center of the debate. Tertullian too reacted with great animation against the church of the bishops in the matter of the power of the keys, contrasting that church with the church "insofar as it is spirit." In Rome, Hippolytus protested against the ease with which Bishop Callistus claimed to be able to grant remission of sins to those who came to him and reacted strongly against the theory according to which a bishop who had committed even a mortal sin should not be deposed.[75] During the first half of the third century, almost every Christian community was troubled by the question of how to know who had the power to remit the sins of others and to purify himself of his own sins.

If we think of the eucharist as the instrument of this purification, then at least that aspect of the eucharist was bound to be taken over by one minister who had been given the power to remit sins. Taking part in the eucharistic synaxis could, in that case, no longer be the same for everyone. There could no longer be simply a difference between clergy and laity in the practical distribution of roles. That difference between them came inevitably to be seen in the distribution of powers within the eucharistic assembly, and this meant that all the Christians taking part in that liturgy were no longer equal.

At the same time, whereas the bishops asserted and strengthened their power in the question of the remission of sins, lay people gradually ceased to exercise one of the rights—and it would be better to speak here of one of the duties—of all baptized Christians, namely the right or duty publicly to express, explain and hand on their faith. The functions of teaching, in other words, the functions of the doctor and the catechist, were made offices and handed over to the clergy.

Despite this, however, the gulf between clergy and laity was not total at that time. They were not regarded by everyone as definitively separate, because the earthly titles could possibly be called into question by the heavenly titles. Nor was their separation seen by all Christian thinkers as absolute, because, at least according to Tertullian, a layman could, in the absence of the clergy, carry out priestly functions. The separation between clergy and laity was in fact based on a distribution of roles which operated, as Tertullian was very careful to point out, with the full consent of the people.

Insofar as this distribution of roles was not regarded as untouchable and as long as Christians were aware that it could be changed, even though changes were in fact quite exceptional, members of the clergy and lay people continued to associate with each other on a basis of equal dignity and to share the same tasks and duties. This is certainly what seems to have happened in the first stage of the history of the laity. In his insistence that they should all remain monogamous, Clement of Alexandria associated laymen quite naturally with presbyters and deacons. Again, both in reminding lay people that they were priests and that they could, under certain circumstances, carry out priestly functions, and in pointing out that members of the clergy might have to be recruited at certain times from among the laity, Tertullian concluded that neither the clergy nor the laity should be permitted to remarry. Both in Carthage and in Alexandria, the reappearance of the term "lay" was as unexpected as the occurrence of discussions about second marriages, and we are bound therefore to ask whether the word "lay" was not employed there with the essential aim of galvanizing Christians by reminding them that they belonged to a priestly people and that they had certain obligations resulting from this.

Tertullian continued to point out that those obligations had to be fulfilled by everyone and not simply by the clergy or by a small elite acting as a reserve for the clergy. Origen, on the other hand, merely regretted that there were married people in the church who had married for the second and a third time. Without taking part in a battle that he knew in advance he would lose, he consoled himself with the thought that only those who had married once were really part of the church without spot or wrinkle.

In the case of Origen, the frontier between clergy and laity began to close and the inequality also began to enter the way of life of the Christian people and even penetrate into their attitudes. This inequality was justified by a metaphor—that of the high priest who alone was permitted to enter the holy of holies and who alone was entitled to offer the sacrifice that purified. It was also relativized by a metaphor—that of the heavenly hierarchy which did not correspond exactly to the human hierarchy on earth. The first of these two metaphors added strength to the historical tendency to make more and more Christians without being too concerned about quality, apart from confining both the ideal of perfection and power in the church to a small number of "chosen" members of the people of God. At the same time, the second metaphor, which might possibly have acted as a challenge to the formation of an elite within the chosen people of God, soon came to act as an anesthetic, since it was, according to Origen, after all possible to become a priest in heaven without having been one on earth.

The result was that the laity, who belonged to the chosen people of priests, very soon became the people of their priests.

CHAPTER 5

Clergy and Laity:
An Institutional Barrier

The Beginning of the Third Century:
A Decisive Time

In the history of Christian institutions, this time was one of the crucial turning points. We have very little information about the life of Christian communities and their organization during the whole of the second century and what we have is often enigmatical and difficult to situate in time and space. At the beginning of the third century, on the other hand, the churches can be seen clearly as well structured and firmly situated in the Roman empire.

At that time, the local Christian community, the *ecclesia*, was at the basis of every institution. Each church was a self-sufficient living organism that was able to create all the specific ministries that it found indispensable. There was only one exception to this principle of the autonomy of the local churches: the consecration of the bishop. Each bishop had to be consecrated by three existing bishops, and these were usually bishops of neighboring communities. This acted as a safeguard for the bond between the local churches.

In addition to this, apart from a certain identity in the matter of faith, there were also, at the beginning of the third century, several institutional constants in each local church. Christian communities almost everywhere were governed by a monarchical episcopate. One bishop and only one per city was regarded as sufficient to guarantee orthodoxy and unity. Nowhere was a bishop allowed to move from one community to another. Each bishop held his post for life and was the bishop for his own local church and for no other. He was not a bishop in an absolute sense. This monarchical episcopate was strengthened by the principle of the apostolic succession. Finally and most importantly, there was what can be regarded from this time onward as a constant aspect of the Christian churches, namely the distinction between *ordo* and *plebs*—in other words, between the clergy and the laity.

This last observation may strike the reader as surprising, since we have spent a long time in a vain search for traces of the laity in the second century. Should we therefore conclude that the silence of the documents is deceptive? Did a slow development, on the basis of particular local characteristics which have left no trace behind in the history of the period, really take place during the second half of the second century? It is possible, but why should we postulate that history necessarily takes place in the form of a slow and regular evolution? Could attitudes not have been transformed quite quickly and the creation of a clergy and a laity have been brought about suddenly? This hypothesis would certainly be more in accordance with the situation reflected in the available documents. Or is it quite unacceptable? There are many cases of times in history when events have speeded up and change has occurred quite abruptly. Do those who were born in 1965 remember the time when mass had to be said in Latin, when it was forbidden to eat meat on Friday, and when to receive communion, which was in itself seen as a purely individual act, in the hand was regarded as sacrilegious? Would a young person of eighteen know that not very long before he was born no one turned round to stare at a priest wearing a soutane and a biretta, but that a young Roman Catholic curate who was bold enough to dress in the dark gray suit of an Anglican clergyman would arouse curious glances? So, if the twentieth century church has experienced changes in its way of life in less time than it takes to sit for an examination, why should Christian communities at the end of the second century not have been transformed in two decades?

At the beginning of the third century, then, the impression that we have from all the Christian authors—Tertullian writing for the church of Carthage, Hippolytus writing for the Roman church and Clement and Origen teaching and writing for the church in Alexandria—is that there was at that time a frontier within the baptized people of God dividing the Christian social group into two—clergy and laity. Within each of these two groups, various functions lived side by side. Attempts were made in documents specifically dealing with this question to define and justify the outline of this frontier separating the clergy from the laity and to define the duties and the roles within each of these two groups. This is usually called the "canonico-liturgical documentation." The text of the *Apostolic*

Constitutions that we have already discussed in connection with the question of the uneducated bishop and the reader forms part of this documentation.[1] Other texts that are generally included within it are the *Apostolic Tradition* and the *Didascalia*, both of which supply us with important information about different aspects of the relationship between the clergy and the laity and enable us to give an exact content to the concept of the laity in contrast to that of the clergy.

A "NORMATIVE" TEXT: THE APOSTOLIC TRADITION

The canonico-liturgical texts contain precepts of a moral and disciplinary order. These precepts are presented as having been established by the apostles or by Jesus himself. The way in which these writings are grouped under the generic heading of church regulations describes their nature very well—they are longer or shorter series of canons and constitutions. Some of the texts claim to provide an integral and organic church rule of law. All of them in fact contain a continuous mixture of a description of real practices and an expression of their authors' desire for reform.

One of these canonico-liturgical documents which appeared at the beginning of the third century is the *Apostolic Tradition*. There is no certainty with regard to the date when it was written or edited, its author or compiler or the place where it originated, but we can be fairly sure that what we have is a document that claims to describe what was taking place in the author's church and to define what should be done in that church. It also gives the clear impression that improvisation was still the rule in the liturgy. For the historian, the *Apostolic Tradition* also reflects many of the questions that were being asked by Christians at the beginning of the third century. Even when it is obscure, the text also gives us glimpses of the conflicts that the author or compiler was trying to overcome.[2]

For several reasons, the *Apostolic Tradition* has an exceptional place in the enormous canonico-liturgical literature. First of all, it is exceptional because it presents its data so clearly. It is the first document to provide us with exact criteria by which we can define membership of the clergy. It is also exceptional because it was successful. This success is obvious from the number of times that it was copied and introduced into all the great canonico-liturgical collections and from its frequent reinterpretations. Even today, thanks largely to the work done by B. Botte, it continues to inspire liturgical reforms.[3]

The Clergy—A Basic Structure

The *Apostolic Tradition* does not give us any positive definition of the whole of the laity. All that it does is to enable us to define it negatively, that is, by tracing the outline of its frontiers in the impression left on the whole of the Christian people by the ministers. In 200 A.D. or thereabouts, the clergy consisted exclusively of one bishop with his presbyters and deacons. This does not mean that these were the only ones to carry out a permanent function that was necessary for the spread of the Christian community. All that it means is that all the other functions or states that may have existed at the time in the Christian communities were categorically excluded from the clergy. On what criteria was this exclusion based?

If we are to understand this frontier between the clergy and the laity and how it was justified, we must go back to the classical text in the *Apostolic Tradition* on widows, which represents the first attempt to use technical language to justify this frontier.

> When a widow is instituted (*kathistasthai*),
>> she is not ordained (*cheirotonein*),
>> but is called by (that) title.
>> If her husband has been dead for a long time, she should
>> be instituted, but if her husband has been dead for only a
>> short time, she should not be trusted. But, (even) if she is
>> aged, she should be tested for a time. For often the
>> passions age with the one who gives them a place within
>> herself.
> The widow should be instituted (*kathistasthai*)
>> by the word only
>> and she should join the other widows.
> But the hand should not be laid on her (*cheirotonein*),
>> because she does not offer the oblation (*prosphora*)
>> and she has no liturgical service (*leitourgia*).
> Ordination (*cheirotonia*)
>> is done for the clergy (*kleros*)
>> with liturgical service (*leitourgia*) in mind.
> The widow is instituted (*kathistasthai*)

for prayer,
which is (the shared role) of all.[4]

There must have been a good deal of pressure exerted on behalf of these widows to be ordained and thus to form part of the clergy. The author of the *Apostolic Tradition* rejects this solution and takes advantage of the situation to define the different Christian groups. The members of the clergy (*kleros*) receive the laying on of hands (*cheirotonia*) because they have a role to play in the liturgical service (*leitourgia*). The functions that have no cultic role to play do not have to receive a laying on of hands. An installation or institution (*katastasis*) is sufficient for the community to recognize a service carried out within it. The conclusion is also curious. These widows are to be instituted, but that "institution" simply enables them to dedicate themselves to what all Christians should do, namely to prayer. There is, then, a certain ambiguity in the status of the widow, which is already present in the first letter to Timothy.

This restriction of the *kleros*—which is a term that was not often used at the beginning of the third century—to the ministerial triad of bishop, presbyters and deacons is found in all the Christian writings of the same period—those of Origen, Hippolytus and Tertullian. It is interesting, however, to note that, in the case of Tertullian, the term *clerus* does not apply to the whole of the *ordines*. Widows were for him a special ordo within the Christian community and they did not form part of the *clerus*. Were they therefore lay people? The texts referring to widows are not explicit and such subtle questions are not asked in them.

Although not a word is said about it in the *Apostolic Tradition,* the question of the frontier between the clergy and the laity is in a sense a repetition of that between man and woman. We only have to look at the text edited by the *Canons of Hippolytus,* a new version of the *Apostolic Tradition* made about 340 A.D. According to this text,

> Widows who have been established should not be ordained.
> . . . For them, there are the precepts of the apostle. . . . They
> should not be ordained, but they should be prayed over, for
> ordination is for men. The function of widows is important
> by virtue of everything that is incumbent upon them: fre-
> quent prayer, the care of the sick and frequent fasting.[5]

"Prayer, which is the shared role of all"

Photo by Leonard von Matt
Rome, Catacomb of the Jordani

The great merit of the *Apostolic Tradition* is that it was able to justify this ambiguous status by means of a single logical explanation. This justification is the same both for men and for women: it is the carrying out of the *leitourgia* which justifies ordination (*cheirotonia*), which is the indisputable sign of membership of the clergy. The author of the *Apostolic Tradition* seems to have been prepared to maintain this position, despite all the storms raging around him. It presupposes a limited conception of a leitourgia closely connected with the offering of an oblation (*prosphora*). The terms had developed since, for example, the time of Clement of Rome, who had recommended all Christians, including lay people, to exercise their function or *leitourgia*.

Should the Doctor Be a Member of the Clergy or a Layman?

The author of the *Apostolic Tradition* believed that there could be no objection to the functions that were not directly concerned with the liturgy being carried out by laymen. He expresses his view about this quite clearly in the text referring to the doctor: "When, after prayer, the doctor lays his hand on the catechumens, he should pray and send them away. Whether the one who teaches is either a member of the clergy or a layman, he should do this."[6]

Hermas believed that the doctor walked according to the Holy Spirit and, as we have already seen, Justin felt no need to justify his activity as a doctor by being ordained or by any special status.[7] He traced that activity back to the grace that had been given to him. We have, however, observed in the case of Origen that it was not at all easy at the beginning of the third century simply to be both a layman and a doctor. We know too that, since that time, the bishop came to be the doctor *par excellence* of his church and that all the heads of the school of Alexandria seem also to have been ordained presbyters. Tertullian, on the other hand, seems to have known independent doctors who were gifted with the charism of knowledge and that he situated these men alongside those other charismatics who were virgins and martyrs.[8] From the middle of the third century onward, however, Cyprian was to speak of doctor-presbyters as a firmly established institution. From then onward, the function of the doctor seems to have been totally assimilated into a clerical function.

The text in the *Apostolic Tradition* dealing with the doctor has to be situated, then, at a time when there was a strong tendency to demand that the doctor should be a member of the clergy. It is significant, however, that the author of the *Apostolic Tradition* was discreetly opposed to this tendency. This is clear from his observation that the doctor could be "either a member of the clergy or a layman." All the same, it has to be stressed that the function of the doctor is presented in the *Apostolic Tradition* as being exercised within the context of baptismal instruction and is therefore closer to the function of the catechist as outlined in the *Pseudo-Clementine Literature* than that of the doctor as exercised by a man like Origen.[9] The doctor described in the *Apostolic Tradition* did not provide teaching at a advanced level for highly educated Christians anxious to increase their theological knowledge, but was introducing catechumens to truths established by the rule of faith that they would confess when they were baptized. That teaching, obviously at a more modest level, was still important for the Christian community, and it is understandable that certain members of the clergy wanted to supervise it. On the other hand, however, the context of baptism, in which the doctor described in the *Apostolic Tradition* played his part, seems also to have led him to carry out a number of para-liturgical functions such as prayer and the laying on of hands. The distinction that the author of the *Apostolic Tradition* apparently continued to make between the ministers of the liturgy who took part in the oblation and the doctor was therefore all the more significant and demonstrates how strictly he applied his theological criterion of distinguishing between clergy and laity.

A Recognized Lay Function: That of Reader

There can be little doubt that the lector or reader was originally very close to the doctor. He was an educated member of the community who enjoyed a certain prestige. According to the *Apostolic Church Order*, he may even have been better educated than the bishop.[10] There are indications in the *Pseudo-Clementine Writings* that there was a time when the reader, who was the custodian of the books, was also the custodian of orthodoxy.[11] We have the impression from these texts that this situation might well have become dangerous as soon as power came to be concentrated in the hands of the bishop surrounded by his presbyters. But, from the time when the reader worked alongside the doctor, it is clear that the prestige of the latter's function began to diminish once it had been dismantled.

This is certainly the case in the *Apostolic Tradition*, where the reader is presented as exclusively responsible for reading, but not for interpreting the text: "The reader is instituted (*katistasthai*), when the bishop gives him the book, because he does not receive the laying on of hands (*cheirotonia*)."[12]

It should be noted that the author of the *Apostolic Tradition* is very careful to point out that the reader did not receive the laying on of hands. Following the logic defined above, he included him among the laity. The readers, then, as Christians who were most concerned with the cultic aspect of the function of teaching, were also anxious, it would seem, to be included among the ministers of the altar. This indicates how dominant the clergy had become by that time and how all those who fulfilled any service in the community were drawn to the clerical status. The readers must have tried to come closer to those involved in the liturgy rather than to the doctors because the place occupied by the former seemed to them to be more prestigious.

Another Frontier: Ordination and Installation

The Greek text of the *Apostolic Tradition* is lost. The different versions that we possess and the various changes in the text, however, enable us to reconstitute a text which is probably quite close to the original. A text reconstructed in this way, on the other hand, will always contain at least some hypothetical elements. In addition, for several decades now, research into the Christian ministries has pointed with increasing clarity to the frontier between ordination (by a laying on of hands known as *cheirotonia*, reserved for the three "orders" of bishop, presbyter and deacon) and simple "installation" (by *cheirothesia*, reserved for the functions). This frontier was strengthened by the statement made in the motu proprio *Ministeria quaedam* of 15 August 1972 that only the church's bishops, presbyters and deacons were clergy and that the other functions were regarded as "lay ministries."

What is interesting, however, is that this distinction between clergy and "lay ministries" had already been made in the *Apostolic Tradition*, a document containing the earliest rituals of ordination and in which a technical terminology was beginning to form. The bishop, the man who is chosen by all the people, receives "ordination" (*cheirotonia*). According to the text, which was visibly changed, the deacon is "instituted": "When a deacon is instituted (*katistasthai*), he should be chosen in the way described above, the bishop alone laying on hands (*cheirotonia*)." The language was not firmly established at this time, but it is obvious that the laying on of hands (or of one hand) was reserved for the triad of ministers (the bishop, presbyters and deacons). The others, as we have seen in the case of the widow and the reader, did not receive this laying on of hands.

Quite logically, the virgin was also not ordained, since she carried out no cultic function: "The virgin should not receive the laying on of hands, but her decision alone makes her a virgin."[13] In the case of the sub-deacon, the laying on of hands is contrasted with nomination: "The sub-deacon will not receive the laying on of hands, but he will be named so that he may follow the deacon."[14] This distinction seems to have been associated with an intention to give the function of sub-deacon a lower status.

Finally, the author speaks about the gifts of healing. He relies in this case on the ability of Christians to discern between the various charisms: "If anyone says: 'I have received the gift of healing in a revelation,' hands should not be laid on him. The facts themselves will show whether or not he is speaking the truth."[15]

These short texts provide us with different ways of recognizing a non-clerical function. They all make one very obvious point, namely that ordination should not be conferred routinely on all those who claimed to exercise a function in the church. The theme is essentially negative. But in making this negative point, these texts have a certain inner logic. The reader is instituted when he is given the book, which is the sign of his function. Virginity is a state of life, and the title "virgin" is exclusively dependent on a personal decision made on the part of the person concerned. The sub-deacon is the one who follows the deacon, and his name is a sufficient designation in itself. Finally, it is logical to expect those who claim to have the gift of healing to show their ability to heal by healing.

An Extreme Case: The Confessor

The same logic is also to be found in the well-known passage about confessors. Here is the text as established by comparing the eastern versions:

> If a confessor has been arrested for the name of the Lord, the hand should not be laid on him for the diaconate or the presbyterate, since he possesses the honor of the presbyter-

ate by virtue of his confession. But if he is instituted as bishop, the hand should be laid on him.

If, however, there is a confessor who has not been taken before the authority and who has not been arrested or put into prison or condemned to any other punishment, but who has been mocked for the name of our Lord and punished with a household chastisement, if he has confessed (his faith), the hand should be laid on him for every order of which he is worthy.[16]

If we are to interpret this text correctly, we must put ourselves in the position of Christians of that period and try to think as they did. A person who confessed his faith to the point of suffering martyrdom and dying, for it was regarded as "possessed by the Spirit." As a martyr, he was imitating Christ perfectly and filled with the Spirit. Christians of the time therefore did not see why, since he already possessed the Spirit, that Spirit should be given to him again by a laying on of hands. The man who had suffered in order to bear witness to his faith, then, "possessed the honor of the presbyterate by virtue of his confession." There was simply no need to lay hands on him for him to be a presbyter or a deacon. It is, moreover, known that these confessors were a kind of "reserve" for these functions and that the oldest confessors undoubtedly became presbyters while the others became deacons.

The logic of the palaeo-Christian church also enables us to understand why this *cheirotonia* (by means of a laying on of the hand or hands) could not be extended to include the bishop. We have in fact already seen that there could be only one bishop for each community as the sign of the unity of that community. Since the Spirit could not be divided and therefore be the source of division, confession did not, *ipso facto*, make one a bishop, since this would call the unity of the church into question. It was therefore necessary to ordain by a laying on of hands the one whom the community chose as its bishop, even if he was a confessor of faith.

A Portrait of the Troubled Life of a Slave Who Became the Bishop of Rome

At the beginning of the third century, Callistus was the first slave to become the bishop of Rome. He owed his career in the church as much to his management skills as to the fact that he was a confessor. His case is clear evidence that a humble origin was not an obstacle to becoming a bishop.

The *Apostolic Tradition* in fact contains a list of professions and activities that were forbidden to Christians, but apart from these cases of impediments to baptism, the church seems to have been very tolerant and democratic. According to the author of the *Apostolic Tradition*, anyone aspiring to baptism should not be the proprietor of a house of prostitution, an actor, a gladiator, a *bestiarius* (a fighter of wild beasts) or a public servant working in the sphere of the Roman games, a priest or a keeper of idols, a magistrate of a city, a prostitute, a sexual pervert or a favorite. If the candidate for baptism was a sculptor, he should not make idols. If he was a charioteer, he should not take part in the games. If he was a soldier of subordinate rank, he should not kill. The catechumen or the full believing member of the church was not to enlist as a soldier. The author of the *Apostolic Tradition* was more tolerant, however, in the case of teachers whose profession obliged them to impart profane learning to their students. He allowed them to continue to exercise their profession so long as they had no other skills.[17] The *Apostolic Church Order*, on the other hand, forbade the teaching of profane or pagan doctrines. It also refused to allow the Christian to be an augur, a sorcerer or a purifier.[18]

All these prohibitions can easily be explained on the basis of Christian morality, but it should not be forgotten that they also had economic implications. In the middle of the third century, Cyprian, the bishop of Carthage, asked one of his colleagues, for example, to forbid a Christian to open a school for acting. It is worth noting in this context that he also advised his colleague to provide the actor in question with other means of subsistence or, if the local church lacked the funds to do this, to send the man to the church of Carthage, which would take care of him. Such moral prohibitions, then, often led the church to add its grain of salt to the economic system.[19] As the church grew in size and numbers, money began to occupy an increasingly important place in its life.

To return to Callistus I, however, it may seem paradoxical that a slave should reach the episcopate in these conditions. But then, Callistus was not a slave like other slaves. He was a special case, but not so much because he was a slave and a Christian, since many slaves were also Christians, either because they had been converted personally or simply because they had been baptized at the same time as all the other members of their master's household. We do not in fact know which of the two kinds of convert Callistus was. What we do know, however, is that he was very capable in financial matters and that it was this skill, together with his confessor's crown, which he acquired later, that enabled him to pass from slavery to the episcopate. But this rise from lowly status to high office was not achieved without difficulty. All the information that we have about his career comes to us from Hippolytus, the Roman presbyter who was his rival and sworn enemy.[20]

These, then, are the data supplied by Hippolytus. Callistus' master entrusted his slave with money so that he could devote himself to banking transactions, but Callistus became insolvent and, when his creditors complained about the money that he owed them, he tried to run away. This attempt failed and he was condemned by his master to work in the mill. In the hope that he would eventually pay his debts, he was allowed to leave the mill. The next that we hear of him is making a disturbance at the synagogue on the sabbath when he was demanding his money from his Jewish debtors. These Jews protested to the authorities and Callistus was condemned to work in the mines in Sardinia, this time, however, as a Christian. He was set free, thanks to the intervention of Marcia, the concubine of Emperor Commodus. Callistus' return seems to have embarrassed Victor, who was bishop of Rome at the time and who apparently did not want him back. He gave a discreet pension to Callistus, who was now the proud possessor of the title of confessor.

In 199 A.D. Victor was succeeded as bishop of Rome by Zephirinus, whom Hippolytus calls a "simple and uneducated man" and who certainly lacked Victor's discretion. Zephirinus entrusted Callistus with the task of arranging burials and burial places. Like all citizens, Christians were able to organize themselves in burial associations and to acquire and manage property used for this purpose. Callistus carried out this task very efficiently, and when Zephirinus died in 217, he succeeded him.

Callistus, the slave who became a bishop, always took human weaknesses into account. Hippolytus, the conservative presbyter who defended tradition in the church, was always strenuously opposed to what he regarded as laxity. In his opinion, Callistus welcomed sinners as members of the church and was ready to grant them remission of their sins. He accepted men who had contracted a second or a third marriage into the clergy and even allowed existing members of the clergy to marry. It is interesting to note that the question of second and third marriages is not mentioned in the list of impediments to baptism in the *Apostolic Tradition*, and what caused offense to Hippolytus was only that such marriages could be tolerated in the case of the clergy. As Origen was to comment regretfully later, it was a simple fact that there were within the church Christians who had remarried once or even twice. Unlike Tertullian or Clement of Alexandria, Hippolytus did not try to impose the ideal of monogamy on the laity in spite of all opposition, but simply strove to maintain it among the clergy.

He seems to have been less hostile to the claim itself to remit sins and more opposed to the ease with which Callistus remitted sins. In indulging in the power to remit sins, the latter was undoubtedly following a tendency that was common at the time. Tertullian was reacting violently against this tendency when he made a sharp contrast between the spiritual church and the "church of the bishops" which usurped the power of the keys. How would Tertullian have reacted, then, if he had been introduced to the bishop of the *Didascalia?*

THE DIDASCALIA OR THE OMNIPOTENCE OF THE BISHOP

The Syrian church has left us with two major literary legacies. These are the first Christian novel—the *Pseudo-Clementine Writings*—and a vast canonico-liturgical document dating from the period around 230 A.D., the *Didascalia*. Whatever its literary genre may be, it is obvious that the monarchy was regarded as the ideal system for Christians of that time, both for civil society and for the church. It was a system that eliminated all conflict from the life of society. One of the *Pseudo-Clementine Homilies* is attributed to Peter, who, it is claimed, delivered it before ordaining Zacchaeus as bishop of Caesarea. He justifies the institution of the monarchical episcopate in the following way:

> "The great number of believers," he said, "must obey one leader if they are to live in harmony together. For the means of government which, based on the model of the monarchy, results in one leader being in command enables

all that leader's subjects, through good order, to enjoy peace. But if all men want to be in command and they all refuse to obey one leader, they will all, because of their very divisions, inevitably be lost. Do we not have convincing proof of this truth in the spectacle that is before our very eyes? There are so many kings now from one end of the earth to the other that war is being waged continuously. For each ruler has the pretext that he is making war against the power of the other. But if only one ruled over the whole earth, he would no longer have any reason to make war and would therefore live in permanent peace. In the end at least, in the age to come, God will establish one king of the entire universe over those who will be judged worthy of eternal life, so that certain peace will prevail, thanks to the monarchy. The whole community must therefore follow one man as its guide and honor him above all others as the image of God."[21]

The Bishop as the Father Hen of His Lay Chicks

This conception of the structures of the community that is considered and developed in the *Didascalia* within an Old Testament context was bound to lead to the laity being treated, at least collectively, as infants.

The bishop should love his laity like children. He will make them grow and will warm them with the zeal of his love, as (happens in the case of) eggs, so that chicks will emerge from them, or else he will care for them and make them grow as chicks, so that he will make them reach the size of chickens.[22]

This episcopal paternalism was, according to the *Didascalia*, to be practiced essentially with penitence in view. If a Christian deserved to be reprimanded, the bishop had to carry out that task, but only in order to lead him back on to the right path and to prevent him from being lost. In a long comment on Ezekiel 34, the bishop is invited to be a "sympathetic shepherd, full of love and tenderness" and to be continually concerned for his flock. He was to be the physician of his church and should "never cease to give medicine to cure those who were ill because of their sins." He had above all to avoid being proud of his power and becoming guilty of the word of the Lord: "You shall not lord it and have authority over them."[23]

"You shall not be quarrelsome and bad-tempered," the section in the *Didascalia* on the bishops concludes. "You shall not be scornful, haughty or arrogant."[24] This points clearly to the dangers and distortions of which all power used in an absolute way is capable. The author of the document was so aware of this risk that he felt compelled to insist on the right way for a bishop to exercise his power over his laity: "You must not be violent in your guidance of them. Do not be hard. Do not judge too quickly. Do not be without mercy. Do not despise the people who are in your hands. Do not conceal from them the words of repentance."[25] The bishop should not deal harshly with the sons of his people because they were in danger of leaving the church and the bishop himself would, in the opinion of the author of the *Didascalia*, then be responsible for their leaving: "The one who drives someone out of the church without mercy is simply killing him wickedly and shedding his blood without mercy." If the bishop refused to remit a penitent's sins, God would hand him over like food to the eternal fire.[26]

This appeal to treat lay people gently did not prevent the author of the *Didascalia* from insisting firmly that they should be submissive to their bishop. "Just as the layman should love his fellow layman, so too should he love, honor and revere his bishop as a father, a lord and God, after the almighty God, for it is to the bishop that it was said to the apostles: 'He who hears you hears me and he who rejects you rejects me and he who rejects me rejects him who sent me.'"[27]

Honoring: Honor and the Tithe

The word "honor" is very ambiguous in many languages, and this ambiguity is reflected in most translations of the *Didascalia*. Chapter 26 of Book II is entitled in the Syriac text, following the Greek text: "An exhortation to the people to honor the bishop." This heading was rendered by the later Arab and the Ethiopian translators as: "The laity are obliged to offer gifts to the church according to their resources." This change is evidence of a development in the relationship between the bishop and his people and emphasizes the increasingly financial role of the latter. "Honor" had by that time become the contribution of an "honorarium," in this case a tithe.[28]

The text in which the author of the *Didascalia* exhorts lay people to contribute their tithe to the bishop is at the same time paradoxically the one that contains possibly the finest, most lyrical and most theologically accurate definitions of the laity of the period. "Listen, then, all of you," the author writes, "lay people, the God's chosen church! For the first people—the Jewish people—were called church, but you (are called) the holy and accomplished Catholic Church, the holy multitude, the people (adopted) as an inheritance, the great church, the bride adorned for the Lord God."[29]

The same text goes on to remind those who have been called to this high vocation of their very concrete duties: "Everything that has been said so far—listen to it now, set aside the offerings, the tithes and the first-fruits for Christ, the true high priest, and set aside for his ministers (especially) the (saving) tithes of life, to him the beginning of whose name is the ten."[30]

The theme of the tithe allows the author of the *Didascalia* to make a comparison between the earlier people of God and his new people and to provide a description of the various ministries that existed at the time in his community:

> Listen, Catholic Church of God, you who have escaped from the ten plagues and have been given the ten commandments and have learned the law and kept the faith— you have kept the yod at the beginning of the name (of Yahweh) and have been made strong by the fullness of his glory. Instead of offering the sacrifices of that time, offer prayers now, petitions and thanksgiving. Instead of first-fruits, tithes, oblations and gifts, there are now offerings made to the Lord God by the bishops who are your princes of the priests. The priests and Levites are now the presbyters, deacons, widows and orphans.[31]

This section in the *Didascalia* ends by returning to the first theme of honoring, giving honor and manifesting one's submission and respect. Those who are to be honored by the laity are presented in typological and symbolic language:

The Levite and the prince of the priests is the bishop. He is the minister of the word and the mediator. For you he is also after God a doctor and a father. He has begotten you by water. He is your leader and guide. He is a powerful king who leads you to the place where the almighty God lives. Honor him as God, because the bishop is for you in the place of almighty God. The deacon occupies the place of Christ and you should love him. You should also love the deaconess, who is in the place of the Holy Spirit. For you, the elders represent the apostles. The widows and orphans should be seen as the altar.[32]

"It Is for You Lay People That It Was Said:
'Judge Not, That You Be Not Judged' "

The bishop of the *Didascalia* was omnipotent. He possessed a heavenly power. He ruled over the souls and bodies of the members of his flock and had therefore to be loved as a God.[33] One passage which has, as so often is the case in the *Didascalia*, been badly edited reveals a very equivocal relationship between God's benefits and the gifts that the laity had to make to the bishop. In order to "do honor" to their bishop, the lay people had in fact to bring him the fruits of the work of their hands for him to bless them:

Give him your first-fruits, your tithes, your offerings and your gifts and he must feed himself with them and also distribute them to the needy, each according to his need. Your gift will therefore be acceptable in the presence of the Lord your God, in an odor of peace in the heights of heaven in the presence of the Lord your God. He will bless you and increase for you the good things of his promise, for it is written in Wisdom: Every simple soul will be blessed and a blessing will be on the head of the one who gives.[34]

In this exchange between man and God, this sacred commerce in which the *do ut des* is present, the bishop's function is given a social and theological value. From the point of view of the theology of the bishop's function, the exchange made the bishop the priest of the new people of God, on the model of the high priest of the Old

Testament, and he was regarded as the intermediary between man and God.[35] This intermediary was given such a high value that lay people were advised not to trouble the bishop, but to approach the deacons:

> In every place, then, (the bishop) should be honored by all the laity, as is proper, by gifts, honors and the respect of the world. (The lay people) should have great trust in the deacons and should not be constantly troubling the leader, but they should tell him what they want through the *hupeterai*, that is, the deacons, for no one can approach the almighty Lord God if it is not the Christ. They will therefore teach the bishop, through the medium of the deacons, everything that they want to do and then they will do it.[36]

This theological overevaluation of the function of the bishop had an institutional consequence, namely that the lay person had not to call the bishop to account for the goods that he gave him. He had not to judge the way in which the bishop

> ruled and managed his stewardship, or when he gave, to whom, where, for better or for worse, or with justice. It is the Lord God who will call him to account, he who has entrusted him with that responsibility and who has judged him worthy to hold the priesthood of such a place.[37]

The author of the *Didascalia* seems to be describing the exact opposite of what some Christians are claiming now, at the end of the twentieth century. They want to share in the management of the church's goods and finances or at least they want to be able to give their advice. "You are commanded to give and it is for him to dispense"[38]—this is the categorical statement made in the document that was promulgated in the hope of managing the lives of Syrian Christians in the third century. "Do not watch over the bishop and do not call him to account, so that you will not speak evil of him, resist God and offend the Lord."[39]

The logical consequence of this attitude is that the laity came to be treated as inferior. The laity had therefore always to bear in mind what Jeremiah told them: "Does the clay say to the potter: 'You are not working and you have no hands'? Like the one who says to his father and his mother: 'Why have you begotten me?' "[40] The fact that laymen possessed the good things of this world compensated for making them theologically inferior in this way: "Your power is in the good things of this world."[41] But since this treasure can lose its value, it is better to invest in treasure in heaven:

> You shall not love the Lord only with your lips, like the people whom he reproached when he said of them: "This people honors me with their lips, but their heart is far from me." No, you must love and honor the Lord with all your strength. Be faithful in bringing gifts and do not remove yourself from the church. When you have received the eucharist of the sacrifice, throw away what you have in your hand (what you have at your disposal), in order to be associated with strangers, since that is gathered for the bishop, for all the strangers.[42]

The layman, then, who possessed the good things of this world, had to give to the bishop. He had, in other words, to honor him and give him an honorarium or fee. He was not to "appear before God empty-handed."[43] What the *Didascalia* was saying to him, in other words, was: Do good deeds and you will store up an eternal treasure in heaven "where neither moth nor worm consume and where thieves do not break in and steal."[44] The layman should not, however, believe that, if he gave in this way, he would gain power over the bishop. He would have his reward in heaven. On earth, he had to honor the bishop without judging him:

> While you are acting in this way, you are not to judge your bishop or your companion, because it is for you, lay people, that it was said: "Judge not and you will not be judged."[45] If you judge your brother and condemn him, you believe that your brother is guilty and it is yourself whom you are condemning, for you will be judged with the sinners. It is the bishops who are permitted to judge, for it is to them that it is said: "Be good stewards."[46]

The Place of the People in the Liturgical Space

The lay people are put firmly in their place in the *Didascalia*'s treatment of the relationships between the bishop and the laity in the question of material and spiritual goods. It was the bishop's task to persuade them to come together in the church,[47] where he had to take care that each lay person stayed in his proper place. The presbyters had a special place reserved for them on the east side of the house, and the bishop's throne had to be placed in the middle of the presbyters. The way in which the lay people were distributed in the assembly was fully in accordance with the accepted good conduct of the period. First the men and second the women and the old people were seated separately. Then the young people were allowed to sit down if there was room; otherwise they remained standing. The children were assembled together and supervised by their parents.

In the description of this organization of public worship given in the *Didascalia*, three groups are mentioned. There are the "leaders" of the people (the bishops and possibly also the presbyters), the "seculars," and finally the women.[48] If the word "secular" is translated as "lay," then one is obliged to exclude women from this group. "The deacon will ensure that each person who comes in goes to his place and that he does not sit down elsewhere. The deacon must also ensure that no one speaks, sleeps, laughs or makes signs."[49]

The aim of this excellent cultic arrangement was to make it possible for the part played by each person in the community to be respected. Woe above all to anyone who dared to take over the priestly functions of the bishop:

> Just as it was not permissible for the stranger, that is, anyone who was not a levite, to approach the altar or to offer anything without the high priest, so too must you do nothing without the bishop. If anyone were to do anything without the bishop, he would be doing it in vain, since it would not be imputed to him as a work. It is not in fact admissible for anyone to do anything outside the prince of priests. Bring your gifts, then, to the bishop either by yourselves or by means of the deacons, and when they have been received, he will share them out with justice.[50]

This text may, in its final form, go back to about 230 A.D., but it certainly contains earlier levels. It shows clearly that the bishop's "priestly" function was not presented entirely within an exclusively cultic or eucharistic framework. On the other hand, this same text from the *Didascalia* appears much later, in 380, in the *Apostolic Constitutions*, where the prohibition against taking over the priestly functions is developed and extended to include the layman who dared to do anything without the priest, that is, without the bishop:

> Just as Saul was told by Samuel, "You have acted foolishly," after having offered sacrifices in Samuel's absence, so too does the layman act in vain if he does something without the priest. And just as King Uzziah, who carried out the function of the priests, was struck down by leprosy because of his sin, so too will the layman, who has scorned God and insulted his priests by attributing to himself their dignity, not remain unpunished. He is not imitating Christ, who did not attribute to himself the glory of becoming a pontiff, but who waited for the Father to tell him: "The Lord has sworn and will not contradict himself: Thou art a priest for ever after the order of Melchizedek."[51]

This reinterpretation of the text in the *Didascalia* continues in the *Apostolic Constitutions* with a return to the Old Testament text underlying the passage in which the word "lay" appeared for the first time in Christian literature, the epistle of Clement to the Corinthinans:[52]

> If Christ did not, independently from the Father, attribute glory to himself, how, then, can a man appropriate the priesthood to himself without having received that dignity from a superior, and how can he carry out what only priests are permitted to carry out? Although they were of the tribe of Levi, were Korah's men not burned by fire because they had risen in revolt against Moses and Aaron and had taken part in affairs that did not concern them? Did Dathan and Abiram not go down alive into Hades? And did the rod that budded not confuse the multitude of foolish men and point to the pontiff chosen by God?[53]

The Family Duties of Laymen

The bishop, who is at the center of all the directives contained in the *Didascalia*, was above all, like God, the father of his church. In his image. Christian fathers—laymen—had the task of managing their families well. They had above all to teach their children a trade and, if possible, a trade that would be useful to religion. To achieve this, they were not to spare their children, who had both to be educated and to be made obedient. With this in mind, they ought not to hesitate to punish them physically if that was necessary:

> Teach your children the word of the Lord, strike them with blows and, from their infancy, make them listen to your pious words. Do not give them the power to rebel against you (and) against their own (people). They should do nothing without your advice. Do not let them meet together and amuse themselves with those of their own age, because in that way they will learn vanity, will seek sensual pleasure and will fall.[54]

Christian fathers not only had to bring up their children well. They had also to take care to choose wives for their sons and to ensure that they married, "so that they will not, in their youth and because of their age, fornicate like the pagans and so that you (fathers) will be able to give an account of it to the Lord God on the day of judgment."[55]

The author of the *Didascalia* also advises the Christian who has no children to accept a Christian boy or girl who has become an orphan into his home: "It will be good for one of the brethren who has no child to take a boy as his son and for anyone who has a son to take a girl and to give her to him as his wife when the time comes, in order to accomplish his work in the service of God."[56]

It would seem that, if no one wanted to take care of these orphans—something that may have happened frequently—that task had to be taken over by the bishop: "You, bishops, take care of their upbringing, so that nothing is lacking. And when it is the time of the girl, marry her to one of the brethren. In the same way, when the young man grows up, he should learn a profession and, when he becomes a man, he will receive a salary that is in accordance with his trade, acquire the tools that he needs and no longer be dependent on the charity of the brethren—a charity that has been without any ulterior motive or hypocrisy."[57] It is possible that the bishop had to make up for the deficiencies of Christians by acting as their substitute because the group of Christians had fulfilled their main task as lay people by giving him their tithe. "Blessed is he who, being able to help himself (that is, being able to make gifts), does not tread on the place of the orphan, the widow and the stranger."[58]

Was the Widow an Odd Kind of Lay Person?

There are long passages in the *Didascalia* devoted to the "widow," which was a state of life that must have given rise to many problems for the leaders of Christian communities at the beginning of the third century. We have already seen that the first definition of the Christian clergy was provided in the *Apostolic Tradition* within the context of the widow. If we are to understand the situation at that time correctly, we must take into account both what was implied by the state of widowhood and what we have learned about the management of wealth in the community. The widow was a woman who had lost her husband. As a marriageable woman, she might therefore be thinking of remarriage, but from the purely material point of view and especially if she was a woman with a humble origin, some means had to be found for her to remain alive. If she had a more wealthy background, she might well be a desirable object.

We know that, for theological reasons, remarriage, that is, digamy or a later second marriage, was not favored by third century Christians. This meant that it was regarded as necessary to use all possible means to prevent widows from being obliged to remarry simply for economic reasons. A careful reading of the text of the *Didascalia* shows that the widow appears remarkably frequently in the list of those whom the community had to help. In fact, she was, with the orphans, the poor and the strangers, one of those for whom the bishop, who was the community's steward, had to care more than anyone else.[59]

Among those requiring assistance in this way, the widows and orphans were regarded as the altar,[60] because it was to them that part of the offerings made by the faithful went. It also provided the author of the *Didascalia* with an opportunity to use this comparison to urge widows not to continue to move about:

A widow should know that she is God's altar and she should remain all the time in her home. She should not wander or go about in the houses of other believers in order, as it were, to receive, since the altar of God never wanders or goes about in a place, but always remains in the same place.[61]

On the other hand, those who were sustained by the gifts made by other believers had the task of praying for those who gave: "With regard to the altar, the widows, after being sustained by an altar of justice, should offer holy and acceptable service (should pray for the giver) in the presence of almighty God, through the intermediary of his beloved Son and the Holy Spirit, to whom glory and honor be given for ever and ever."[62]

It is also important to note, in connection with those who made gifts, how troubled the *Didascalia* is about their behavior. This is clear from the author's insistence on this theme. There was always the possibility that the money may have been gained dishonestly and the bishop, who was the steward of these "treasures of God," had to be alert to the giver's situation. He had to avoid accepting money "from the hands of the rich who had put men (who may have been innocent) into prison or from those who behaved badly toward their servants or in their own towns or who oppressed the poor, from the unchaste or from those who did evil with their own bodies, from the wicked, from those who reduced or increased, from iniquitous lawyers, unjust accusers or judges who take account of persons, from those who paint in color or make idols, from thieves who manufacture gold, silver and bronze, from iniquitous tax collectors, from those who see visions, who change weights or who cheat treacherously, from innkeepers who mix water (into the wine), from soldiers who live iniquitously, from murderers, from executioners, from any magistrate in the Roman empire who has defiled himself in the wars, has unjustly shed innocent blood, has changed judgments and, in order to steal, has behaved iniquitously and cunningly with pagans and the poor and worshipers of idols and from impure people, usurers and misers."[63] Reading a list like this, which shows us how little human nature has changed, we are bound to wonder from whom the widows could have received their food and sustenance.

It was only if the widow was "filled with the bread of righteousness" that she would be able to offer her service and prayer with purity in God's presence. Helped and fed by the community, she had above all to devote her time to prayer for her benefactors and indeed for the whole church. The author of the *Didascalia*, however, seems to be impelled to insist at great length on the way in which widows ought to behave.[64] He says, for example:

> The woman who is widowed must be gentle, quiet, moderate, without malice or anger and not talkative or quarrelsome. She should not have a long tongue and should avoid arguments. If she sees or learns about a bad deed, she should behave as though she had neither seen nor heard.[65]

This advice was obviously hardly ever followed. The portrait that the author of the *Didascalia* paints of false widows shows that the reality was very far from his wishes. Widows clearly "wandered and went about in the houses of other believers" and were like "blind people who only wanted to receive."[66] "Because they are talkative and without shame and love scandal, they cause quarrels and are bold and without modesty."[67] Above all, these bad widows seem to have benefited from their status as people receiving assistance by in fact receiving more than they should have done and, what is more, receiving directly without going through the intermediary of the bishop or the deacons:

> We see widows for whom widowhood has become an industry. They receive greedily and, instead of doing good works and giving to the bishop, so that strangers may be received and the poor given relief, they lend their money to usurers. They are only concerned with money, these women whose gods are the purse and the belly. Where their treasure is, there is their heart.[68]

These miserly, lying and jealous widows of the *Didascalia* were a great problem to the bishop. They were really a very odd kind of Christian! But is it possible to call them an odd kind of lay person?

The Role and Status of Women in the Church

Although many books and articles have been written recently about the place and the role of women in the church, no author has to my knowledge asked whether women ought to be included among the laity.[69] Some authors have, by forcing the texts to some extent at least, wanted to make them members of the clergy, especially when they were "deaconesses," but no one has ever been further from the evidence than the contemporary reader, namely that anyone who is not a member of the clergy is of necessity a lay person! It may be that the situation of Christian women, especially their situation since the first centuries of the church's history, should lead us to put the questions in a different way.

Let us begin, then, by looking at the roles that women were able to fulfill in the church of the *Didascalia*. We shall not, however, reconsider the state of the widowed woman who was helped by the community, the widow, that is, who was normally aged and who was expected to devote herself to prayer and to serve the community in certain small ways. We must examine what the *Didascalia* says about two other groups of women who had a part to play in the church—the instituted widows and the deaconesses.

The "instituted" or "established" widows formed a separate group—the group of widows, the *cherikon*. Certain conditions had to be satisfied if a woman was to be accepted into this group. She had to be at least fifty years old. That age was regarded as a guarantee that she was not seeking remarriage. Young widows, then, were not included within this group. They were helped, in the hope that they would not take a man in a second marriage because they were in need. Apart from prayer and fasting, the older widows who were established in the order of widows were expected to visit the sick and lay hands on them. They were not, however, to do anything without the authorization of the bishop or the deacon. These older women must have been strongly tempted to play an important part in the community and at least in the community of women. The author of the *Didascalia* is insistent that widows should not, for example, baptize and teach, and this must be because some widows were inclined to do this.

According to the *Didascalia*, then, widows, like all other women, had no right to baptize:

> We do not allow a woman either to baptize or to let herself be baptized by a woman, because this is contrary to order and it is dangerous both for the one who is baptized and for the one who baptizes. If baptism by a woman were allowed, our Lord and master would have been baptized by Mary, his mother. But he was in fact baptized by John, like many

others among the people. Do not, then, brothers and sisters, be led into danger by going outside the law of the gospel.[70]

A century and a half later, the compiler of the *Apostolic Constitutions* was to develop this ban by a two-pronged argument based on the nature of man and that of woman on the one hand and the institution of Christ on the other:

As for the question of women baptizing, we would point out to you the great danger in which those women who act in this way place themselves. That is why we do not advise it, for it is uncertain, or, rather, it is illicit and impious. In fact, the head of the woman is the man and it is also the latter who was chosen for the priesthood. It is not right to scorn creation and to leave what is first to go toward the body that came last, for the woman is the body of the man. She came from his side and is subject to him. She is also distinct from him with procreation in mind. In fact, it is said: "He will rule over you. For the man is the head of the woman, because he is the head." Above, we have forbidden women to teach. How, then, is it possible to consent to let them exercise the priesthood, contrary to nature? For that aberration, which consists in instituting priestesses for female goddesses, comes from the atheism of the pagans and not from the institution of Christ.[71]

The *Didascalia* also forbade the widow to teach or even to reply to questions that might be asked "about justice and faith in God." This reservation, however, placed the widow on an equal footing with the layman, who also did not have the right to teach:

Neither the widow nor the layman is permitted to speak about them (the unity of God, punishment and blessedness, Christ's kingdom and divine providence), for, if they speak about these things without any knowledge of doctrine, they will blaspheme against the word. . . .

In the gospel, our Lord also said to the widows and the laymen: "Do not throw your pearls before swine, lest they trample them underfoot and turn to attack you."[72]

But even though most instituted widows were not allowed to baptize and to teach, their age, their experience and their situation in society gave them a status and an independence that must have been an embarrassment to the bishop. It is not difficult to sense this situation underlying this kind of criticism made of rebellious widows: "You should blush with shame, all of you who are like that, who think yourselves wiser and more prudent not only than men, but also than the presbyters and the bishops."[73] Reading these prohibitions and criticisms, it is possible to understand why the author of the *Didascalia* was in favor of the deaconess, who exercised a female ministry that was more easily subjected to the hierarchy of the period.

The *Didascalia* is the first document in which the function of the deaconess is presented. In what may be regarded as the original text of the *Didascalia*, this female function appears only in two clearly defined places and in both cases in a form that is still by no means fully developed. We have already encountered the first reference, in connection with the honor that the people were to give to the bishop. This text presents the deaconess as a person "honored (by you) in the place of the Holy Spirit."[74] This female typology should be understood within the context of a language in which the Spirit was feminine. It tells us very little about the role and the place of the deaconess.

The other text referring to the deaconess is much longer and has been the object of many commentaries. In it, the role of deacons and the institution of deaconesses are placed in parallel.[75] The original Greek version of this text is lost, but there is general agreement that the terms employed should be "the deacon," in the feminine form *he diakonas*, and "the woman deacon" or *gune diakonos*. It was not until the First Council of Nicaea (325) that the term "deaconess" (*diakonissa*) was commonly used in the eastern church. This linguistic development shows that this female ministry had its earliest beginnings with the *Didascalia* in the third century. By creating a fairly close parallelism between the deacon and the woman deacon, an attempt was probably being made to neutralize the pervasive and embarrassing intrusion of widows into church life. "That is why, bishops, you should become workers of justice, helpers who will lead your people toward life. You will choose and establish as deacons those who will please you from the whole of the people, a man who will carry out numerous tasks that are necessary or a woman to serve women."[76]

The reason given for the creation of this female ministry is a reason of convenience. This is clear, for example, from the following statement: "There are houses where you cannot send a deacon to the women, because of the pagans." If they were sent into the houses of the pagans "where believing women lived," these deaconesses accomplished a spiritual work of prayer and at the same time the material task of giving first aid.

Deaconesses were also employed in the baptismal liturgy for reasons of propriety, since ritual nakedness was required in the rite of baptism and it was "not good for women to be seen by men." Consequently, the deaconess had the task of anointing the woman who was going to be baptized with holy oil. This did not, however, lead the author of the *Didascalia* to mitigate his "anti-feminist" attitude, for he goes on to say that it was only the bishop or the deacons and presbyters who had the power to baptize. The deaconess, who was, after all, a woman, had simply to receive the woman who had been baptized after her baptism and "to instruct her and feed her, so that the unbreakable seal of baptism might be (preserved) with purity and holiness."[77] Her role, in other words, was that of godmother or sponsor to women. Should we, then, conclude from this that she was relegated to the rank of "lay" woman?

The author of the *Didascalia* does not ask this question, but a careful study of the document allows us to situate his idea of the status of women in the church. It is important to note first of all that the term *kleros*, clergy, does not occur at all in this long canonico-liturgical document. The frontier between clergy and laity is, in other words, not recognized. On the other hand, the term "lay" is used quite frequently. It is, however, never employed to describe female members of the community. Whenever it is a question of defining instructions concerning women, the author simply uses the terms "women," "Christian" in the feminine form, "Christian woman," "widow," "instituted widows" or "women deacons." But he certainly had reasons for never speaking about the "lay woman" or "lay" in the feminine form.

The fundamental reason is to be found in the attitude that prevailed at that time. The woman had to be subject to her husband.[78] He was the head of the woman, as Christ was the head of the man.

The same monarchical structure that is found at the level of civil or religious society of the period can also be found at the level of the family, but not totally, since the Christian woman shared in the eucharist and in Christian worship,[79] where she had a separate place. She formed part of the chosen people, then, and was entirely a Christian, without in fact being a lay Christian, but also without being regarded as similar in every detail to the woman member of the people of God of the old covenant. She could even exercise the ministry of deacon, like the women who "served" Jesus: Mary of Magdala, Mary the daughter of James and the mother of Joseph and the mother of the sons of Zebedee.[80] If, however, we are to understand why the woman was not a member of the clergy rather than a member of the laity, we have to go back to the material organization of the wealth in the Christian community and to the way in which the bishop, the only high priest of the new covenant, had to manage the gifts that the laity sent to him.

The Bishop as the Steward of the Christian Community

According to the *Didascalia*, the bishop ruled "over the soul and the body to bind and loosen a heavenly power on earth."[81] He was regarded as the priest and intermediary between man and God and, as we have seen, members of his church were told: "You are commanded to give and it is for him to dispense."[82]

It is within this theological context of the economic function of the bishop that the author of the *Didascalia* developed the theme of judgment as the province of the bishop.[83] In this he was reinterpreting earlier traditions in a more or less coherent way, and it is possible that a consideration of what he says may enable us to understand the fundamental reasons that led these early Christian communities to describe certain functions, beginning with that of the bishop, as "priestly," and at the same time and by contrast to define the first characteristic of the "laity" as not exercising that priestly function.

This Old Testament typology is developed at great length in the *Didascalia*, the bishop also being presented as the priest and levite of the new people of God: "Today, bishops, you too are priests of your people and levites in the service of God's tabernacle, which is the holy Catholic Church."[84] Like the levites, the bishops were also able to feed and sustain themselves and their families from what was brought to God as a gift by the whole people: "With the help of these gifts that are offered to you by the people, who depend on you, you must also feed the deacons, the widows, the orphans, the poor and the strangers."[85] This is an interesting statement, in that we find side by side those who serve at the altar—the bishop and the deacons—and those who are served by the altar. In fact, in the third century, most local churches possessed detailed lists of all those who were fed, sustained and aided for various reasons.

The bishop, then, became the only manager or steward of the wealth of the community and had therefore to play the part of the *patronus* for his Christians. It is not difficult, then, to understand how and why this episcopal function became "monarchical" and the reasons that led the authors of the canonico-liturgical documents to moderate that absolute power: "Like a faithful overseer, bishop, you must take care of everyone. Since you bear the sins of all those who are in your hands, as a consequence, more than everyone, you will be honored by God."

The frontier between the different groups of Christians was defined, then, by the economic function of the bishop, reinterpreted in these priestly and levitical categories in the *Didascalia*. First of all, there was the bishop himself who was the high priest of his community and who, following the model of the levites, received "no earthly inheritance."[86] Then, within the community itself, there were those who gave their tithe—the lay people, who were essentially Christian men who were the financial managers of their households.

Within this context, it was difficult for the Christian woman to find a place. If she was young, she depended on her father and, if she was married, on her husband, with the result that she could not carry out the function of lay person as defined here. She could not, in other words, give her tithe. If she was widowed, she raised a problem, and an attempt was made to solve it by giving the bishop the task of feeding, sustaining and caring for her so that she should not be driven by economic reasons to contract a second marriage.

Unlike the layman, she received from the altar, instead of providing for the needs of the ministers of the altar. At the age of fifty, she could become an "instituted widow" and enjoy a certain prestige. She would then no longer have any trace of "lay" status and, according to the *Didascalia*, it would seem that the bishop feared her initiatives. This was undoubtedly the reason why he introduced the idea of a ministry of women deacons who would depend more closely on his good will as their bishop. The fact that he probably feared the domestic intrigues of women is evidence of the existence of a certain form of female power, but the social image of women that was generally accepted at the time does not seem to have been absorbed easily into the image of the lay person responsible for giving a tithe. Women were situated apart from both groups—the laity and the clergy. They were also undoubtedly on the periphery both of the definition of the Christian social groups and of the economic roles.

The bishop—the high priest—possessed, on the other hand, both the economic power and all the functions. He had the authority to name deacons and deaconesses to help him in his management function. He fed and helped those—the widows, the orphans, the poor and the strangers—who were in difficulty. He also had the sovereign right to decide on how the wealth that the community had entrusted to him should be used. In such conditions, it was inevitable that what was originally a service of the community should be seen as a power by lay people who no longer had any right of inspection with regard to the destination of the subsidies that they provided. One has the impression that the community became an instrument at the service of the extension of a monarchical episcopate and that the episcopate, on the other hand, had only to be an instrument at the service of the community.

This concentration on the bishop and this change in finality points to a complete revolution in Christian attitudes. This transformation is also revealed in the reversal that took place in the most traditional metaphors. In the epistles to Titus and Timothy, the good father of his family who was able to manage his household in a worthy manner was given to the episkopos as a model. In the *Didascalia*, on the other hand, the bishop is given as a model to fathers of families.

CHAPTER 6

The Life of a Church
in the Middle of the Third Century

The Pope of Carthage

Callistus only succeeded in becoming the bishop of Rome after experiencing many vicissitudes. Cyprian's career in the church seems to have been much less adventurous. He was converted to Christianity by a presbyter and baptized in 245 A.D., and by 249 he was already the bishop of Carthage. Little is known about his life during the years preceding his conversion, but it is generally believed that he taught rhetoric. What is certain is that he lived in a very wealthy environment. When he became a bishop, he drew on his own resources to help the victims of persecution, and he also withdrew for a time to his own villa and its gardens outside Carthage. Because of his own background in society, he was not only free and at ease in hierarchical relationships. He also had a natural authority and a gift for management, so that he was able to administer the church of Carthage with the skill and confidence of a proconsul.

His circumstances as the bishop of Carthage soon gave him the opportunity to exercise that organizational dexterity that was inherent in his character. Emperor Decius began to persecute Christians from 250 onward, forcing them to offer sacrifices to the gods of the Roman empire. Many bishops preferred to suffer martyrdom, with the result that Christian churches lost their heads and became disorganized and decimated by the tribute of blood that they had to pay. Without their leader, many churches lost confidence and were weakened by internal quarrels. Cyprian sensibly decided to take shelter from these storms, trying to maintain the unity of the church by standing at a distance. The unity that he had in mind was not only that of his own community in Carthage, but also the unity that he wanted to exist between the local churches. He engaged in a voluminous correspondence, dealing in a very concrete way in his letters with questions of church organization. Decius' persecution came to an end in 252, but from 257 onward Christians were persecuted again. Cyprian himself was martyred in 258.

A WELL-STRUCTURED CHURCH

The second and the beginning of the third centuries was a period of prosperity for Africa. Agriculture was economically successful. Carthage was an important commercial center and acted as a bridgehead for Gaul, Spain, the east and especially Italy. Christianity flourished in this favorable economic climate. There were as many as sixty Christian communities in the province of Africa. Possibly almost half the population was Christian and Roman Africa was on the way to becoming Christian Africa. It was this flourishing church that the Decian persecution struck like a whip.

A Member of the Clergy Is Not a Layman

During the persecutions, Cyprian had to administer his church at a distance. His letters are full of teachings on the subject of the concrete organization of the church. His first letter, for example, contains a definition of the clergy and refers to earlier conciliar decisions, providing evidence of the fact that the African church had for some time been affected by a certain juridicism. This letter was written to the clergy of Furni and dealt with the testament of one Geminius Victor who had appointed a presbyter called Geminius Faustinus as his children's guardian. In it, Cyprian points out that an earlier church council had already prohibited the choice of members of the clergy as guardians. He goes on to justify this conciliar decision,

> in view of the fact that those who have the honor of the divine priesthood and are employed in the duties of the clerical office should only use their ministry for the sacrifice and the altar and should only devote themselves to prayer.[1]

Cyprian bases this theory on the example of the levites. He recommended all Christians to avoid becoming too involved in the activities of this world. For the clergy, however, this recommendation was an imperative:

> This is the discipline that was observed by the levites in the old law. The eleven tribes divided the land between them, each one having a share. The tribe of Levi, whose members were dedicated to serving in the temple and at the altar, was not included within this sharing. The others devoted themselves to cultivating the land. The tribe of Levi devoted itself exclusively to cult. To support this tribe, the eleven others contributed a tithe of the fruits of the land. God wanted everything to be regulated in this way so that those who dedicated themselves to the divine service would not be turned away from it and forced to give their attention to profane occupations. This is the same rule that is still followed today for the clergy.[2]

At about the same time as this letter was written, Origen had been putting forward more or less the same ideas, but with a slightly different emphasis. Whereas, for Cyprian, the levitical activity was centered on the sacrifice and the altar, for Origen it was focused on a study of the law. This difference between the doctor, who had devoted his life to teaching, and the bishop, who was above all concerned with the liturgy, should hardly surprise us. It is, however, the only subjective note. What is more important is that Cyprian wanted those "who had been raised by ordination to the rank of the clergy in the church of God should not be turned away from the divine service and run the risk of becoming involved in the activities of the world." Origen, on the other hand, insisted on the need to free the "levites" from every material care and on the dangers that would occur if this were not done. "In fact," he said,

> the law of God has been entrusted to the priests and levites so that it might be the only aim of their activity and so that they may remain aloof from every external preoccupation and devote themselves exclusively to the word of God. In order that they may be able, however, so to dedicate themselves, they have to make use of the ministry of the laity, since, if lay people do not provide the priests and levites with what they need, those preoccupations—I mean those

material cares—will prevent them from giving themselves totally to the law of God. And if they do not give themselves to that and if they do not dedicate their entire activity to the law of God, then you are the one who is in danger. It will in fact grow dim, that light of knowledge that is in them, if you do not provide the oil for the lamp.[3]

Whereas Origen regarded gnostic illumination as the benefit that lay people derived from the material contribution that they made to the activity of the clergy, Cyprian thought that "the man who wanted to hold himself aloof from the altar of the priests and from the ministries of God did not deserve to be named at the altar of God in the prayers of the priests."[4]

For Cyprian, a member of the clergy was someone who was set aside for the service of the church and who had to devote himself totally to his religious tasks. For this, he received his sustenance from the church, in other words, from the brothers. The clergy benefited from the *sportula*, that is, from the gift or offering. This word was taken from profane vocabulary and originally meant the basket into which masters put what they wanted to give to their dependents. (This was often the equivalent of a meal.) The gift could be made in kind. But the church of Carthage was organized and its clergy had not been reduced to waiting day after day for an offering made regularly by the laity. Speaking about a sub-deacon and an acolyte who had left their functions during the persecution, Cyprian deferred judgment on them and simply asked whether they "should abstain for the time being from claiming the monthly remuneration (*divisio mensurna*)."[5] It is clear from this, then, that the Carthaginian clergy was assured of a remuneration each month. This probably came from the kind of "common money chest" described by Tertullian.

But what kind of people were regarded as belonging to the clergy? The term *clerus* might, according to the circumstances, point to various groups. It could be used in a very general and vague sense to indicate all those male individuals who had a function in the church. More frequently, however, it was used to describe the presbyters and deacons. It was also sometimes employed for the group consisting of the bishop surrounded by his *presbyterium*.[6] In certain cases, it could even include all the minor ministers who worked for the Christian community—the sub-deacon, the acolyte or the lector or reader[7]—and who received the *divisio mensurna*. In Cyprian's church, the *sacerdotes et levitae* seem above all to have constituted the clergy, but, by extension, the term was also applied to the minor ministers who also benefited from financial support.

Although all members of the clergy received subsidies from the church, not all those who received such subsidies were members of the clergy. The church had people whom it assisted, but who were not necessarily members of the clergy or indeed of any particular group. We have already seen how Tertullian protested against the idea of including within the *ordo* of widows a young woman in need and recommended that she should simply be helped. We know too that Cyprian suggested that an actor should be provided with sufficient means for him to survive if he were to give up his profession, "on condition that he was satisfied with simple food and did not take it into his head that he should be paid a pension, in view of the fact that it is not us whom he serves by no longer sinning, but himself."[8] This points to what must undoubtedly have been, for Cyprian, an essential difference from the clergy, who, by their service at the altar, enabled all believers to benefit from their prayers.

At the same time, however, Cyprian was also very concerned for the victims of the Roman persecution, whether these were Christians who had already confessed their faith or whether they were simply poor and deprived. He clearly believed that he was, as bishop, responsible for these charitable works. During the Decian persecution, he wrote, for example, to his clergy: "I would to God that the rank that I hold enabled me to be present there! I would very willingly carry out all the good offices of charity among my dear brothers while exercising my ordinary ministry."[9] But, being absent, he made available to his clergy the sums collected and even the funds that belonged to him personally.[10] And whenever he made financial resources available in this way, he always gave advice or recommendations about how to practice charity.[11]

Although he was above all concerned that the poor should not abandon their Christian faith,[12] he was also very anxious that they should not enjoy being dependent on receiving assistance in this way. In one letter, he even directly quoted Saint Paul's words to the Christians of Thessalonia: "We did not eat anyone's bread without paying, but, with toil and labor, we worked night and day, that we might not burden any of you."[13]

There was obviously a risk, then, that Christians might become dependents. This was undoubtedly the reason why he made it clear that those Christians who were being aided should not let this situation, in which they were receiving assistance, make them lazy. Following the same line of thought, he wrote to several of his presbyters: "I have sent you as my representatives to provide for the needs of our brothers from our resources, to aid with the necessary funds those who would like to carry out their profession and at the same time to consider their age and their condition and thus to know what they are worth, just as I, who am responsible for this care, would like to know everyone and to promote to the functions of the ministry of the church all those who are worthy to carry them out and who are humble and gentle."[14]

It is interesting to note that the main qualities required for future members of the clergy—and, what is more, at a time when they were becoming dependent on their bishop, who was enabling them to receive assistance—were humility and gentleness. Felicissimus, who was Cyprian's main opponent, obviously had no illusions about this, because, at the same time as he examined those being considered for the church's ministry, he also put an end to the distribution of assistance.

The holiness of a Christian community could be measured by its prosperity and the number of its members. This meant, in other words, that it had to be visible through the number of those supported by the church. This was the argument that seems to have been developed by Cornelius, the bishop of Rome and Cyprian's contemporary, and used by him against the schismatic Novatian:

> Does this avenger of the gospel not know that there must be only one bishop in the Catholic Church? He must know— how could he not?—that there are, in that church, forty-six presbyters, seven deacons, seven sub-deacons, forty-two acolytes, fifty-two exorcists, readers or lectors and doorkeepers and more than fifteen hundred widows and needy people, all of whom are fed and sustained by the grace and philanthropy of the Master. Even such a multitude as this, so necessary in the church, which, by God's providence, constitutes a great and abundant number, with a very great and numerous people, has not turned him away from his error and his failure to understand, nor has it led him back to the church.[15]

The danger in the middle of the third century was not so much of that the people seemed to buy God's grace for themselves by buying a clergy, but rather that the bishop seemed to buy a clergy and faithful for himself, even if he needed lay people's money and God's grace to do it!

Faithful, Laity or Church People

Cyprian's first letter may give us quite a clear understanding of what he meant by "clergy," but it is more difficult to know the exact meaning that he gave to the terms "laity" or "lay people." He used this concept very little, preferring the terms "faithful" or *plebs*. He gave great consideration to the people, claiming to have made it a rule for himself from the beginning of his episcopate to make no decisions without consulting the clergy and obtaining the consent of the people.[16] The faithful therefore had a part to play which was, according to V. Saxer, "not to let themselves be fleeced for the benefit of their pastors."[17] Cyprian did not hesitate to threaten rebellious members of the clergy with judgment in the presence of the bishop, confessors and "the entire people."[18] Going over the heads of his clergy, he even wrote directly to the people to ask them to be patient while the bishops investigated the matter of the *lapsi* in the presence of the confessors and the people.[19]

The members of the Roman clergy, who had been without a bishop since the martyrdom of Fabian,[20] were probably alluding to this last communication when they replied to Cyprian: "In a case that is as important as this (the case of the *lapsi*, that is, of those who had fallen away during the persecution), we like what you have said, that is, that it is essential to wait for peace to be granted to the church before dealing with the matter of the *lapsi*, after having consulted with the bishops, the presbyters, the deacons, the confessors and the laity who have remained faithful."[21]

Later, Cyprian was to recall the terms of this agreement word for word in another letter.[22] It is also the only time that he ever used the term "laity" in the case of a consultation. Whenever he had to deal with a delicate case, he preferred it to be regulated in the presence of "the entire people."[23] The term "laity" (or "lay")—especially with a positive connotation—did not flow naturally from his pen. It would seem that it was much more commonly used in Rome.

In a letter written to Fabius of Antioch about Novatian's ex-companions, Cornelius, who was Fabian's successor to the Roman see, pointed out: "They have come back to the holy church and have revealed all his plotting and evil actions in the presence of many persons: bishops, presbyters and lay persons."[24] It is worth noting that the deacons are not mentioned in this text after the presbyters and before the laity. It is also worth trying to understand what Cornelius meant by "lay persons."

In a letter written to Cyprian about the same matter, the bishop of Rome described the "enthusiastic approval of the faithful people" at the time of this scene of reconciliation.[25] Ought we, then, to identify the laity mentioned in the letter to Fabius of Antioch with a heterogeneous group of people including all those who from far and near claimed for themselves the name of "Christian"? Probably not, since the letter written to Fabius of Antioch presents these lay people as "persons," which means that men were involved, possibly married men and certainly men who were regarded as mature, both in age and in moral qualities. It was certainly in the presence of laymen of this kind that the ex-companions of Novatian made their confession. It was equally certainly among laymen of this kind, who had been given the authority to make their views about certain important points concerning life in the Christian community known, that the first signs of opposition to the ordination of Novatian appeared. According to Eusebius, the historian of the early church, Novatian was a man who had been "honored with the priesthood according to the grace of the bishop, who had laid his hands on him to give him rank among the presbyters, despite the opposition of the whole of the clergy and of many lay people."[26]

All the texts with a Roman origin contain evidence of the positive aspect that was attached to the lay person. In all these texts, lay people are presented as those who had some say in the running of the church and those who were asked for their views. Cyprian, on the other hand, never used the term in this sense, although he claimed to consult the people on every important matter. It is difficult to say whether this difference in vocabulary conceals theological nuances or whether it simply comes from a difference in linguistic usage. The use of Latin became general in Rome only toward the middle of the third century, and the Romans of that period might have been more inclined than their African colleagues to retain and to continue to use originally Greek terms such as *laikos*.

As far as the "negative" use of the word "lay" is concerned, however, both Romans and Africans were in agreement, the "lay communion" was regarded as a lesser evil and a fallen state for unworthy members of the clergy. In the same letter to Fabius of Antioch referred to above, Cornelius also speaks of the bishops who had ordained Novatian to the episcopate and writes that, a little later, one of these bishops came back to the church complaining wretchedly. He also adds: "We have received him into the lay communion. All the people present interceded for him." In the same way, in connection with the bishop, Trofimus, who had done penance, Cyprian also states clearly: "Trofimus has only been admitted to our communion as a layman and not, whatever you may have been told in malicious writings, with the episcopal dignity."[27]

Although it may have been the commonest form of punishment for erring bishops at the time, this lay communion was certainly not the most severe. Cyprian tells us, in connection with a bishop who had defected during the persecution, that "having of his own accord renounced the honor of the episcopate, in order to obey his conscience, which was tormented with remorse, he began to do penance, being only too glad to be able to receive communion as a layman."[28] The bishops who did not submit to this and remained rebellious were regarded as going too far in a fallen state. This was why Cyprian, following Cornelius' warnings, accepted the responsibility of making it known that Evaristus, Novatian's companion, "had previously been a bishop, but was now no longer even a layman."[29] This was, of course, implicitly the same as excommunication. In a very general way, Cyprian and the African bishops believed that those presbyters and deacons who had become heretics as well as those who had been ordained by heretics should only be received into the church on condition that they shared in communion only as laymen.[30]

This last statement is clear enough evidence that, even though Cyprian never made a direct contrast in his written works between the clergy and the laity, he certainly did not regard deacons as laymen. This statement may seem to be obvious, but it is nonetheless important to recognize that the bishop of Carthage tended, as we have already seen, to "forget" the deacons in his classification and that he consequently made a contrast only between those who carried out a priestly function and laymen and distinguished simply between bishops and the laity.[31] In this respect he was like Cornelius, who tended to make a contrast between laymen and those who were regarded as fulfilling the priestly functions in the strict sense of the word, that is, in the case of the church of Rome, between the laity on the one hand and the bishop and the presbyters on the other.

The idea of the clergy as such, then, began to be determined almost exclusively by the concept of "sacerdotalization." In this process, the deacons, who, it cannot be denied, belonged to the category of the clergy whose members were fed and sustained by the church and which were a group that was distinct from the laity, similarly began to become a "minor" group compared with the *sacerdotes*, that is, the priests or "sacerdotal" group. At this stage, then, the laity could be defined in two ways. Laymen could be defined either positively as those who fed and sustained the ministers of the altar, symbolized by the levitical hierarchy, or negatively as those who were not priests. This second definition allowed the precise situation of the diaconate to remain to some extent vague. This vagueness is even increased if an even lower function than that of the diaconate is taken into consideration—the function of the lector or reader.

There is the case of Celerinus, whom Cyprian took it on himself to ordain. The bishop of Carthage said of this man that he had been associated with the "ministries of the church." Cyprian also claimed that it was not right for a confessor of his kind to remain "without a church honor."[32] What do these statements really mean?

There Are Different Kinds of Readers

Tertullian seems to have regarded readers as laymen rather than as members of the clergy.[33] The lectorate was often presented as a temporary function for young men who were capable of reaching the higher grades of the clergy. It would seem that the African authors to some extent liked to apply the description "church" or "ecclesiastical" to readers or lectors. More than a hundred years after Cyprian, Augustine spoke of "church readers."[34]

From the time of Cyprian onward, however, readers were certainly members of the clergy. The confessor Lucianus claimed to write to Cyprian in the presence of two members of the clergy—a reader and an exorcist.[35] Cyprian himself informed his clergy that he had to go ahead with the installation of a reader and a sub-deacon to remedy a shortage of clergy.[36] In the same letter, however, he also wrote that it was possible to exercise the functions of reader without necessarily belonging to the clergy. That was so in the case of Saturus, who had been "brought close to the clericature" when he had been given the responsibility of doing the reading twice on Easter Sunday. The reader's functions, then, could sometimes be carried out by laymen.

At the end of the fourth century, Augustine made a distinction between the church reader, who read the canonical scriptures, and the reader who read the church's non-canonical scriptures. This second type of reader could only have been a layman.[37] It may have been because of this persistent ambiguity surrounding the functions of the African readers that the Council *Sub Grato* decided that a bishop was forbidden to accept readers or laymen who had come from another bishop into their ministry without previous authorization.[38]

Even when there was no doubt that the reader was a member of the clergy, Cyprian still found it necessary to make a distinction between the status and the honor of the function in the strict sense of the word. On the subject of the confessors Saturus and Celerinus, he had, for example, this to say: "Know, however, that we have established them as readers only while we look forward to something better. . . . We have, moreover, nominated them for the honor of the presbyterium. They will receive the *sportula* as presbyters and will have an equal share in the monthly remuneration. They will sit with us later when they are more advanced in years."[39]

Clearly, then, young readers also benefited from the financial advantages attached to the status of the presbyters. The reason for bestowing a favor such as this might have been the exceptional merit and popularity of these martyrs. On the other hand, it might have been because of the infirmities and the after-effects resulting from their confession.

These were, of course, probably rather exceptional cases. What, then, were the most usual functions of these readers who remained on the frontier between the clergy and the laity? The main one was undoubtedly that of reading the precepts and the gospel of the Lord.[40] This reading took place in the course of the liturgical synaxis.[41] Like any other member of the clergy, however, the reader might also be called to serve as a messenger and bear letters.[42] Because of his education, he was also a secretary and an archivist.[43] Finally, he could also become an auxiliary teacher of catechumens, helping the doctor-presbyters in this task. His function in this case was that of lector audientium, which probably means that he intervened to read the text that the presbyters explained even during the celebrations. This function seems to have enjoyed a certain prestige and to have led to promotion.[44]

Was a Heretic a Layman?

As we have already seen, a heretical bishop, presbyter or deacon could be readmitted to the church if he came back and did penance, but only to the lay communion. It is, however, important to recognize that this was only possible if the member of the clergy concerned had already been baptized in the Catholic Church before he had become a heretic. If he had not been previously baptized, it is highly likely that Cyprian and his African colleagues would have felt constrained to rebaptize him. What is certain is that Cyprian regarded baptism administered by heretics as invalid. He fiercely opposed Stephen, the bishop of Rome, when the latter claimed that second baptisms should be forbidden in the name of tradition. The bishop of Carthage convened a conciliary assembly to discuss this question and wrote numerous letters about it. He obtained support from every part of the church, the most notable of his supporters being Firmilianus, the bishop of Caesarea.[45]

Cyprian's thesis was quite simple. Only the church had the power to baptize, and the church could not be divided. Those who had placed themselves outside the church could not on any account baptize.[46] Whether the form under which the church's baptism was given seemed to be regular was not very important. The questions asked at baptism in any case included a reference to the church. It was not possible to ask as a valid question "Do you believe in the remission of sins and in eternal life through holy church?" if one was outside the true church.[47] What counted, then, for the bishop of Carthage was not the form, but the "full and complete faith of the one who gives and the one who receives."[48] From this point of view, it was therefore not very important whether clinical baptism was given by simple sprinkling or whether it was given by complete immersion. Cyprian was convinced that the Holy Spirit came entirely into the one who believed and that all believers received, at the beginning of their life in the church, an equal distribution of heavenly grace, "without difference of sex, without distinction of age and without respect of persons."[49]

This thesis appears in his conciliar letter of 255 A.D., together with a number of other arguments of a liturgical nature—Cyprian, for example, states that the water used for baptism should first have been purified and sanctified by the bishop.[50] The one who had been baptized should also have been anointed with oil consecrated at the altar during the celebration of the eucharist. It was undoubtedly this oil that is called "the oil of thanksgiving" ("eucharistic oil") in the *Apostolic Tradition*—the oil, in other words, that accompanied the laying on of hands by the bishop and the petition for the Holy Spirit for the one baptized.[51] The blessing of this oil probably took place in the course of the eucharist, just after that of the bread and the chalice.[52] It is therefore not difficult to understand that this oil could not be consecrated by those who were not in communion with the church.

If heretics coming back to the church were to be admitted to communion as laymen, it was obviously not enough for them simply to repent. They also had to be "rebaptized." This rebaptism was moreover regarded as the only real baptism. The practice of rebaptizing heretics had been established in Africa about 220 A.D., during an assembly held under the episcopate of Agrippinus,[53] and in Asia at about the same time, during an assembly held at Iconium in Phrygia.[54]

Cyprian justifies this quite recent practice by saying that the church had never intended to rebaptize the first heretics, who in fact only fell into heresy after having received baptism. This was, he claims, in fact the practice still followed by the church of Carthage: "If those who, we know with certainty, have been baptized here and who have left us to go over to the heretics come back later, acknowledging their mistake and abandoning their error, to the truth and to their mother's bosom, it is enough for us to lay hands on them and receive them as penitents."[55] For those who have been deeply involved outside the church and have been polluted by profane water, on the other hand, "it is not enough for us to lay hands on them so that they may receive the Holy Spirit."[56] As for Novatian, he proved to be even more intransigent than Cyprian, rebaptizing all those from the Catholic Church who came over to him.[57] There was, then, mutual disagreement about what constituted a member of the people of God or a baptized Christian.

Confessors—The Last Charismatics

In this context, it is worth recalling the text in the *Apostolic Tradition* referring to confessors quoted earlier in this chapter:

> If a confessor has been arrested for the name of the Lord, the hand should not be laid on him for the diaconate or for the presbyterate, since he possesses the honor of the presbyterate by virtue of his confession. But if he is instituted as bishop, the hand should be laid on him.[58]

How did the church conform to this rule a few decades later? When Cyprian established the two confessors Saturus and Celerinus as readers, he was careful to make it clear that he had established them as readers "only while looking forward to something better" and to add that he had, "moreover, nominated them for the honor of the presbyterium."[59]

The honor of the priesthood was, however, at that time presented essentially in its financial aspect, as a fee or honorarium or as a right to receive the *sportula* or the *divisio mensurna* or monthly remuneration. The reference in the earlier *Apostolic Tradition* to the honor of the presbyterate, on the other hand, emphasizes above all its spiritual aspect and implies the reception of the spirit of grace and counsel of the presbyterium, since it made the laying on of hands accompanied by the invocation of the Holy Spirit unnecessary. It is obvious that Cyprian did not for a moment want to see these confessors sitting on the presbyterium, since he adds: "They will sit with us later when they are more advanced in years." It is clear that he was embarrassed, because he goes on to say at once, "although the one who has consummated his age by an eminent glory should on no account be regarded as less because of the small number of his years."[60] If Cyprian had really wanted to recognize the charism resulting from this confession of faith, he would have been able to let confessors sit on the presbyterium. What we in fact have here is a voluntary reduction of the charismatic privilege recognized in the confessor.

Cyprian's attitude toward confessors did not, however, remain unchanged throughout the course of his episcopate. This is clear from his correspondence. His Letter 6 is an exhortation to reach the glory of martyrdom. His Letter 10 is an enthusiastic and lyrical celebration of the glory of confessors. In his Letter 12, he urges the clergy to watch over those who are in prison and insists that "nothing should be lacking with regard to the care taken of those in whom nothing is lacking with regard to glory."[61]

Letter 13 is addressed to those who have confessed their faith, and he exhorts these confessors to maintain their glory with courage and perseverance. Cyprian was obviously afraid that persecution would make some Christians give way, because he urges them to be prudent with these words in the same letter: "It is not very valuable to have been able to acquire something. It is much more important to know how to keep what one has acquired. It is not the result that he has achieved that will save a man, but his ultimate success."[62]

Again in the same letter, he calls on his readers to be an example of irreproachable virtue to their brothers and begs them to take great care of the honor of the group of confessors by expostulating with those who "make a stain in the mass."[63] He also has in mind those who are excessively proud, those who break the laws and even those who celebrate their return to the country after having triumphed for Christ by drinking too much. He even criticizes those who sleep in the same premises as women. He ends this Letter 13 to confessors by giving them an account of the sending of funds to provide for their food and clothing.

In Letter 14, he exhorts confessors to remain "humble and gentle," reminding them that more than they have already done still remains for them to do, "for it is written: 'Call no man happy before his death.' "[64] At the same time, Cyprian also discreetly suggests to these witnesses to Christ that they should not continue to let themselves be supported and to claim arrogantly and as due to them the help provided by the church. This is clearly a relativization of the charism of confessors. They have above all to "remain humble and gentle"—in other words, they have to respect the discipline of the church.

The church's martyrs, then, were venerated and regarded as glorious. Cyprian himself clearly accepted this in making use of the prestige acquired by the presbyter and confessor Numidicus and in adding weight to the condemnation of Novatian by the bishop of Rome by recalling the martyrdom of Cornelius. However venerable and glorious they might be, however, it was essential that they should not upset the established order. The problem of the *lapsi* and the way in which some confessors tried to use their prestige to have those who had failed during the persecutions readmitted to communion simply strengthened Cyprian in his conviction. His letters show that he increasingly made a distinction between good and bad confessors, contrasting Mappalicus, whom he described as "prudent and discreet," and Celerinus, who was, in his view, "moderate, prudent and reserved in a manner that is suitable for our religion," with Lucianus, "who has hardly . . . any understanding of scripture and displays an indiscreet easiness."[65] It is quite certain that Cyprian chose from among those who were both worthy and "humble and gentle" men whom he intended to appoint to functions in the church's ministry.[66]

WHERE THE PEOPLE MADE THEIR VOICE HEARD

Despite the authoritarianism that sometimes makes itself felt in his correspondence, Cyprian always regarded it as important to consult the people. He says himself that this was something that he had done from the very beginning of his episcopate.[67] He thought of this as a personal resolution. But was this resolution really in accordance with a truly African tradition? Or was it rather the result of exceptional circumstances that Cyprian encountered in his episcopate and therefore a way of bringing his community, which was shaken and even divided by persecution, more closely together? Should we even see this appeal to the people as a sign of weakness on the part of the bishop of Carthage, who felt that he had to play the power of the people off against that of members of his clergy who were challenging him?

Part of the truth can be found in each of these hypotheses. The instructions that he had given to his clergy in the case of the *lapsi* had proved to be useless and Cyprian, disappointed, had gone over the heads of the presbyters and deacons, making a direct appeal to the people. Although consulting the people in this way is known to have been especially important in the church of Carthage, this does not mean that it was an exclusively African procedure.

The questions that we have to ask are: How and about which matters were the people consulted? Did the people only have a right to approve or did they really take part in open discussion? Were they all or were only their representatives consulted? And, finally, what was the importance of this faithful, believing people consulted by their bishop, Cyprian, after the Carthaginian community had been torn apart by Felicimus' schism?

Penance and Reintegration into the Community

What share did the people have in the penitential procedure followed by the church of Carthage when a faithful member of the community lapsed? According to Cyprian, "when it is a question of less serious faults in which God is not the object, there should be first penance for a fixed time and then exomologesis after the penitent's way of life has been examined, and he is only admitted to communion after the bishop and the clergy have laid hands on him."[68] In this case, then, only the clergy and the bishop were involved. In the case of a serious fault, however, and especially in such a case, the people also had a word to say during the time of penance and when the penitent is readmitted to communion.

In the first place—and this would have been natural in the case of the *lapsi*—the confessors were called on to play a certain part. Those who had failed would turn to those who had suffered to ask them both to intercede for them and to forgive them. But the final decision would be with the bishop. Cyprian's answer with regard to the *lapsi* who were not in danger of death was quite categorical: "Despite the letters that I have received from the martyrs, I have said that their case should be postponed until later and kept for the time when we shall be present, so that, when the Lord has given us peace, we shall be able to meet with several bishops and, not without reaching agreement with you (that is, the Roman clergy), to regulate or reform all things."[69] The Roman clergy was to approve of Cyprian's authority by affirming that the martyrs and confessors, pressed hard with questions, should appeal to the bishop.[70]

Like the confessors, the clergy was also called upon to submit to the bishop's decision. Cyprian did not hesitate to threaten with excommunication those presbyters and deacons who shared communion with the *lapsi* before he had pronounced his verdict.[71] In the sphere of penance, he also established a parallel between the authority of the bishops and that of God.[72] But, despite the supreme authority that he possessed in this sphere, he still regarded it as important to consult the people.

This approach is, of course, not always free from ambiguity. The bishop of Carthage began by threatening to remove from the sacrifice, at least temporarily, those members of his clergy who refused to submit to his instructions, until they plead their cause in his presence and in the presence of the confessors themselves and of all the people.[73] He then wrote directly to the people. In his letter, he expressed the wish that the *lapsi* would wait until he returned so that he could study the letters written by the martyrs together with his colleagues, the other bishops, in the presence of the martyrs, at the same time hearing the people's opinion.[74] On this occasion, Cyprian praised his people's modesty and their restraint. For him, it was now a question of letting the people's power be asserted in opposition to that of the recalcitrant members of his clergy, so that he could ultimately make his own authority felt more firmly.

It would, however, be quite wrong to see this case of the bishop's consulting his people as a purely political maneuver. This consultation was for Cyprian a general rule. He even criticized his colleague Therapius for having given a presbyter who had erred peace without due consideration: "without having waited for the usual lapse of time, without the people's having known it or having asked for it or without its having been caused by illness or any other necessity."[75]

Cyprian consulted his people above all when the case in question was likely to make case-law. This might happen in the case of members of the clergy who had gone into hiding for a time during the persecution. "In such cases," the bishop of Carthage wrote, "I do not think that I have to be the only one to give my opinion. There are many members of the clergy who are still absent and who have not thought it necessary to return to their posts even belatedly. On the other hand, I am bound to recognize that there are special cases and I am looking with great care for a solution to this problem, not only with my colleagues, but also with all my people. There is an urgent need to weigh and balance everything before pronouncing a rule in any matter, a rule which may in the future constitute a precedent for the church's ministers."[76]

In a very general sense, this prudence and this practice were in accordance with those of the Roman clergy, whose advice was to wait until peace had returned before regulating the matter of the *lapsi* and then only acting after having consulted with the bishops, the presbyters, the deacons, the confessors and the lay people who had remained faithful believers. Why was this procedure followed?

The reason is that it was and is always risky and unpopular to be the only one to pass judgment against the majority. In this case, the sentiments expressed by the clergy reveal feelings that are almost democratic: "A decision cannot be very binding if it does not seem to reflect the votes of a majority of those voting in favor of the resolution."[77]

The Roman confessors were also to approve of Cyprian's prudence in terms that were very similar to those used by the clergy. When he had reintegrated some of those who had followed Novatian into communion with the church, Cornelius explained how he had gone about the task. After first making contact with those sent as envoys by the schismatics, he sent for those concerned with the aim of making sure of their intentions. Then he convoked an official meeting of the presbyterium. Five bishops were present at this meeting, taking part in the debate and receiving the entreaties of the penitents. Finally, he informed the people about the proceedings. This was something that he regarded as natural, and he did it, it would seem, not so much in order to ask them for their advice as to reassure himself that they approved and to make the forgiveness of the penitents public. The latter repeated their confessions in the presence of everyone and were granted forgiveness with the enthusiastic approval of the faithful people.[78]

There were, however, other cases which were not settled so easily and in which agreement was far from unanimous. In these cases, it proved necessary to rely on the people's opinion, since scandal had at all costs to be avoided. Cyprian himself wrote, for example: "Some have had such serious complaints made against them or have encountered such firm and indeed absolute opposition on the part of the brothers that it is absolutely impossible to receive them. . . . But if you could be here, my dear brother, and near to us when these men who have erred and gone astray come back to us from schism, you would see how difficult it is for me to persuade our brothers to be patient and to be less indignant, so that they might be able to receive the guilty ones and to work for their healing. They may well be happy and they are ready to be pleased about the return of those who can be endured and who are in fact less guilty, but they complain, on the other hand, and are opposed to the return to the church of those who are incorrigible, hot-headed, defiled either by adultery or sacrifices and still proud, since their return may mean that honest souls will be corrupted by them from within."[79]

Cyprian, then, claimed that it was very difficult for him to obtain the readmission of certain people. He also admitted that he was sometimes wrong not to take seriously the people's opposition, since those whom he had readmitted to communion did not always persevere in their good intentions. What we have here, then, is a clear indication of the precise extent of the people's power. In law, the bishop was always free not to heed their opinion or follow their advice, but, in general, the voice of the people counted for a great deal and the bishop would be reluctant to go against it.

The Election of the Bishop

The part played by the people was even more important in the election of the bishop than in the question of penance. According to Cyprian, a bishop had to be elected in the presence of the people, in the sight of everyone and to everyone's certain knowledge. He was, moreover, convinced that the source from which this practice in the election of the bishop came was to be found in the teaching contained in the scriptures and that it therefore went back to the very origins of the church's life.

"We must be careful," Cyprian wrote, "to preserve the divine tradition, the apostolic practice, and to observe what is observed among us and in almost all the church's provinces. Wherever a leader has to be ordained for the people, the bishops of the province must gather together and the election of the bishop must take place in the presence of the people, who are acquainted with the life and who are able to appreciate each person's behavior because they live close to each one."[80] This, then, was the criterion for the regular ordination of a bishop, and this practice of electing a bishop by the people was not peculiar to Africa. It was practically universal in the church.

Cyprian recalls the time when he was regularly elected by the suffrage of the whole people.[81] He seems to have had a very happy memory of this enthusiastic election.[82] Writing in some detail about the regularity of Cornelius' ordination, he was very careful to note that this bishop had also been elected by the people.[83] What is more, he also insisted on the importance of this fact each time that he wanted to point to the regularity of this particular ordination: "Cornelius was elected bishop by the judgment of God and his Christ, by the favorable testimony of the virtually unanimous vote of the clergy, by the agreement with them on the part of those of the people who were present, by the community of the venerable bishops and the honest people, no one having been elected in preference to him to replace Fabianus."[84]

What was the exact meaning of this presence and this suffrage of the people? Cyprian's Letter 67 would lead us to think either that the people had to choose between different candidates who had already been selected and recognized as able and suitable or that they had to confirm the good testimony provided by the clergy, according to whom the candidate put before them deserved to be elected. This approval was not just a formality. It gave the people "the power to elect worthy bishops and to remove those who were not worthy."[85]

The part played by the people in the election of a bishop could therefore be decisive, especially when social conventions and other unforeseeable factors made themselves felt. This was probably what happened in the case of the unexpected election of Cornelius' predecessor, Fabianus. According to the church historian Eusebius, the latter was quickly installed on the bishop's throne by a movement on the part of the people inspired by a divine spirit.[86] In the case of the election of a bishop, then, when the voice of the people made itself heard unhesitatingly and unanimously, it was believed to be the voice of God. In this sphere, the intervention of the people went far beyond the mere consensus which was for Cyprian a duty to take seriously whenever he was dealing with any matter of importance.[87]

When Christians Provided an Example of Democracy

As we have seen above, the tradition of episcopal elections went back, according to Cyprian, to the scriptures and the apostolic age. But what was the situation in reality? Had Christianity not been influenced in this matter by the way in which civil society appointed men to carry out public functions? This does not seem very likely. At the time of the republic, the Roman magistrates may well have been appointed by the people, but this had ceased to be the case in the empire. There is no doubt that the people could still express their opinion and could still be invited to approve by acclamation the man presented to them, but the superior or the order concerned was also able to make a personal appointment, without the intervention of the people, choosing the man whom they wanted to appoint. This so-called *adlectio* was a system that could only increase in importance as the government of the empire became more and more centralized.

There is also the case, more than a century after Cyprian, of Lampridius, a pagan who was concerned that his fellow pagans should have certain freedoms in an empire that was becoming increasingly Christianized. He suggested, as a model for civil society, the electoral procedure followed by Christians. He was able to put his argument convincingly by citing the example of Alexander Severus, who was emperor from 222 to 235 A.D. According to Lampridius, Alexander wanted the imperial magistrates to be chosen on the model of the Christian and Jewish sacerdotes and following the procedure of an election.[88]

This story probably does not date back to the first half of the third century, that is, to the time when Alexander was emperor, and was undoubtedly forged by Lampridius himself in an attempt to express his own personal aspirations. But it had to be a plausible story if it was to convince his contemporaries. In other words, it had to satisfy two conditions. First, it had to be in accordance with the way in which people reacted in the second half of the fourth century, and, second, it was important that it should be in keeping with what was known at the time when Lampridius was writing of civil institutions and church practice in the third century.

The Transfer of Powers

Letter 16 contains a good definition of Cyprian's fundamental principle that no decision should ever be made without consulting the presbyters and deacons and without the consensus of the people. This excellent resolution could, however, hardly be maintained in the presence of schisms and the dispute over the *lapsi*. As we have already seen in Letter 17, Cyprian did not follow the procedure of consulting his clergy, whose view was very different from his own, and instead went to the people for support.

This was, however, an uncomfortable and unsatisfactory situation for the bishop of Carthage. As he was not able to make unity prevail in his own community, his response was to try as quickly as possible to strengthen his links with the other churches. The result of this was a horizontal communion, extended geographically to the "Catholic" Church, which gradually modified the local vertical communion, that had in any case already been led in the wrong direction by the internal conflicts resulting from the persecution.

It was not long before Cyprian was asking for the approval, if not the support, both of the local churches[89] and of the Roman church.[90] Rome responded broadly to his request.[91] The consultations between the bishops continued and bore fruit, thus enabling Cyprian, who was strengthened by this support, once again to approach his people directly with the statement that the decision had been taken —by himself, by the confessors and the clergy of the city and by all the bishops living either in the province or beyond the sea—not to make any new regulations with regard to the *lapsi* until they had been able to meet, share insights and then come to a decision.[92]

Consultations were held in this way both within and outside the church province because the problems raised by the persecution were so serious and so widespread. The persecution had, in other words, been so general within the Roman empire that almost all the local churches were confronted with similar problems. Whenever one of them was put to the test by the martyrdom of its bishop or some of its clergy, the other churches whose members were able to do so naturally enough bore witness to their solicitude.

Above all, however, persecution made the local church break out of its narrow confines. Those expelled by one church would go from one community to another and there would inevitably be an exchange of information and news, for example, about those who had left and the identity, nature, character and quality of those who had joined. In addition to this, there were the confessors, who perhaps did not feel bound, as the clergy did, by any obligation not to go beyond the frontiers of the local community, and the Carthaginian *lapsi* who were anxious to obtain remission for their error. For these men, the letter written by a Roman confessor might be equal to the severe penitential discipline imposed by their bishop. Finally, it is very likely that some Christians were moved to the most important administrative posts and perhaps even to Rome when they were condemned. It goes without saying that new links were in this way formed between people.

What did the people gain and lose as a result of these consultations between local churches that were soon to become more specifically consultations between bishops? It would appear that nothing was in fact gained or lost by the people. Cyprian continued to approach them directly and to keep them informed. He never ceased to respect his people and continued to work for their votes. The reality of the situation was, however, clearly that the people could not participate directly and that they could only be informed later about what had taken place between the bishops in their discussions. It is also clear that it was impossible in practice for the people to call into question the solutions that several bishops had already decided to apply. The principle of lay participation in all the important decisions that had to be made regarding the life of the church may have persisted in theory, but its practical application tended on many occasions to become purely symbolic.

CONCLUSION

The Third Century:
A Century of Change for the Clergy

The term "lay" became more widely and more generally used throughout the course of the third century. This rapid expansion was semantic as well as geographical. The term first appeared, as we have seen, in Alexandria in the writings of Clement and in Carthage in those of Tertullian. Later, it emerged in Syria, in the *Didascalia*, and in Rome, in the letters exchanged during Decius' persecution. To begin with, "lay" indicated a clearly defined group formed by those who were the "husband of only one woman."

At this period, then, the laity was not contrasted with the clergy. The term "lay" was a name that was intended to remind Christians that they were called to the same dignity and—at least at the level of morality—to the same duties as the presbyters and the deacons. Clement did not spend much time attempting to prove something that seemed to him to be obvious. Tertullian, on the other hand, was a polemicist and a moralist and therefore regarded it as important to demonstrate that the distinction between the clergy and the laity was based exclusively on the authority of the church. He also insisted on the fact that the layman had always to remain sufficiently worthy to carry out the priestly functions that he might be called on to fulfill in the absence of a member of the clergy or in the case of a regular promotion.

It was not long, however, before the laity was totally opposed to the clergy and all men who were not members of the clergy and belonged to the church became laymen. To Origen's deep regret, they were far from being as perfect as Clement and Tertullian would have liked. For the author of the *Didascalia*, these lay people were only children whom he had to watch over. The idea of the layman was in no sense elitist, and when the word "ministry" was used for the first time in the history of the Christian communities in association with the term "lay," it was to give the laity the essential task of ensuring the upkeep of the ministers of the altar. This role should in theory have been fulfilled by any Christian, and the laity seems from this time onward to have been confused with the whole of the Christian people. Finally, we have noted that women were never, throughout the whole of the third century, explicitly regarded as "lay."

It is, moreover, very difficult to define with any degree of precision the frontiers of the group of lay people. Was it not implicitly restricted, for example, to men only? Did it extend to include all the male people of the church? Were catechumens, penitents, children and young people excluded? Was the lay category open to include all the people or was it confined only to the most worthy, the most wise or the most active members? Was the Carthaginian plebs really, as Cyprian seems to suggest, equivalent to the Roman laity? This may have been the case, as it was obviously the mass of the people whom the bishop of Carthage seemed to consult whenever he wanted to confirm a decision about the penitential discipline or a promotion in the clergy. On the other hand, however, reading Cyprian's letters, one has the definite impression that the laity consulted by the Roman clergy were notable people or at least selected Christians, even though, in important instances, the acclamation of the people was sought once the decision had been made.

Whatever the case may be, and whatever precise name should be given to those who intervened when decisions were made, what cannot be disputed is that the local churches made use of a clearly democratic principle and regarded it as important to listen to the people's opinion in the case of matters of some delicacy. It was in the way in which this democratic principle was applied that variations occurred. Were all the people to be consulted, for example, or only representatives of the people? Should the consultation take place before or during the decision-making process or should the people or their representatives only be consulted after the decision had been taken?

The consultation of the people's representatives may seem to be a more serious way of dealing with delicate matters than simply having recourse to the people as a whole for their acclamation. During the first half of the third century, however, consulting the whole of the Christian people represented a power which was not in any way purely formal and which could in fact prove to be very effective. This is why it occasionally happened that the people would raise to the episcopal throne a candidate of whom no one had previously thought as a suitable bishop. In the same way, the opinion of the great mass of the people might also be the determining factor in the case of the penitential discipline, even though it was the bishop who, as high priest, had, by virtue of his priestly character, the power to remit sins.

Paradoxically, it was the principle of universalism which was gradually to weaken this principle of democracy. Eminent laymen were often actively present at the preliminary discussions that took place in preparation for meetings between bishops and regional councils and during the editing of the texts that had been adopted. Direct intervention on the part of the mass of the people during the debate between the bishops was, however, almost impossible. It was only when their bishop returned that the people could be invited to express their approval or disapproval once the decisions that had been made at the bishops' meeting had been put into effect.

Neither a true form of popular democracy nor individual charisms could be encouraged by the emergence of a church with a rapidly growing membership. The increasing number of believers made it necessary for Christian communities to have a firm organization in which chance and unforeseen events were as far as possible eliminated. This meant that confessors of the faith gradually lost the position of eminence that they had previously held in the communities. The author of the *Apostolic Tradition,* who was, of course, himself a traditionalist, reminded his readers that those who had suffered for their faith possessed ipso facto, by virtue of their confession of the Christian faith, the honor of the presbyterate. An administrator like the bishop of Carthage, on the other hand, was much more prudent. He cautiously supervised the admission of confessors to the clergy and was careful not to let them sit directly on the presbyterium. Centralization at the local level meant that it was only the bishop who could distribute the duties (*kleroi*) and that powers coming from elsewhere became less and less acceptable.

Cultic functions that were quite distinct and different from liturgical and disciplinary functions had for a long time been tolerated in the Christian communities, even when those functions had been "sacerdotalized." When all the powers became centralized and were, in other words, in episcopal hands, however, the bishops found it increasingly difficult to accept this independence. Some functions, such as that of the catechist, just disappeared without a trace. In the case of others, such as that of the reader or lector, the social image was reduced in stature and the role was reduced first to a bare living and then finally to a position at the bottom of the ladder of clerical functions. Other persons exercising functions in the church and especially the doctors and teachers or *didaskaloi* had simply to accept that their functions were taken over by the clergy.

There were certainly laymen who played a cultural part in the life of the church, but either this role was to be marginalized or it was to be taken over by men who were already distinguished by civil honors and could combine political power with religious power. The man who enjoyed the highest prestige of all was, of course, the emperor, but this introduces a new chapter into the history of the church and its laity.

PART III
FROM THE FOURTH TO THE
SIXTH CENTURY

THE NEW RACES
OF CHRISTIANS

CHAPTER 7

When the Civil Authorities Went Over to Christ

The "conversion" of Constantine has always raised a great number of questions for historians. Was he, for example, the saint that Eusebius of Caesarea called him, a man totally preoccupied with his own salvation and the kingdom of God? Or was he a subtle politician who recognized that it was not possible to obtain absolute power without the help of the religion that was beginning to become dominant? Between these two extreme views, every possible hypothesis has been suggested.

What is beyond doubt, however, whatever answer may be accepted to these countless questions, is that the age of Constantine opened new perspectives for the institutions of the church. The part played by these changes has often been exaggerated, and accusations, many of them wrongful, have been made against the Constantinian church. It is often claimed, for example, that it was from this period onward that bishops began to play at being princes, that power phenomena began to figure prominently in the Christian communities, and that the idea of hierarchy and clerical cursus began to absorb men's thoughts. All these "evils" existed, however, before Constantine. It is possible that they have simply been systematized by our knowledge of Christianity.

After the conversion of Constantine, Christianity, from having been an illicit religion, became a religion that was first tolerated and then, with almost breathtaking speed, a privileged religion. The ease with which this new state religion forgot the very recent past, when appeals had again and again been made to the emperors to put an end to the persecution of Christians and to be tolerant, and, as soon as it was officially recognized, became in its turn the intolerant persecutor of others, is quite astonishing.

Did these changes, implying, as they did, close collaboration between the civil and the religious powers, influence the idea and the position of lay people in the church? Some scholars[1] have suggested that the conversion of Emperor Constantine in the fourth century inaugurated a new era in the role of the laity in the church. Is this claim justified? Did Constantine, who was converted after making a long and complicated politico-religious journey, himself become the first "lay" emperor in history? Our reply to this question has to be quite subtly shaded.

Can a God Become a Layman?

It is worth bearing in mind at the outset that politics and religion could not be dissociated from each other in the Roman empire. They were two aspects of the same social reality. So, when Tertullian declared: "The emperor is only great insofar as he is below heaven,"[2] he was going directly counter to the dominant ideology of the third century. From the time of Caesar and Augustus onward in fact, a complete aura of divinity had grown around the person of the emperor. He was deified by apotheosis when he died, but he could also be already deified during his lifetime. He was the "son of God" or "close to the gods."

In his attempt to restore the state after the many different political crises that had shaken it during the first half of the third century, Diocletian began by setting up a tetrarchy based on a theological hierarchy. In this order, the emperors were regarded as "Jovians" and the caesars held the rank of "Herculeans." Were these titles simply a means of affirming the conviction that the gods acted as protectors and that the emperors and the caesars held their powers? Or did they express a real "epiphany" of the divine presence as something that was part of the function of the emperor? Was this epiphany only effective as long as the emperor's function lasted or did it impress a permanently divine character on the person of the emperor?

Diocletian's abdication in 303 A.D. would seem to provide us with an answer to this question, because the ex-emperor was ranked among the gods after his death, although he had become a simple citizen after his abdication. According to the historian Eutropius, this solution appears to have surprised his contemporaries. Eutropius was himself obviously astonished too, since he says: "Since the foundation of the Roman empire, Diocletian is the only man who has, of his own free will, descended from the highest peak of honors and returned to the rank of a simple citizen. And what has happened to him has happened to no one since there have been men—he died as an simple private citizen and he has been included among the gods."[3]

Since the mere fact of having fulfilled the imperial functions, even for only a time, therefore conferred a divine character on a man, we may be quite certain that an emperor still carrying out his functions must have been regarded as divine in reality and not merely as metaphorically divine. How, then, was Constantine able to descend from this divine state to the lay state?

We should note first of all that there is no contemporary document that might allow us to say that either Constantine himself or those around him ever described the emperor in this way. What, then, was the meaning of the term "lay" at the beginning of the fourth century? Whether it pointed simply to those Christians who were male adults or whether it was applied to all the baptized, Constantine certainly only became a "layman" on his deathbed in 337 A.D. That was, after all, when he was baptized by an Arian bishop, Eusebius of Nicomedia. When he intervened in the affairs of the church, what he did not fail to do from 314 onward, when he convoked the Council of Arles, and in 325, when he summoned the First Council of Nicaea, was to reestablish the unity of the empire, which was in the process of becoming Christianized.

He intervened in fact as pontifex maximus, but he did it in quite a new way—a way which made Julian the "Apostate" describe him as the "innovator and violator of the early laws and customs received since time immemorial."[4] Eusebius of Caesarea, the theologian of this new imperial power, called him, on the other hand, the thirteenth apostle or the bishop from outside. During the first half of the fourth century, a Roman emperor had hardly any chance of being regarded as a simple layman. The church was, however, only too delighted, at least to begin with, with this change to be offended about the authority of the emperor.

This was no longer the case at the end of the century, especially in the west, when the troubles caused by the Arian controversy had led some bishops to distance themselves from an imperial power that was at times capricious and when the emperor had to deal with a "Christian priest" of the caliber of Ambrose of Milan.[5] In the west at least, the time seemed to be ripe for a relative distinction between powers to be accepted. Emperor Valentinian I (364–375), who was probably weary of his involvement in the internal quarrels that were tearing the church apart at the time, replied tersely to the eastern bishops who had come to him to ask him to hold a synod: "I am only a layman and so I do not have the right to be concerned with such matters."[6]

The same emperor also decreed: "In the question of faith and in every matter connected with the church's hierarchy, a judge must have equal dignity and similar rights."[7] He was also to insist that it was not within his authority to settle differences between bishops. His successor Gratian (375–383) abandoned the title of pontifex maximus. This meant that, from then onward, there was, theoretically at least, no obstacle in the way of regarding the emperor as a layman. The match had, however, still not been won.

When Valentinian II (383–392) called on Ambrose, the bishop of Milan, to let himself be judged by laymen, the latter angrily reminded the emperor of the decisions taken by his father Valentinian I: "When have you ever heard it said, most clement emperor, that, in a matter of faith, laymen have pronounced a verdict on a bishop? Do we have to debase ourselves by adulation to the point where we forget the rights of the priesthood and hand over to others the privilege with which God has honored us? If a bishop has to receive lessons by a layman, what will be the result? The layman will have only to discuss and the bishop to listen and to become the layman's pupil. But if we question the divine scriptures and past history, who would dare to disagree with what I say, namely that, in a matter of faith, it is the bishops who are customarily the judges of the Christian emperors and not the emperors who are the judges of the bishops?"[8] This letter to Emperor Valentinian II is dated March 386 and it points very clearly to the development that had taken place by the end of the fourth century in the relationships between political and religious power.

The bishop of Milan went so far as to convince the young emperor, who was sympathetically inclined toward the Arians and was still only a catechumen, that he had fewer rights than a layman. We should not, however, make any mistake about this: in this particular context, the term "lay" points to individuals holding secular power and wanting to impose the yoke of that power on the church. Ambrose may have refused categorically to be judged by such laymen, but he was certainly ready to submit to the judgment of the people. Paradoxically, the people was therefore confronted by laymen and

Valentinian I
"I am only a layman"

Ambrose was naturally tempted to contrast in a very Manichaean way the temporal authority of such powerful laymen with the spiritual power of the poor and the needy who were in his care as their bishop.

Ambrose was convinced that he was and that he had to remain a "free priest." He would never compromise when this conviction was at stake. The public penance that Ambrose made Emperor Theodosius I do after he had massacred the inhabitants of Thessalonica is a striking example of how the church could increase its authority when it did not compromise in the question of its independence. This case provided Ambrose's contemporaries with clear evidence that the emperor was, from the religious point of view, no more than a layman who had to submit to the church's priests.

A century later, Theodoret of Cyrrhus expressed his admiration for what Ambrose had done and even embellished his account of it with an anecdote. Adding that Theodosius had made an offering after his penance and had remained in the choir, he also pointed out that Ambrose had given a lesson on the places in the church and told the emperor that the choir was the place reserved for the priests. Theodosius asked to be forgiven according to the eastern custom and took his place among the people. When he had returned to the east, he was invited by a bishop to sit in the choir. "I have learned to my cost to distinguish between a priest and an emperor, because I have found to my cost a master of the truth."[9]

It was to prove easier to keep the powers of the church and those of the emperor separate in the west, where the power of the emperor was becoming weaker, than in the east, where caesaropapalism was to produce a hybrid form of legislation which gave canonical force to the imperial laws.

Constantine, the Bishop of External Affairs

The fact that, in the east, these two powers were not kept distinct suited Emperor Constantine far better than the situation that finally came to prevail in the west. The idea of separating the two powers was not, as we have seen, acceptable to the leaders of that time. The pontifex maximus could not be interested in the affairs of the state without feeling that God had invested him with that mission. "Guided by you," he wrote in an edict, "I have begun and ended my undertakings for the good of men. Everywhere I have had

"I have learned to my cost to distinguish between a priest and an emperor"

Ravenna, San Vitale. Photo André Held-Ziolo

your sacred sign carried before me, leading the army in this way to glorious victories. And if the state is in distress and has to appeal to me again, I shall once more follow the same sign and march against the enemy, to such an extent that I feel that I am driven to give myself to this task in order to restore your holy house (the church), which ungodly and atrocious men have criminally laid waste and profaned."[10]

The secularization of the emperor's power was not in fashion at the time of Constantine, who, in setting the church free, was quite convinced that he was the instrument of divine power. This was something that he made known in the still ambiguous text of the inscription that is found on the triumphal arch that he had erected in about 350 A.D.: "In honor of the pious and blessed Emperor Caesar Flavius Constantine, the great Augustus, who, inspired by the deity (*instinctu divinitatis*) and in his greatness of spirit, took revenge, with his army and with righteous weapons by means of a decisive act, on behalf of the state, on the tyrant and the whole of his party, the Senate and the people dedicate this arch as a sign of his triumph."

This text and others express the theology of victory that had been an essential element of the politico-religious thinking since the beginning of the Roman empire. Victories were regarded as a kind of manifestation of the deity. They were evidence of the divine power that was at work in the victorious emperor. When this virtus favored the church, Christian authors regarded the emperor as the one who had been providentially sent by God. These victories were, in a curious and fleeting sense of harmony, the point where Constantine's theological options and the historical views of Christians came together.

Both Lactantius and Eusebius developed this providential view of history, each in a rather different way. Lactantius, for example, wrote: "All our adversaries have now been crushed, peace has been restored to the universe, and the church, which was only a short time ago dejected, is once again standing upright. The mercy of the Lord is again raising up God's temple, which godless men had ruined, but which is now more glorious than ever. God has aroused princes who have done away with the criminal and bloodthirsty empire of the tyrants by dispersing the cloud overshadowing that sinister time and filling all hearts with the joy and sweetness of a serene peace."[11]

Constantine I
The Bishop of External Affairs

In the *Life of Constantine*, which is attributed to Eusebius, the emperor himself is made to express a theological view of history that is very close to that of Lactantius. According to this author, Constantine stated that "a great godlessness was pressing down on men, and the state was threatened with total ruin, as though by a plague. There was an urgent need to find an effective remedy for these evils. What, then, was the remedy found by the Deity? God called on me to serve and swore that I was capable of carrying out his decision. So it was that I left the sea of Brittany and the country where the sun sets and, commanded by a higher power, agreed to drive out and disperse the terror that was reigning everywhere, so that the human race, informed by my intervention, might return to the service of the holy law and the blessed faith might become widespread under the power of the Most High."[12]

Invested with this divine mission, the Christian emperor gradually set aside the title of pontifex maximus, which was too closely associated with pagan religiosity, but at the same time also kept to the theology of the great pontifex and remained God's chosen one, exercising a priesthood which placed him outside any distinction that might have been made between clergy and laity.

Constantine was equal to the apostles—indeed, he was the thirteenth apostle. He had such a distinct and separate place that he was able to convoke councils of the church—at Arles in 314 and Nicaea in 325. He was to treat the bishops who came to Nicaea so magnificently that Eusebius believed that he was contemplating a beatific vision. "No bishop was absent from the Lord's table," he wrote. "Some were lying on the same couch as the emperor, while others were resting on nearby couches. The whole scene could easily have been taken for an image of the kingdom of Christ. It was thought to be a dream rather than a reality."[13]

When Constantine promulgated edicts, he did not hesitate to use the formula "God's providence acting hand in hand with me." And when he became convinced that Christians were divided for "futile reasons" (these reasons arose because of the dispute over the Trinity) and that they were therefore threatening the unity of the empire, he summoned a full assembly of bishops and, even though he was not yet baptized, did not hesitate to take up his place among them, as one of them. "This is why very many bishops gathered together," we read in the *Life of Constantine*, "and I was also among them, as one of you, because I did not want to deny what gave me such joy, namely that I ranked among you—you who are the servants of God."[14]

This is a theme that is developed more fully later in the same *Life of Constantine*: "God has instituted you as bishops for everything that forms part of the internal affairs of the church. As for me, I have apparently been nominated to be the bishop of external affairs."[15] Eusebius even goes so far as to include the wishes of his emperor: "His solicitude was quite especially directed toward the church of God. As soon as a dispute arose in any country, he would therefore call the servants of God together in an assembly, acting as though God had appointed him to be the bishop of all."[16]

It is clear, then, that Eusebius was not in any way offended by the service provided by the power of the emperor and equally clear that Christians were at that time a long way from sharing the attitude of the bishop of Milan later in the fourth century.

These texts also show above all that it would be quite wrong to regard Constantine as a model for "lay power." One of his much later successors, Leo III, the "Isaurian," wrote in a letter to Pope Gregory II in the eighth century: "Do you not know that I am a priest and a king?" Like the emperors, the church was to continue to be tempted to form a collusion between spiritual and temporal power. The "Christianization" of the imperial structures did not take place in a day, if it ever took place at all. Nonetheless, the model of Roman organization certainly played an important part in the church's concept of power and influenced the relationships that were to develop between the members of the Christian *plebs* and the various *ordines*.

Civil Authority and the Authority of the Church: Mimicry and Its Limits

Recent research has tended to overestimate the influence of the changes in civil society on the structures of the church. This reaction is quite understandable, of course, when the way in which so many histories of the church have been written is borne in mind, but it is not a valid reason for making such unshaded affirmations. Mimicry of civil society and its powers by the church has certainly played a part, but it has its limits and it above all has its own history.

Constantine I
"God's providence acting hand in hand with me"

Christianity's territorial organization is possibly the most striking aspect of its intrusion into civil society in the fourth century.
Christian communities were an urban phenomenon at the beginning of the third century, but, during the century that followed, they
tended to become organized according to the geographical structures of civil administration.

The first stage in this reorganization undoubtedly took place
before Constantine's time. At the end of the second and above all
during the third century, the bishops' meetings tended to take place
according to civil districts. The principal reason for this was convenience.[17] The First Council of Nicaea (325 A.D.) confirmed what was
already current practice in the church in calling, in its fourth canon,
for the bishop to be established by all the bishops of the province
(the provincia or eparchy). The main result of this first type of reorganization was that the bishops began to be "hierarchized." In other
words, the bishop of a metropolis would supervise what was happening in the bishoprics of his district.

It is worth noting, however, that this geographical structuriza-
tion was not uniform and that a different development took place in
the west. In Africa, for example, the preeminence of the bishop who
was the first to have been ordained was maintained and not the
bishop of the civil administrative center. The canonical legislation of
the Councils of Nicaea (325) and Trullo (691) bear witness to the
later history of this reorganization. From the Council of Nicaea onward, there were great senior metropolises in the east, governed by a
"patriarch" and based on the civil dioceses. When Constantinople,
the new Rome founded by Constantine, became the real capital of
the east, it at the same time became the capital of the church, with
an ecumenical patriarch. This geopolitical mimicry was officially
recognized as normative by the Council of Trullo, which stated in its
canon 38: "If a city is founded by order of the emperor, the hierarchical order of the church (established in that city) will follow the civil
and public order resulting from that foundation."

This geographical hierarchization of the local churches meant
that it was not long before the effects of these changes were felt in
the bishops' attitudes toward and their relationships with the people
who belonged to their churches. Nicaea had condemned the movement of bishops from one bishopric to another as a serious error, but
the authors writing at the end of the fourth century regarded this
condemnation as superseded, it frequently happened that the bishop

of a small community would try to make a career for himself by becoming the bishop of the administrative center of the province and even of the diocese or the capital.

One consequence of this movement of bishops was that the close bond that might have existed in the third century between a bishop and his church would be broken. The image of the bishop as a man who was as closely tied to his church as a husband was to his wife lost its meaning. Another was that Christians began to regard their bishop simply as a "prince" of the church who associated closely and almost exclusively with other leading public figures and administrators and who often acted as they did. The laity became people who were the subjects of the bureaucratic administration of the church.

Some bishops quickly developed a taste for temporal power and showed such a tendency to leave their churches that their actions were criticized by the Council of Sardica in 343 A.D. as being unjustified, out of place, badly timed and too frequent, and they were forbidden by the council to go to the emperor's court. The council was especially opposed to the attitude of those African bishops who were only concerned with their "dignity and profane affairs" and did not "help the poor, the laity and the widows."[18]

Such changes in attitude were not, however, exclusively confined to the level of the bishops of the church. The fourth century was the golden age not only for civil administration and bureaucracy, but also for the clergy generally. Both in civil affairs and in the church, there was a great increase in the number of well paid and highly regarded administrators on the one hand and, on the other, in the number of clergy enjoying special privileges, not required to pay the taxes that were a crushing burden on so many categories of citizen and exempt from obligatory military and civil service.

There were in fact so many such members of the clergy that a hierarchical organization was formed within each of the Christian communities, parallel to the geographical hierarchization alluded to above. In an attempt to justify this hierarchization, Christian authors writing at the end of the fourth century naturally enough used contemporary civil models. In fact they took all their metaphors from the spheres of civil administration, the navy, the army and the educational structures. These comparisons were employed not only to show the need for hierarchization in the life of the church, but also to demonstrate the value of preparing the way to higher functions and of an ascending scale within the church's "orders." Pope Damasus, for example, wrote at this time: "It has never been known for anyone who was not a conscript to have been made supreme commander of the armed forces."[19]

To take one example, the word *stipendium* was originally used to indicate the pay or the number of years of service that enabled a soldier to be given the status of veteran, in which he was semi-retired and received an endowment. This word was taken over by the church and became the technical term either for the remuneration received by the clergy or more frequently for the number of years spent in the service of the church which entitled a man to promotion to the higher functions.

The way in which administrators were appointed also changed in the public sphere. It became more and more common for them to be chosen directly by the imperial power and therefore for them to share in its quasi-divine authority. Christians had not waited for this development in the structures of the state machinery before affirming that all power comes from God. But, by mimicry, all Christian authority came gradually to be regarded as having a directly divine origin. This meant that this same authority ceased to be at the service of a religious end and very quickly became a religious end in itself.

The theological justification for this was also changed. Authority, it was argued, was no longer exclusively at the service of the unity of the religious group, but was in itself religious, with the result that Christians ought to place themselves at its service. The civil administrator or the member of the Christian clergy therefore shared in the authority of those who were hierarchically higher than himself. He would be respected and obeyed only if he himself displayed these attitudes toward those who had instituted, nominated, appointed or ordained him.

A good example of this can be found in the writings of Lampridius. Fearing the arbitrary nature of the emperor's appointment of public officials and administrators, this pagan author cited the election of Christian bishops as a model of democratic procedure. This can be compared with the text of Pope Damasus, giving as an example to his junior clergy the organization and discipline of the army. But these comparisons in which each person only finds what he wants to find in the example of his neighbor ought not, of course, to be trusted.

It is above all a question not of sociological data or explanations, but of arguments to facilitate the introduction of an institutional organization into social practice. This mimicry may only have been apparent, of course, and, when Pope Leo I claimed that it was both iniquitous and absurd that ignorant men should be chosen in preference to masters, that new men were appointed rather than older men, and that recruits were favored more than veterans,[20] we should not automatically conclude that the church based its organization on that of public administration, the armed forces or the official educational structures.

Whatever the situation may have been, the result was the same for the layman. He found himself at the bottom of the ladder, even more completely separated by a weighty machinery from his bishop, who was probably a complete stranger to him. The bishop had probably simply dropped for a while into his community and intended to stay there long enough to further his own career. He had not originally come from that community and he hardly knew it, its problems or the individuals who belonged to it.

The First Stages in the Clerical Career:
The Laity at the Bottom of the Ladder

During the period beginning at the dawn of the third century and ending with the death of Gregory the Great (604), a frontier that was increasingly difficult to cross was established in the church's structures between the clergy and the laity. There were several stages in this development, each of them leading to a different position occupied by the group of lay people.

At the beginning of the third century, there were still, as we have already seen, church functions that were not clericalized. There were, for example, readers or lectors and doctors carrying out a real function in the church and not necessarily being members of the clergy. The frontier ran between the ordained ministries (the bishop, presbyters and deacons) for the *leitourgia* and all the other functions or states of life. Curiously, however, according to the prayer for the ordination of a deacon in the *Apostolic Tradition*, God was asked that "in service that is beyond reproach and in leading a pure life, he (the deacon) may reach a higher state."[21]

This is clearly, in embryo, the first sign of a clerical career and it points clearly to a very important change in Christian religious attitudes. At almost exactly the same time, the distinction between clergy and laity began to appear and the whole idea of "service"— *diakonia*—began to be transformed. From having been a generic term characterizing every function in the Christian community, it became a much more specific term describing a function, one of the aspects of which was to be a stage in the clerical career. The growth of the Christian social group and that group's need to persist and have a stable structure may be one possible explanation of this change, but this is not a satisfactory theological justification for the change.

The simplest way of justifying this change theologically is by the argument of good sense. A man has to provide evidence of his ability to carry out a function and has to be prepared for the task. This is clearly what underlies Canon 2 of the First Council of Nicaea in its legislation concerning "those who become members of the clergy immediately after baptism." This must have been current practice, because the church's rule had to be recalled:

> Either because of necessity or for other reasons, several things have occurred that are contrary to the rule of the church. The spiritual bath and, immediately after baptism, the episcopal or presbyteral dignity have been given to men who have barely ceased to be pagans and entered the life of faith and who have only been instructed for a very short time. It is therefore right and proper that this should not happen in the future, since the catechumen needs to be put to the test for a time and, after baptism, for an even longer time. The words of the apostle are quite clear: "The bishop must not be a recent convert or he may be puffed up with conceit and fall into the condemnation of the devil."[22]

The demand that the candidate should be "put to the test for a time" between baptism and the episcopate is quite logical. But should the same be required of a candidate who was rich, had a good position in society and was known by everyone? Hosius gave the following reply to this question at the Council of Sardica (343–344): "I believe that, if a rich man or a jurist of the forum makes a claim to the episcopate, he should not be installed until he has carried out the functions of reader, deacon and presbyter, so that, from being promoted from one to the other, if he is judged worthy, he may go to the peak of the episcopate. Promotion in each order should clearly take some time, so that his faith, his firmness, his goodness and his uprightness of character may be made known and that he may, considered in this way to be worthy of the divine priesthood, be able to enjoy this great honor."[23]

In the last quarter of the fourth century, the bishops of Rome developed this legislation concerning admission to and promotion within the clergy. The frontier dividing the clergy from the laity tended to be greatly strengthened and even more clearly—and negatively—defined by the decretals (letters in which a precise outline was given to questions of church discipline) sent at this time by the bishops of Rome to the other bishops.

The first of these decretals, addressed to the bishops of Gaul, called for "care in the choice of bishops from among the clergy." The earlier functions that had been carried out at the beginning of the third century by the laity became at this time clerical functions. These previously lay but now clerical functions also tended to lose their real content and become no more than a period of probation, during which the "lower clergy" could gain experience of service in the church and, even more importantly, could provide evidence of their chastity. It was in fact at the end of the fourth century that the idea began to be developed in the legislation of the Roman church that a member of the higher clergy had to be chaste. If this period of probation (*tempora*) proved conclusive, the candidate could then be admitted to a higher grade of the clergy. The more senior function was therefore regarded as a well deserved reward. At the same time and almost inevitably, then, the layman came to be regarded as a person who had not deserved this promotion because he was not worthy of a higher status.

This legislation concerning the *tempora* was developed and defined more precisely in the decretals of Siricius (384–399), Innocent I (401–417) and Zosimus (417–418). In all these decretals, there is broad measure of agreement in calling for two stages of preparation or two periods of training or probation. During the first of these periods, the candidate was to be an exorcist or a reader or lector and, during the second, he was to become an acolyte or sub-deacon. If he performed good service during these stages, he could then become a deacon, presbyter or bishop. From that time onward, he was obliged to remain chaste.[24]

At the end of the fifth century, circumstances outside the

church—the barbarian invasions—played an indirect part in changing the Christian ministries once again. The shortage of clergy made it necessary for Pope Gelasius (492–496) to find quick solutions, while at the same time observing the rules defined by his predecessors. He therefore reduced the *tempora* or time of preparation and probation during which a candidate exercised a minor function and at the same time required him to serve in three stages instead of two. This "compensation" tended to ritualize the clerical career by making it known that the order received rather than the function exercised was the important factor.

The desiderata of the lower Roman public servants expressed in the Symmachian Apocrypha (ca. 501–508) have to be situated within this context. The clerical career, which was, it was hoped, to take place *per gradum*, by steps, and not *per saltum*, became a guarantee of the moral and religious perfection of the one who had followed its course. At the same time, however, it also became the symbol that the man who was to become a priest or a bishop had been properly prepared. If he had received all the minor "orders," he would be able to exercise all the functions that were needed for the life of the church.

This ritualization of the clerical career therefore culminated in the principle according to which one power could be substituted for and fitted into another and the senior member of the clergy could do everything that was done by the member of the lower clergy. This way of looking at the Christian ministries was, even at the beginning of the sixth century, still no more than desire to reform, but it reflects very well the way in which Christian attitudes had developed. What is particularly clear from it is that the layman was still at the bottom of the ladder of perfection and powers and that his state was quite different from that of the clergy. The appearance during the sixth century of the clerical tonsure, as a liturgical rite giving a sacred value to the transition from the lay to the clerical way of life, was a striking manifestation of this difference between those two states.

At the end of the palaeo-Christian period, Gregory the Great was therefore able to make a distinction between three categories of Christian—the *conjugali* (in other words, married people), the *continentes* (who were essentially monks) and the *rectores* (those in responsible positions in the church). Married lay people were in the lowest position. The ideal position was occupied by those who led a mixed way of life, that is, the contemplative life coupled with pastoral activity. A council that took place in 595 went so far as to forbid the employment of the laity in the personal service of the pope. Offices of this kind, this council insisted, had to be fulfilled by the clergy or by monks.[25] Being a member of the clergy therefore became synonymous with being an active member of the church.

Finances: Lay Stewards and Clerical Stewards

The "sacralization" of Christian ministers and its counterpart, the "religious devaluation" of the ordinary believers, does not date from the fourth century. It is possible to detect an increase in the social value or status of the person and function of the bishop as early as the end of the second century. The problems raised by the administration of the church's wealth and property formed part of this phenomenon. The bishop was in fact obliged to administer the church's finances, which were becoming increasingly important. This function led him to play the part of the powerful leader in the Christian community. It is in fact possible to say without exaggeration that he played the part of *patronus* with regard to his customers, who consisted of all the members of his church, but particularly to the clergy whom he fed and sustained.

The fathers of the Synod of Antioch (341) left it to the bishops to dispose of the church's wealth in order to provide for the poor and the needy. They also agreed to let them use it for their own personal needs if that proved necessary and for their brothers who received their hospitality. The fact that bishops were able to leave the management of all or part of the church's wealth to next of kin, servants, relatives, brothers or sons was, however, offensive to them.[26]

According to Canon 24 of the same Synod of Antioch, the administration of the church's wealth had to be done under the supervision and authority of the bishop, and the presbyters and deacons had to know clearly and precisely how it was administered. The bishop had to give an account of his administration to the provincial synod, the members of which would probably appoint an administrator in cases where the reputation of the presbyters and the bishops had become compromised.

The bishop might have found it difficult to carry out all the tasks entrusted to him in large cities. He therefore delegated his administrative functions to others and usually to deacons. We have already seen what an important part was played by the ex-slave Callistus, who was skilled in dealing with quite large sums of money and who was later made a deacon and finally became the bishop of Rome.

The misappropriation of funds was, however, quite a common practice at this time. In a letter written to Cyprian, Cornelius mentions an ex-deacon named Nicostratus who was "accused of several crimes." The bishop of Rome goes on to say: "Not only has he defrauded and stolen from the woman who employs him and whose affairs he manages, but, having also received very considerable sums of money from the church, he has carried them off."[27]

In his reply to his fellow bishop, Cyprian develops this accusation in terms that are very close to those employed by Hippolytus in the case of Callistus, writing that "we have learned that, having lost his holy office of deacon after having purloined the church's money by sacrilegious larceny and having refused to return the funds of the widows and orphans, Nicostratus has not even tried to come to Africa, but has fled from Rome, terrified because of his thefts and his infamous crimes."[28]

When he left his episcopal city for a time to retire to his villa outside Carthage, Cyprian clearly regarded the task of settling these financial matters himself as important, possibly because it was essentially a question of his own personal money. The fathers of the Council of Antioch, on the other hand, wanted to make a distinction between the bishop's private patrimony and the wealth of the church in order to avoid an injustice to the heirs or causing a scandal. This is illustrated in the canon prohibiting the seizure of a bishop's wealth and property after his death promulgated by the Council of Chalcedon (451).

We do not know whether it was precisely the intention of the Council of Antioch to proscribe in every case the choice of a lay steward or whether the fathers of the council simply aimed to prevent abuses in cases in which the bishops entrusted the administration of the church's wealth to next of kin or close relatives. More than a hundred years later, however, all ambiguity was removed by the Council of Chalcedon, which insisted that every bishop should have a clerical steward to administer the wealth of his church, while he himself would remain responsible.

According to this Chalcedonian Canon 26, "having learned that, in certain churches, the bishops have administered the church's wealth without employing a steward, the council has decreed that every church which has a bishop must also have a steward taken from the clergy of that church, who will administer the wealth of that church according to the advice of his bishop. In this way, the administration of the church will not be unsupervised, the church's wealth will not be dissipated and the dignity of the priesthood will be protected from accusations. If the bishop does not do this, he will be subject to canonical penalties."[29]

The canons preceding this canon point to the importance of the part played by the steward in the case of the bishop's decease, and Canon 25 in particular calls for "the income from a pastor's private church to be kept integrally by the steward of that church."

The function of steward seems to have been an obligatory institution from the fourth century onward in Egypt. In his instructions to the delegate whom he sent to reorganize certain communities, following the Arian crisis, Theophilus of Alexandria recommended him to choose "another steward" after consulting with all the clergy and with the approval of Bishop Apollos (who seems to have been in communion for a while with the Arians).[30]

We do not know whether these stewards were necessarily members of the clergy or whether it was possible for them to be laymen. In any case, we do know that it was not necessary for them to be presbyters. In his letter written in 458 about simony, Gennadius I, the patriarch of Constantinople, makes a distinction, on the one hand, between the ordination for money of a bishop, a *chorepiscopus*, a presbyter, a deacon or someone inscribed in the catalogue of the clergy and, on the other, the promotion for money of a church steward, syndic or tutor. We are apparently confronted here with two parallel and not very strictly coordinated hierarchies. In the sixth century, the wealth and property of Pope Gregory the Great was administered by a sub-deacon in Sicily.[31]

> The qualifications possessed by laymen, who were used to business life, made them very suited to act as the bishop's valuable assistants in the administration of the patrimony. They certainly misused this ability. There is clear evidence in the fourth and fifth century texts that there was more insistence on preserving the bishop's prerogatives than on extending the part played by the laity.[32]

This is a correct statement, but it requires amplification, and a few details have to be added. From the beginning of the third century onward, the bishops enjoyed absolute moral prerogatives with regard to the management of the church's wealth and property. This management, however, was not exclusively dependent on moral or theological imperatives. Even if it is true that certain laymen were able to betray the trust placed in them, the deacons and the bishops themselves were certainly not immune from the same temptation. That is precisely why the institution of the steward was justified.

Then there is the fact that the problems differed according to the importance and the nature of the church's wealth and property. The situation in which the community was placed also played a very important part. If, for example, the Christian church was not tolerated in society and there was a constant threat of renewed persecution, forcing it to become clandestine, there was a strong case for having the wealth of the Christian community or at least part of it administered by a layman, since he would be less directly aimed at than the bishop. Finally, there was the legal position of the church. This played perhaps the most important part of all.

The Clergy's Civil Privileges

At the beginning of the fourth century, the Council of Elvira suggested that the bishops who wanted to make bargains outside their own provinces should entrust their business dealings to the care of a son, an emancipated slave, a servant or a friend.[33] Some forty years after this council, the Council of Antioch severely warned those who entrusted the church's wealth to servants, next of kin or close relatives against doing this. What was the reason for this change of attitude?

Two important facts occurred in the interval between these two decisions: Constantine the Great had been "converted" and certain privileges had been granted to the church and its clergy. As a result, the church no longer had to conceal its wealth under the official lid of funeral companies, as it had needed to do during times of persecution, nor did it find it necessary to entrust the management of that wealth to laymen. The Council of Antioch was therefore able to insist that the bishop's private wealth should be systematically separated from the church's.

Above all, however, the church benefited from the favors of power and was able to increase its patrimony considerably. Throughout the course of the fourth century, moreover, the clergy was also made exempt not only from many taxes, but also from more and more tasks. The greater importance of the patrimony also increased the need for this to be administered and, what is more, for that management to be entrusted to members of the clergy. They, after all, had the advantage of being exempt from many taxes and were therefore free to carry out certain tasks without difficulty. These clerical exemptions were important at a time when the needs of the empire both for public administrators and for military personnel and precious metals were leading to a crushing burden of taxation.

Quite apart from the directly economic consequences of these clerical privileges, the new and favorable legal position granted to the church had some influence on the formation and the definition of the clergy. From what tasks was the clergy exempt? They were first of all not obliged to exercise any public function such as the *munera civilia* in which the *curia* or municipal assembly participated and which it was bound to distribute. This included duties that were as different from each other as public works, the levying of taxes, the tasks of the scribe and contributing to the provisions of the armed forces.[34] Members of the clergy were also not obliged to pay trade taxes. They were also exempted from payment of the *chrysargyria*, a tax on silver. This exemption, which was really very important, also included the servants of the clergy who were engaged in trading. The clergy was also not required to carry out the more menial tasks or *munera sordida* such as preparing bread for the soldiers of the imperial army.[35]

To all these many exemptions can be added one final and very important tax exemption. Not only members of the clergy, but also their wives, their emancipated slaves and their servants were not obliged to pay either land tax or any emergency taxes. We may therefore conclude that the tax exemption of the clergy was almost total.

It was not long before these measures had a very striking effect —there was a rush to join the ranks of the clergy. Basil of Caesarea expressed his deep regret that unworthy men had been accepted for service in the church without any examination of their conduct and simply on the basis of their family connections or of sympathy. He was quite outspoken, saying: "Because of this, every little town has a great army of clergy, but none of them is worthy of the altar."

Basil's decision was radical: "Because, in my opinion, the situation has become intolerable, especially at present, when very many men who are afraid of being called up for military service have enlisted in the service of the church, I am obliged to renew the canonical instructions of the fathers. I therefore order you to send me a list of the clergy serving in each town. . . . If, then, there are any men whose names have been included by the priests on this list since it was first published, they shall be rejected and included among the laity, and their canonical examination will be reviewed by us."

He also felt obliged to state very firmly that he alone had the power to decide in this matter. He ordered his *chorepiscopi*: "From now on, you must examine those who are worthy and admit them to the clergy. But do not enter their names on the rolls of the clergy until you have referred to us. If you do not do this, then the man who is accepted for service in the church without our consent will be regarded as a layman."[36] This centralization of authority in the hands of the bishop means that the latter had the sovereign right to decide on who was to belong to the group of the clergy and who to the lay group.

The bishop was not the only one to supervise the admission of laymen to the clergy. The emperor, overwhelmed by the success of his laws, was also to try to control this flow from one group in the church to the other. In 329, Constantine published a constitution forbidding the recruitment of clergy from the ranks of his *decuriones*, the sons of his *decuriones* or persons who were sufficiently wealthy to be able to contribute to the public offices. What he wanted to do was to reduce those who went beyond this decision to the lay state and to the curia.[37] In keeping those who paid the most tax within the ranks of the taxpayers, he also restricted recruitment to the clergy to the lower middle class. In addition, the threatened return to curial obligations was only generally applied in the case of the lower clergy and not at all to the deacons, the presbyters and the bishops. It was also always possible for the law to be twisted. That was what some laymen attempted to do by entrusting the management of their affairs to members of the clergy and in this way having their wealth and property made exempt from tax under the clerical exemptions.[38]

Following the example of Basil of Caesarea, the bishops tried to eliminate certain types of servant and service that were a cause of scandal. It is, however, difficult to understand why they deprived themselves of good servants and why they also deprived those servants of the benefits that went with the clerical status. But it was in this way that the idea gradually gained ground that all those who played any part at all in the service of the church were able to benefit from the title of "clergy."

In the middle of the third century, the bishop of Carthage, Cyprian, had, it will be remembered, called on members of his church to provide for the needs of those whose attention ought not to be distracted from the service of the altar. Less than a hundred years later, the *chorepiscopi* of the bishop of Caesarea, Basil, were unable to find, among the names of the individuals inscribed on the catalogue of the clergy, anyone who could carry out any function in the service of the altar. Between the two lies an enormous change had taken place. The group of the clergy no longer formed an elite. It had in the meantime grown in numbers and had lost at least part of its distinctive character. The lay group, on the other hand, had become slimmed down or at least modified and it is very likely that it no longer included, at least as far as the middle and lower classes are concerned, anyone who carried out functions or performed any real service in the church. Any Christian who wanted to exercise a function in the church and at the same time do without the advantages of the clerical state would have had to be unusually stoical. From this time onward, the lay people with a socially lower status had no active share in the religious life. It was only people belonging to the most leisured classes, that is, laymen of a higher status, who played an important part in the church.

It is worth noting that Christians who belonged to the more lowly categories were also able to benefit from the generosity of the emperor. Servants of the clergy were able to enjoy their masters' good fortune and profit from the exemptions which the law granted to those masters. Slaves also benefited, because the clergy and the church assembly could exercise an almost total right of emancipation, with the result that it was much easier for a Christian slave to achieve full citizenship.[39] Finally, from 321 onward, all workers were obliged to observe the rest day known as the *dies solis* or "Sunday."[40] Agricultural workers were the only exception to this rule of Sunday rest, insofar as they were bound by their seasonal work. Trials were also forbidden on Sundays. The emancipation of slaves, on the other hand, was permitted because of its positive character.

Constantine also bestowed a legal privilege of considerable importance on the church in about 320, when episcopal jurisdiction was officially recognized. Like the emperor's authority, the bishop's laws could not be repealed. They also apparently applied to every Christian and even to all pagans insofar as the latter were party to a lawsuit with a Christian.[41] What is, however, particularly interesting is the change of attitude that these new regulations brought about in the Christian way of acting and reacting. It became quite different for a Christian to have voluntary recourse to the arbitration of a bishop from whom he expected moral advice, or to be transferred to his defending body by a bishop whose judgment was without appeal and who had at his disposal means of civil coercion in order to make his verdict apply. The laity must therefore have felt increasingly insignificant and impotent in the presence of the bishop and the clergy, while the latter became more and more like an army of official administrators.

The Lay State as a Punishment:
Laica Communione Contentus

When a public administrator makes a mistake or commits an offense, he is suspended and ceases to exercise his function. This applies particularly in the case of a man who belongs to any special civil or public body and, if the mistake or offense is serious, he may be demoted and even excluded from his profession.

The same applied to the clergy in the fourth century. If a member of the clergy was found to have made a mistake or to have committed an offense, he was also "suspended" from his ministry and, if that mistake or offense was regarded as serious, he was demoted or even "deposed" from his office. It is not difficult to find, both in the canonical documents and in the legislation that appeared from the fourth century onward, many canons in which this type of language occurs: "deposed," "removed," "demoted," "downgraded," "ceasing to belong to the clergy," "losing the honor and dignity of the episcopate," "excluded from the clergy," and so on. We do not have to make fine distinctions here or to make a detailed study of the punishments imposed on offending clergy. All that needs to be said is that this legislation points indirectly at least to the lay state as a punishment for the clergy.

From the end of the fourth century onward, there appear in this legislation, alongside precise terms indicating "deposition," removal or exclusion from the clergy, data that help to explain the situation of those who have been punished in this way. In the *Apostolic Canons*, for example, we read that the presbyter or the deacon who has left his diocese and who refuses to obey his bishop, when the latter recalls him, should cease to exercise any liturgical function and, moreover, that "he may receive communion as lay people receive it."[42]

In 343, the Council of Sardica insisted that Eutychian and Museus should no longer be regarded as bishops, but "so long as they claim lay communion for them, it should not be refused."[43] The idea of lay communion thus gives a more precise meaning to the "deposition" of a member of the clergy. It helps to explain the historical change that had taken place, namely that, for a member of the clergy, the lay state was the inferior situation of demotion in which he would find himself if he made a serious mistake or committed an offense.

This punishment also had an important social and civil aspect. A member of the clergy who had been reduced to the lay state lost all the privileges that formed part of his rank. According to the *Theodosian Code* XVI, 2, 39, for example, "deposed" clergy should be employed in public service. From the religious and liturgical point of view, a member of the clergy who had been "deposed" was no longer allowed to take part in the eucharist in his previous place in the church, that is, he could no longer sit in the presbyterium or the choir. He had to take his place among the laity.

The consequence of this was inevitable. Even though a man who continued to be a member of the clergy might be quite convinced that the laity consisted of baptized Christians who were fully a part of the people of God, it would nonetheless have been difficult for him not to regard lay people as a group with an inferior status, to which those who had made mistakes or committed offenses had been demoted. The lay state, then, was really and indisputably, in the minds of the laity and the clergy, the lower state, because it was possible to return to that state by falling and being punished, and the clergy had a status that was higher than that of the laity. No one ever thought that a layman who had made a mistake or had committed an offense would be condemned to the punishment of becoming a member of the clergy!

This idea of punishment, then, was, together with that of "lay communion," one of the basic elements by which an inferior status was given to the laity. For a member of the clergy who was guilty of error, the sanction of being "reduced to the lay state" was regarded as more serious than excommunication. This is partly because excommunication was not usually definitive. It therefore only affected the excommunicated person for a period of time. When the ban of excommunication was lifted, that person recovered the rank that he had previously held—a layman became a layman again and a member of the clergy was able to resume his clerical function. "Deposition" from the clergy, however, was not temporary. It deprived a man definitively of his clerical status, just as members of certain professions are today "struck off the register."

It is interesting in this context to compare the available ways and means of punishing the clergy and the laity, since they all point to the inferior position of the laity. Basil of Caesarea, for example, declared: "The deacon who has committed fornication after his ordination must be suspended from his function as deacon, but, having been reduced to the lay state, he should not be deprived of communion, since there is an early rule stating that clergy removed from their office should not be submitted to this kind of punishment. In that respect, our ancestors conformed, I believe, to the law which states: 'You shall not punish the same offense twice.' Another reason is this. If those of the lay state are excluded from the ranks of the faithful, they can be readmitted to them, whereas the deacon is condemned once and for all time to permanent deposition. In view of the fact that the function of the deacon cannot be restored to him, we must go no further than this one punishment."[44]

The system, then, was totally constituted that, in the church, the lay state was at the bottom of the social and religious ladder. A man could move from this inferior state to the higher state of the clergy, by means of the tonsure, which was visible evidence of that man's change of condition, state and way of life. Just as baptism was generalized and every citizen was a Christian or was at least on the way to becoming one, so too was religious society becoming modeled around the division clergy/laity. A layman might become worthy of the clerical state if his moral conduct was good and he fulfilled certain conditions. A member of the clergy could, on the other hand, be demoted or "reduced to the lay state" if he was found to have made mistakes, to have committed an offense, or to have been guilty of serious faults.

From this time onward, certain laymen could only compensate for their factually inferior status by making use of civil power. With the disappearance of the Roman empire and the rise of the barbarians in Europe, this led to a history of struggles between the two powers of the church and the state. But I do not propose to go as far as Canossa in this study.

CHAPTER 8

Christianity Confronted with Pagan and Barbarian Cultures

Powerful figures entered Christianity with the conversion of Emperor Constantine. But it is difficult for the rich to enter the kingdom of heaven! The empire was proud of its traditions, and it was hard for a Roman to give up his cultural wealth on the threshold of baptism. Nor did the church claim to call for such a sacrifice. So it had to provide evidence that this wealth was compatible with Christianity. If they were to engage in conversation with the powerful leaders of society, Christians had themselves to give up part of the culture that Christianity had acquired in the previous three hundred years and only preserve what was strictly necessary in their faith.

To understand the Roman elite, it is necessary to understand from within its philosophical and pagan culture. The laity played a pioneering part in this inevitable attempt to assimilate another culture. At a time when all the internal functions of the community were beginning to become "clericalized," educated laymen, possibly precisely because they had been rejected at the frontier, were finding in this mission a special territory for themselves. So long as it did not try to intervene in the life of the church by the indirect route of a policy that all too frequently combined religious with secular power, the lay aristocracy had, in literature, a very special way of placing itself at the service of Christian faith. It was in fact to try, sometimes with a greater and at others with a lesser degree of success, to do this, and in the end it was to make it possible for future generations to make use of the ancient culture without any danger of Christianity being swallowed up in a wave of syncretism.

A Layman in Search of a Cultural Synthesis

Lactantius, who was an African trained in rhetoric, was not, like Origen, a true lay teacher or *didaskalos*. He seems to have had difficulties in attracting pupils and founding a real school. It has to be said, however, in his defense that this Latin rhetor, who had been called by the emperor to Nicomedia, the city of Greek culture, was deprived of his chair during Diocletian's persecution. He was in fact more of a writer and tutor than a real "master."

On the other hand, Jerome does not have very kind things to say about this lay intellectual in his *De viris illustribus*.[1] It cannot be claimed that he was entirely without personal ambition. After losing his chair at Nicomedia, he embarked on the task of writing seven volumes of a work entitled *The Divine Institutions* (*Divinae Institutiones*), in which he attempted to refute definitively and for all time the errors of both the philosophers and the persecutors.

"What makes these philosophers, orators and poets pernicious is that they can so easily ensnare spirits that are not on their guard. They do this by the charm of their prose and the rhythms of their poetry with its attractive emphases. But it is honey covering poison! Why I have tried to combine wisdom and religion is because I am afraid that those who devote themselves to study may be hampered by a useless form of knowledge. I have also done this so that a knowledge of literature may not harm both religion and justice in any way, but rather serve it as much as possible, if the one who studies them is more edified in the subject of virtue and wiser in the subject of truth."[2]

Lactantius, who was consciously striving to imitate Cicero, probably wrote more elegantly than any other author of his time. His aim was in fact quite modest. It was to combat the ancient culture with his own weapons and to bring about an "acculturation," in other words, to make it possible for Christianity to assimilate the culture conveyed in Latin literature. He believed that his faith raised him indisputably above those philosophers and other authors of the ancient world who had dealt with the question of God. He also even believed that he was superior to Tertullian.

He thought that Cyprian's writings were quite inaccessible to pagans because he wrote too much about the Christian mysteries. This was for Lactantius a matter of regret, because he admired Cyprian's rhetoric.[3] He criticized him above all for making too much use of scripture and decided to do what the bishop of Carthage had not been able to do. That was to speak directly to the pagans in their own language, making use above all of reason. In this he was very conscious of being a forerunner in this approach and therefore of preparing the way for others who would follow him. He wrote, for example: "If learned and eloquent men respond to our appeal, begin to commit themselves to this way and are ready to use their talent and their energy on the battlefield of truth, there can be no doubt that the false religions will soon vanish and that all philosophy will fade away."[4]

Was Lactantius really equal to this task? It is in fact very doubtful whether he could have achieved what he set out to do. In 317, however, when he was already advanced in years, he became tutor to Constantine's oldest son, Crispus, although this was, at least according to Jerome, after having suffered great poverty. It is difficult to assess what a pagan who was completely ignorant of Christianity could have made of Lactantius' almost too highly organized works, but one is bound to conclude that it was unlikely that they either aroused a passionate response or led to large-scale conversions.

A pagan might have been fascinated by the elegance of Lactantius' style, but would he have learned anything about Christianity from reading his works? Lactantius may have been a very sincere Christian, but what he wrote about it was certainly watered down and sweetened. He says this, for example, about Plato: "He certainly spoke a great deal about the one God through whom the world was, according to him, created, but he does not speak of religion. He dreamed up God, but he did not know him."[5] I am tempted to apply these words to Lactantius himself and say: "He certainly spoke a great deal about religion, but not so much and not really about Christianity. He may have dreamed up his Christianity and presented it in discreet and distinguished language, but without really knowing it."

This was not simply because of the literary genre that Lactantius followed, nor was it due to the demands made by his apologetics. His form is always very carefully constructed, but the fundamental content of his Christian reflection is very dull compared with, for example, Justin's. He sneers, for example, at the man who is scandalized by the apostles' lack of learning and culture: "One would think that he can hardly bear the fact that an Aristophanes or an Aristarchus has not commented on this subject!"[6]

Lactantius would like to have been regarded as wise, but it does not seem to have troubled him that he was in fact regarded as foolish by those who he thought were in error. He defended the existence of God's passion and even of God's anger, but he was himself more passionate about justice than about charity or agape. He wrote a long treatise on the *Divine Institutions*, but it reveals nothing at all about the organization or the way of life of Christian communities. He speaks about "our people," but it is impossible to learn from his treatise how that people was constituted. He never even refers to the ministers of the Christian people!

He does, however, state one principle, namely that, in God's eyes, no one is a slave and no one is a master, declaring that "from the moment that God is for everyone equally a father, we are all his children, enjoying the same rights" and adding: "We have no reason for giving each other the name 'brother' apart from the fact that we believe that we are all equal."[7] And, having said that, he clearly believes that he has said the most important thing and need not trouble himself with concrete details.

What is important for us here, however, is that Lactantius never once speaks in any of the seven books of his *Divine Institutions* about the clergy or the laity. He even gives a little light and shade to his statement about the equality of all Christians by affirming that the righteous man is superior in God's eyes and that the man who humbles himself now will be raised up in dignity on the day of judgment.

Lactantius, then, was obviously an idealistic intellectual who did not want to waste too much time considering everyday realities. He preferred to reflect about what he regarded as the logic of Christianity. The result is a very abstract presentation of Christianity. It is a tour de force, but one that does not contain, for example, a single positive reference in all seven books to the eucharist! In fact, the only Christian "institution" that seems really to have interested Lactantius is penance. He even makes penance one of the characteristic marks of Christianity. This, of course, is fully in accordance with his temperament as a moralist.

In one respect, however, he provides evidence of his originality and makes a positive contribution to Christian theology. This is in his conception of the body. He calls the body good and, with unshakable optimism, provides a detailed description of the structure and the organization of that body, seeing in it a manifestation of God's greatness and power. In the attention and interest that he gives to anthropology, Lactantius clearly rejects all the gnostic tendencies that were current at the time. This was undoubtedly the most original contribution that he had to make to the process of "acculturation" that he was trying to initiate.[8]

It is, of course, regrettable that Lactantius lacked what he called the "wild" eloquence of Tertullian and that he tried to present us with such a wise, civilized and rational form of Christianity that charity seems to have become lost in the process. One question, however, remains and that is: Why did such a calm and level-headed man go to such lengths to write in defense of Christianity?

Lactantius himself answers this question when he announces his intention to write a treatise defending true philosophy and reducing to silence—with their own weapons—the philosophers of error. That announcement of his intention ends with these words: "Having accomplished this task, I believe that I shall have lived long enough and have fulfilled my duty as a man if my work has directed the steps of some men, set free from their errors, on the way to heaven."[9] In the fifth book of his treatise on the *Divine Institutions*, he makes a more modest claim: "Even if it is of no value to anyone else, it will, for us at least, be a valuable work. It will be a joy for our mind and a pleasure for our life to bathe in the light of the truth. In it, the soul finds nourishment filled with a truly unbelievable sweetness."[10]

These statements show how sincerely convinced this lay intellectual was of the rightness of his cause. He made such use of rational argument perhaps because he got emotional satisfaction from it. This may sound paradoxical, but, as an author, Lactantius is characterized by paradox. He vilified the philosophers, for example, but spoke no other language but theirs. He wanted his contemporaries to have a better knowledge of Christianity, but reduced Christ to the dimension of a moral hero. He wanted "truth to give evidence of its value by the force and clarity that it had of itself rather than by a facile, lying and deceitful way of speaking."[11] And, as a final example, he was one of the first writers to put classical poetry at the service of the risen Christ with his *Ave phenix*.

Landowners, Poets and Christians

Lactantius put a very ancient pagan symbol with a universal value to use in the service of Christianity in his *Ave phenix*. In that form of poetry, Christianity was only discernible through the filter of the metaphor. There were also other lay Christians writing in the fourth century who put poetry at the service of their faith—or who at least tried to express their faith in verse—but who never succeeded in separating that poetry from its ancient and pagan form.

The most original and perhaps the most noteworthy attempt was made by Proba, a woman who was a member of the highest level of western aristocracy, writing in the middle of the fourth century. It would not be wrong to call her a lay woman, as this title was coming into use at the beginning of that century. It was also applied to women, and we have the example another woman applying it to Christians of her own sex at the end of the century.[12]

Faltonia Betitia Proba translated parts of scripture into an immense Latin *cento* based on the poems of Virgil. What she did was to cut, change, embellish and alter the meaning of the original Virgilian verse in order to accommodate it to the requirements of the Old and New Testaments. The odds were clearly against her, but she nonetheless succeeded in this exercise, which was acrobatic as well as academic. It was highly praised in her own time.

The difficulties must have been considerable. It could not, for example, have been easy to find Virgilian terms to describe the crucifixion of Christ. But, despite these obstacles, she undertook the risky task. The result was above all verse of a worldly kind written by a lay woman, and Jerome was very scornful of it. It had nothing in common with the poetry written for liturgical use by members of the clergy or the early attempts made by such writers as Hilary of Poitiers or Ambrose to compose hymns in the classical tradition. Nor can it be compared with the work of the noble Spanish priest Juvencus, who, in four volumes, translated the gospels into hexameters.

The form of Proba's *cento* is of such importance that it frequently obscures the content, but her work is not entirely without interest. It was undoubtedly a valuable task to try to reconcile Virgil, who was read by all noble and cultivated Romans, and Christ. For generations, Virgil had formed an essential part of the education of all Romans, and the poetess looked for signs of Christian truth in the master's verses which the author of the bucolics himself would probably have been surprised to discover. Proba accepted responsibility for this in an attempt to prove the truth of what the illustrious "lay" apologist Justin had claimed, namely that it was possible to find in the ancient writers shreds of the truth of divine revelation "more ancient than any of them."

So Proba, the great Roman lady, took material from Virgil in order to rewrite scripture and, in so doing, engaged in a kind of reasoning based on an absurd premise. Even though, a hundred years later, a Theodosian scribe described Proba's Virgil as "better" than Virgil's original work, this proof based on faulty reasoning is hardly convincing, and we are bound to conclude, many centuries later, that it is difficult to know whether Virgil or scripture suffered the greater loss in this poetic exercise.

This purely formal syncretism is difficult for us to accept unless we put ourselves in the place of the Roman noble families who were so proud of their ancient forms. It must have been a great sacrifice to give up the pagan recollections and references associated with those forms, and it was a sacrifice that the illustrious poet and Christian Ausonius did not always make. He was criticized for this by his pupil and friend Paulinus of Nola, when his old master tried to dissuade him from remaining withdrawn from the world: "Can I dream of returning to you, when you breathe barren prayers that are not addressed to heaven and when you are turned away from God and beseech the muses of Castalia?"[13] As a radical Christian, Paulinus would not banter with the muses even if that banter was purely formal and done as a concession to the inspiration of Virgil. But then, the two friends were separated from each other by more than a generation. Who, then, was this old poet who could not choose between his muses and his God?

Ausonius was born at Bordeaux in 310, at a time when the religious powers were in the process of moving in favor of Christianity. He was a member of one of the great landowning and senatorial families. The Ausonii of Gaul were similar to the Symmachi in Italy and the famous "Lord Julius" in Africa. After completing his studies, Ausonius taught in Bordeaux, first as *grammaticus* and then as *rhetor*. Then, in or about 364, Valentinian called him to Trèves to be tutor to his son Gratian. He had a brilliant career there, becoming prefect of the praetorium and later, in 379, consul. When the empress died in 383, however, he decided to return to Bordeaux, where he divided his time between poetry, the country and Rome. It was then, in semi-retirement, that he wrote most of his poems.

In the peaceful environment of his country retreat, this great landowner was able to extol the praises of the balanced life, alternating between the tumult of the city and the tranquillity of the countryside. His writing reflects a kind of rural wisdom, a symbiosis of evangelical inspiration and classical bucolic culture. At a time when great farming estates were beginning to flourish, many members of the influential rural nobility, who were being converted to Christianity, were able to accept this type of rustic philosophy without their consciences being troubled. It was a philosophy that combined both the moderate enjoyment of wealth and detachment from the intrigues of the world. Because of this, it managed to reconcile both a very early Roman tradition and rational Christian moral teaching. What already appears in this blend of literary genres and is visible behind the rural aristocracy that accepted it so readily, then, is the lay figure of the middle ages—the feudal lord.

The peaceful rural life extolled by the poet was also an opulent life. When Ausonius ceased to be Gratian's tutor, he did not enjoy a frugal retirement. He has in fact given us a description of the average estate owned by a Roman of his kind. According to him, it was two hundred and sixty hectares, divided into fifty of fields, twenty-five of vineyards, twelve of meadowland and one hundred and seventy-five of woodland.[14] His own estate was much larger than this. Ausonius also calls the property that his pupil Paulinus inherited from his family "as big as a kingdom."

Fourth century landowners were able to manage very pleasant villas on such vast lands. They almost always had a well stocked library. They often entertained their neighbors. They organized epigram writing competitions, exchanged compliments and circulated poems "in confidence." The same landowners also went up to the nearest big town or city from time to time, although they in fact preferred their own peasants to remain living within a closed economic circuit on their own estates or in their villages.

Retired and living in such a pleasant rural retreat, Ausonius spent much of his time writing precious and mannered verses—epigrams and poems full of reminiscences and mythological allusions. As a Christian, he prayed regularly every morning, rejecting the pagan gods and calling on the dead and risen Christ. At the same time, however, he also developed an idea of the deity and a morality which must have been acceptable to many of his fellow Romans who had not been converted, combining in his poetry Virgilian form and Judaeo-Christian content, including many allusions to the apocryphal writings. He reserved a special place every day for prayers of the most secret and intimate kind. There seems little doubt that he was very sincere in the peaceful wisdom that he expressed in his verses, and there is nothing artificial or shallow in his poetic descriptions of the countryside or of scenes from his own home or

The Ideal of the Wealthy Laity: The Peaceful Rural Life

family life. On the contrary, his poetry is then often moving and really beautiful.

But, of course, Ausonius' form of Christianity is a long way from the ideal of poverty expressed in the early church. The distance was in fact so great that his favorite pupil, Paulinus, could in the end no longer accept it and had to sell all that he possessed and withdraw with his wife to Spain. Both master and pupil reacted to this event by an exchange of poems.

There was not only a difference between the personalities of the two men. There was also a conflict between the two generations. The younger great landowners also felt a need to experience their Christian faith more radically. They were no longer satisfied with a veneer of Christianity covering a noble wisdom and an ancient culture. Ausonius underwent a mutation during his life and, because of it, gives the impression of fragility. He was at the point of transition. For the lay Christians, such as Paulinus, who followed him, Ausonius' rural ideal was transformed into the monastic ideal. Ausonius was aware that the world and its culture that he had loved so much was coming to an end, and there is something very touching in the rather selfishly insistent way in which he continued to remind his most gifted pupil of this fact:

> Our vows, our good omens
> and our prayers remind you:
> Do not delay, while you are still young,
> and may our old age still preserve its strength
> to welcome you with open arms.

When Ausonius died, the worldly poetry that had marked the transition also ceased to exist and a truly Christian form of poetry appeared with Paulinus and Prudentius. Both men were born in the middle of the fourth century into noble families, and both were favored by life and felt themselves drawn to asceticism. The Spaniard, Prudentius, became a lawyer after studying for a very long time and was called to posts of the highest responsibility at the imperial court. He seems to have remained a layman until the end of his life and to have waited until he was about sixty before dedicating his retirement to God. "While the years of my life were flying away," he tells us, "the white covering was appearing on my aged head, reproaching me for having forgotten the distant consulate of Salia. It was under that that I was born. But since then, how many winters has time carried off and how often has it brought back the roses to the fields after the season of frosts? The snow that has now spread over my head shows that! Will either these good or these bad things be of any use to me when my flesh has been destroyed and, in death, this person, whoever it is, that I was, has disappeared? It is time to tell me: 'Whoever you are, the world is lost for your soul, that world that it has served. It is not the things of God that your soul has tasted, but it is to God that you will belong.' "[15]

Paulinus, the man from Aquitaine, did not wait as long as the Spaniard Prudentius. It was in the prime of life, when he was a senator and at the peak of his glory, that he decided to sell all that he possessed and to retire to Spain with his wife. Ambrose had wondered how the Roman aristocracy could have welcomed this scandalous conversion that put an end to the power of a great family. Ausonius' complaints to his pupil sound like an echo in response to such questions. Accusing Nemesis of taking pleasure in persecuting the great men of Rome, he was clearly offended that Paulinus should have taken the curule chair of the Latium and the honors bestowed on him by the fatherland with him into his country retreat.[16]

But his master's appeals did not make Paulinus swerve from his decision to put all his wealth in the treasury of Christ. He wrote no more worldly poetry. Despite himself, Paulinus, the layman who was tempted by asceticism, was ordained and ended as the bishop of Nola, where he put his skill as a poet to use in writing Christian inscriptions, in celebrating Saint Felix, whose relics were at Nola, and in living a very simple life with a few companions.

Prudentius also responded to the same ascetic ideal of Christian life of prayer and fasting. He wrote hymns, several of which found their way later into the Roman breviary. His verse is both lyrical and elegant and more free with regard to the biblical texts than that of Ambrose, for example, but nonetheless totally Christian. He even dealt with strictly theological matters in defense of the Catholic faith against heresies. But, although he apparently remained a layman, he was, like Paulinus, until he became a bishop, really a kind of monk.

Using Profane Culture Well

When he was converted and had decided to dedicate himself totally to God, Paulinus told Ausonius: "God wants us to abandon vain distractions, affairs and leisures and the study of fables so that we may obey his laws and become conscious of his light—that light that shields our eyes from the false arguments of the sophists, the art of the rhetors and the fictions of the poets, who pour false and vain teachings into our hearts and only instruct the tongue without giving us anything that will save us or will cover us with the protection of the truth."[17]

If this seems excessive, we should remember that it was the reaction of a man who had associated excessively with learned literary men and who had only recently been deeply hurt by his master. He did not in fact abandon literature entirely. He simply used it in a less worldly way. He also continued to acknowledge his debt to Ausonius. What he experienced in fact was a need to find a compromise with profane culture.

The teaching of young people was based on rhetoric. Any attempt to prevent young or older Christians from becoming familiar with the works of the ancient Greek and Roman authors would simply have been forbidding them access to culture. In the east, a balanced solution to this problem was suggested by Basil, the bishop of Caesarea, who was Ausonius' contemporary. Basil, the master of eastern monasticism, set himself the task of writing for young people a kind of treatise on how to use Hellenistic culture well. Claiming the authority given to him by his age and experience and the fact that he had spent the last four years of his education at Athens, Basil provided an outline of how young people should behave during their period of study. Like Lactantius before him, he made use of the image of poison with a covering of honey taken from Plutarch. "Familiarity with bad words is like approaching action," he declared. "That is why we have to be careful to protect our souls, to prevent attractive language from making us accept bad principles unknown to ourselves, like those who swallow poison with the honey."[18]

In this way, Basil put pupils on their guard against the licentious stories in Greek mythology and "the art of lying" of the orators. This did not mean, however, that he was simply tolerant of the practice of becoming familiar with profane literature. He certainly put sacred scripture first, but he also believed that profane literature had a positive contribution to make, especially as a preparation for reading scripture. "Poets, historians, orators and all men," Basil insisted. "We must deal with all those from whom some usefulness may be derived for the care of our souls."[19] What is more, Basil also draws on

Old Testament examples to provide a Christian justification for this
curiosity for profane knowledge. Moses, he recalls, was instructed in
Egyptian knowledge and David in Chaldaean learning. The bishop of
Caesarea was therefore able to conclude that it was valuable to look
in the works of the profane authors for examples of the virtues.

Basil's moral teaching also stressed moderation. Temperance
would, for instance, enable the soul to dominate the body. Similarly,
wealth had to be used with moderation, and we should be content to
possess only what was necessary and "to use it only for the necessi-
ties of nature and not for the pleasures that could be obtained from
it."[20] Finally, lying and flattery should be avoided and we should act
in accordance with our conscience.

For each of these moral principles, none of which would have
been rejected by Ausonius, Basil found examples from the classical
works. He even went further than this and found models among the
ancient authors, even in cases illustrating virtues that were strictly
speaking evangelical. A good example of this is his recounting Soc-
rates' anecdote, in which the author was struck again and again in
the face and did not reply, but simply inscribed on his swollen face:
"This is the work of so and so." Finding an analogy between this and
the Matthaean precept in the sermon on the mount, Basil says: "To
the one who strikes on one cheek, it is correct to present the other
and not to take revenge."[21]

As long as they made a selection and did not swallow everything uncritically, young people might therefore—and indeed ought
to—familiarize themselves with classical literature. Their Christian
faith would not be diminished—on the contrary, it would benefit
from this study. Reassured by Basil's suggestion, lay people were
able to overcome their hesitations and experience their own culture
in a Christian way. As Christian lay people living in a profane culture, they were able to feel at ease in both respects and to devote at
least part of their efforts to the spread of Christianity.

"Lay Missionaries"

From the beginning, all Christ's disciples had always been involved in the mission. There was no need for any special instruction
to be given, because it was quite natural that the grace that each
Christian received at his baptism should be offered to and shared
with every member of the human race. The mission, then, was a

duty for every Christian. Sometimes, of course, in the performance of that duty, roundabout ways had to be followed and even subterfuge had to be used with regard to the recognized authorities. Paul himself may have been obliged to change his route in order to carry out his missionary activity and, bearing in mind the need "to preserve his missionary freedom, which was threatened by the way in which his agreement with the 'columns' was interpreted by the Jews of Jerusalem," he felt impelled "to take the gospel into parts of the known world that were remote from the great centers of civilization and from the main communication routes."[22] But at his time, of course, there was no question of making a distinction between the clergy and the laity.

Even when that distinction came increasingly to be made in the Christian communities, all Christians, even the humblest, continued to bear witness in all the places where they were living. According to Origen, Celsius complained about the domestic apostolate that took place among women and children and was carried out by people of very humble extraction. Origen quotes Celsius: "In ordinary homes, there are shoemakers, carders and fullers of wool and ignorant and uneducated people of all kinds who hardly dare to open their mouths in the presence of their masters, who are men of experience and judgment. If these people are able to catch the children in the house or the women at their own level of ignorance, they tell miraculous stories . . . of how they are the only ones who know how life should be lived and of how those who believe what they say will be happy together with their families. . . . Those who are the most bare-faced encourage the children to shake off the yoke, whispering into their ears that they cannot and do not want to reveal anything to them in the presence of their fathers or their tutors. . . . But if they want to learn something, all that they need to do is to leave their fathers and their tutors and come with their wives and their little friends into the women's quarters or into one or other workshop. There they will learn sublime things."[23]

Celsius' haughty criticism did not shock Christians in any way. Athenagoras had already boasted that one aspect of Christian teaching was that it was even offered to the lowliest of people. Origen also accepted that the apostolate included people of all kinds. Going even further, he declared it should not be static.[24] Christians, he insisted, should take the initiative and go out into the villages. The great teacher of Alexandria was, however, in a very good position to point out that people with little education and culture were not the only ones who could help others to believe in Christ. A little later, Lactantius also defended Christianity when the accusation made against it by Celsius was heard again. Christianity was not exclusively something that concerned unintelligent women and vulnerable children. It was above all in order to make it acceptable to educated and cultured men that Lactantius wrote the seven books of his *Divinae Institutiones*.

As we have already seen, from the fourth century onward, the form of the Christian mission began to change. It became necessary to try to convert members of the well-off classes and the nobility who were very proud of their ancient culture and to win their wholehearted support. The mission became a call to conversion to members of the new cultured and leisured classes, and this led to the literary attempts which we have just considered and which proved so valuable.

This was not, however, the only thing that changed in the missionary situation. According to John Chrysostom, there were at least two other changes. The first was that Christians were no longer a minority group in the population. They ceased to have anything to fear from the pagans and could safely associate with them and bear witness to their own Christian lives among them. The second was that miracles no longer played an important part in the apostolate.[25]

Toward the end of the fourth century, John Chrysostom wrote that, during the apostolic period, Christians had been instructed "to hate not only godlessness, but also the godless, in case friendship might become an occasion of sin. That is why all unity and all contact (with non-Christians) were forbidden and barricades were erected on all sides against them. Now that we have acquired a higher philosophy, however, and have been placed in a position that is raised too high for us to be able to suffer harm, we are told to be in contact with them and to help them."[26] So, in mingling with the pagans, Christians would be able to overcome them.

John Chrysostom also pointed to the second new fact in the Christian mission mentioned above—the disappearance of miracles. He might also have added that there were not only no more miracles, but also, with the end of the persecutions, no more martyrs. This source of conversion to Christianity on the part of so many ordinary people had dried up. Chrysostom complained of a lack of zeal on the part of his contemporaries. It is not surprising, however, that missionary zeal should cool off in a church that was beginning to become comfortably established within the empire and that the members of that settled church should tend to rely on a clergy that was now well organized to carry out the work of evangelization.

We should not, however, assume that the people were entirely passive. Augustine, the bishop of Hippo, expressed his faith in the people, for example, in words such as these: "Listen to me! Do you really think that we who are here standing in your presence are the only ones to proclaim Christ and that you do not proclaim him as well? How, then, can it be that we should see people coming to us with the intention of becoming Christians, people whom we have never seen before, people whom we do not know, people to whom we have never preached? . . . The whole church preaches Christ and 'the heavens proclaim his justice.' "[27]

Women continued to play a special part in this church, all the members of which shared in the proclamation of the gospel. At this period, the main task was the Christianization of the elitist sections of society, and this was done above all and very effectively by aristocratic ladies. In Rome, a group of such ladies gathered, for example, around Jerome, while in the country they had pious readings. There is a description by Sidonius Apollinaris, a fifth century statesman who later became a bishop, of the books near to the ladies' seats in the library in a country villa and of those near to the gentlemen's benches. The former were works with a religious content, whereas the latter were books of rhetoric.[28]

Even though these matrons did not always succeed in converting their husbands, they were at least able to instruct their sons in the Christian religion and perhaps persuade them to be baptized or to marry a Christian bride. It was, then, in this way that the Roman aristocracy became Christianized. It is even possible to say that these ladies were able to make some purely nominal Christians quite sincere believers. There is even a suggestion in the work of Ausonius, for example, that Therasia, the wife of his beloved Paulinus, played a decisive part in the latter's conversion. Paulinus seems to have taken his ex-master's allusion amiss. Therasia may not, of course, have forced her husband's hand, but she certainly supported and helped him on his way to conversion.

Later, queens followed in this tradition of the "home" apostolate. Clotilde, Clovis' wife, succeeded in having the children of their marriage baptized, at a time when the proud king of the Salian

Franks was still a long way from accepting Christianity himself.[29] One of his granddaughters, Bertha, married an Anglo-Saxon king on the explicit condition that she would be able to continue to practice her Christian religion. Later, she succeeded in converting her husband.[30]

It would not be difficult to cite further examples of this kind. The popes of this period even went so far as to make a rule of this form of apostolate and wrote letters of encouragement to royal wives. Gregory the Great, for example, wrote to Theodelina, urging her to convert her husband Agilulf, the king of the Lombards.

Gregory was also the first pope to send Christians officially on missionary work. He did this for the first time in 596. Until then, Christians had never felt the need to send missionaries out officially. The mission outside the empire had been regarded as a natural act that could be done equally well, for example, by merchants, traders, prisoners, members of the clergy or monks. Evangelization was a duty which was incumbent on all Christians and which could be carried out by all if the circumstances were propitious.

The people of the kingdom of Axum in Ethiopia were, for example, converted thanks to the efforts of a young Christian captive called Frumentius. While he and his traveling companion Edesius were on their way with their uncle, they escaped being massacred because they were so young. Frumentius was, however, held captive at the court of Axum, where he performed the functions of government that had been entrusted to him so well that, when the king died, the queen asked him to help her continue as regent until the young prince was old enough to rule himself. From that time onward, Frumentius was able to promote the cause of Christianity by letting merchants practice their religion in the kingdom and even by encouraging them to organize themselves in a community and to build places of worship.

The royal child grew, and Christianity spread in the kingdom of Axum, and Frumentius went back to Alexandria, while his friend Edesius returned to Tyre. In Alexandria, Frumentius asked for a bishop to be sent to the Ethiopian Christians. He was himself ordained bishop by Athanasius and returned to Axum, where he continued his work of evangelization. It is hardly surprising that Rufinus, from whom this information about the conversion of the Ethiopians comes,[31] should have given the most prominent place to Frumentius in his account of these events, but we should not forget the part played by all the anonymous Christian merchants in spreading the Christian faith in the kingdom. It was in this way, then, that Christianity began to take root in Axum, as it did in many other places.

Having begun as a layman, Frumentius became a bishop. This was what happened in the case of most of the founders of Christian communities. According to Origen, for example, "if a man arrives in a city where there are no Christians and begins to teach, to work and to lead men to faith, that man will later become the prince and the bishop of those whom he has taught."[32] This rule applied in the third century, when Origen was writing, and it continued to be valid in a general way in the centuries that followed. There were, however, two exceptions—when the principal agent of conversion was either a prince or a woman!

When Princes Converted Their People

Rufinus' account of the conversion of Ethiopia is followed by his story of the conversion of the Iberian tribes of Georgia.[33] He writes of a twofold action performed on the one hand by a woman—whom he describes according to the convention as a prisoner, but who appears to have been an ascetic—and, on the other, by the sovereign rulers of the country. The woman, spending her days and nights in prayer, heals first of all a child and then the queen, who is converted. The king then also embraces Christianity and cooperates with the "enclosed religious" in the building of a church. The woman then sends a delegation to the empire to ask for priests and after this disappears from the religious scene, while the king and the queen continue to further the Christian cause. This story is interesting for two reasons. In the first place, it shows us how individual initiative could be provided by the action of a sovereign ruler and how the king of the Iberians could become a kind of new Constantine. In the second place, it also indicates the precise limits imposed on public evangelization carried out by women.

Rufinus' story in fact points to a clear reservation with regard to the part played by women. When the queen summons the "prisoner," the latter "refuses to go, fearing that she might seem more audacious than her sex would permit." Again, when she is invited by the king to disclose the mysteries of her religion, "she teaches the Christ-God and reveals the rites of prayer and the ways followed in worship, insofar as a woman is allowed to speak of these things." In spite of the importance of the part that she plays in the conversion of these people, she is not regarded as an apostle. Rufinus' reticence with regard to the public and religious part played by women may possibly reflect the customs of Iberian society, but it is certainly also completely in accordance with the position developed in the earlier *Didascalia:* "It is neither suitable nor necessary for women to teach. . . . The Lord God, Jesus Christ our master, has in fact sent us, the twelve, to instruct the people and the nations. There were women with us who were disciples . . . but he did not send them to instruct the people with us."[34] Rufinus, on the other hand, did not hesitate to say of the king that he became the "apostle of his people," even before he had been initiated into the mysteries.

This pattern, according to which the king's conversion was followed by that of the people, was repeated again and again. The most famous conversion story of this kind is, of course, that of the baptism of Clovis in 498, on the instigation of his wife Clotilde, as told half a century later by Gregory of Tours. Summoned by the king, the people's assembly declared in favor of Catholicism. Clovis was then baptized together with three thousand warriors. This event gave Gregory of Tours, the author of the history of the Franks, the opportunity to call the Frankish leader the "new Constantine" and to transform the story of his conversion into the stereotyped account of the defender of the Catholic faith.[35]

What is certain is that, in spite of everything, the baptism of the Frankish leader led to many conversions and eventually to the Catholic Church becoming the national church. A contemporary of Clovis, Bishop Avit of Vienne, even praised the leader of the Franks as the one through whom "God had made the whole nation his own."[36] Even though it may have been politically motivated and, in the spiritual sense, only superficial, Clovis' conversion led to the Christianization of the lesser leaders and their tribes, since the Frankish leader was, like most of the Germanic leaders, almost automatically regarded as a religious leader as well. And above all, perhaps even more than a victory of Christianity over paganism, the conversion of Clovis was a victory over Arianism, giving hope to all those who believed that there was a close bond between being Roman and being Catholic.

The Goths and the Visigoths had, after all, already been converted to Arianism. Clovis, as the only sovereign in the west to embrace Catholicism, was, by this fact, able to have his sovereignty recognized by Emperor Anastasius and to assert his leadership over the Gallo-Romans, who did not expect any further military support from the empire. Clovis in fact became a kind of bulwark of Romanism or of what remained of it. So, even though it is disputable whether Clovis' baptism led to the conversion of countless pagans, we are bound to recognize that it was for the most part motivated by the presence, in the territories that Clovis occupied or wanted to occupy, of a large number of Catholics.

The practice by which the conversion of the prince generally brought in its wake the conversion of his subjects—a superficial or a more profound conversion over a longer or shorter period—was neither initiated nor ended by Clovis. But his history has been emphasized here because it occurred at a time when the Christian mission was changing direction. In the east at the beginning of the fifth century, John Chrysostom was speaking to his flock in terms such as these: "I want you all and I urge you become doctors. Do not simply listen to our sermons! Tell our teaching to others! Go fishing for those who are in error so that they too will enter the ways of truth!"[37] The apostolate was, in other words, beginning to be directed as much toward heretics as toward pagans. This was happening at all levels, from lay people to the bishops and from the humblest to the most powerful. In the west, this new impetus was to be rewarded by the conversion of the king of the Visigoths, Recared, in 586. This resulted in the end of Arianism in his lands and a major movement on the part of most of the Arian bishops and noblemen as well as the majority of the people toward Catholicism.

The Godparent—A "Lay Minister"?

Every member of the church has a missionary duty. Every Christian is called to lead all those he meets to share in the grace of Christ received at the time of baptism. But the believer should not simply convince and convert those who are outside the church— that is not enough. His task of evangelization has also to continue within the church community in connection with those who have recently come to faith. The author of the *Didascalia* therefore recommended in the third century that Christians should encourage converts to be firm in their faith: "So, lay people, be at peace with one another and try, like wise doves, to fill the church. Convert those who are outside, pacify them and make them enter. That is the great reward promised by God if you deliver them from the flames and lead them into the church, full of decision and faith."[38]

Those who brought new catechumens into the church were also among those who led ritually to the bath those who had to be washed and reborn. In the middle of the second century, this rite was described for the first time by Justin. Then, at the beginning of the third century, a more complete outline was given in the *Apostolic Tradition* of the part played by "those who led" the catechumens. They had to bear witness twice in favor of the candidate—first when the candidate was presented to the doctor, "so that he might know that he was capable of listening," and, second, at the end of the period of catechesis, at the time of the catechumen's prebaptismal examination. "When those who are about to receive baptism are chosen, their lives should be examined. Have they lived an upright life while they were catechumens? Have they honored the widows? Have they visited the sick? Have they done all kinds of good works? Those who have led them bear should witness about each one: He has done this, they will listen to the Gospel. . . ."[39]

Those who led the catechumens and bore witness in their favor clearly played the part of godparents, even though they were not called by that name. We should, moreover, not forget that the average length of time between the catechumen's being presented to the doctors for his first instruction and his being chosen, at the beginning of Lent, to be intensively prepared with the community for baptism at Easter was three years. This means that, in the third century, the function performed by the godparent was not a mere formality lasting only a little time. It was a real ministry of supervision, support and help. It was also a ministry of teaching—at least by example. The godparent had to act as a guide. Leading his catechumen to faith throughout the whole period of his instruction, he can be regarded as a true spiritual father.

Describing the liturgies in preparation for baptism that took place in Jerusalem during Holy Week, Egerius explains how "a throne is placed for the bishop at the back of the apse behind the altar and they come one by one, the men with their 'father' and the women with their 'mother,' reciting the creed to the bishop."[40]

At the same period, John Chrysostom exhorts godfathers: "They should not regard the part that they play as insignificant. They should know, on the contrary, that they are sharing in the merit of their godsons and should never cease, in their personal exhortations, to lead them by the hand on the paths of virtue. . . . It is therefore customary to give to these guarantors the name of 'father' in order to let them experience all the affection that, in performing their task, they show, by teaching them spiritual things, to those for whom they have agreed to stand surety. For if it is praiseworthy to inspire a great longing for virtue in those who are completely unknown to us, how much greater merit is there in carrying out this task in the case of those to whom we are committed?"[41]

This spiritual parenthood obviously took a different direction when the godparents had not the baptism of adults, but that of little children in view or when, as was the case from the sixth century onward, the time for prebaptismal catechetical instruction was considerably reduced. The part played by the godparent was changed then in order to project it into the future. The godparent ceased to bear witness to the suitability of the catechumen and to prepare him for baptism and became the guarantor of the recently baptized child's education and future conduct. In the case of little children, then, the "godparents" were almost always the real parents, and it was those real parents who presented the children at baptism. For adults, on the other hand, from the time that the period of preparation for baptism and therefore the period when the candidates for baptism were being observed was reduced, the need for a guarantee was transferred to the baptismal witnesses. According to the *Testamentum Domini*, they had to be adult believers and known to the church.[42]

But however valuable the witness was, "every candidature could be deceptive and therefore disappointing in its expectations."[43] This was the argument that Tertullian used at the beginning of the third century to protest against the practice of infant baptism. At the end of the fourth century, Theodore of Mopsuesta insisted that the godfather could not be the guarantor for the future, but that he could only account for the efforts already made by the catechumen. "This is the part played by the guarantor in the case of those who are baptized," he declared. "It is certainly not for the sins to come that he is the guarantor, because each one of us replies for himself in the presence of God, but, for the one who presents himself, he bears witness to what he has done and for what he has prepared himself. It is therefore with good reason that he is called the guarantor, because it is on his word that it will appear that he (the candidate) is worthy to receive baptism."[44]

Without giving a narrow juridical meaning to the idea of the guarantor, however, it is possible to give it a post-baptismal extension. A little less than a century after Theodore of Mopsuesta, Narsai, a Nestorian from Mesopotamia, stated that, after having borne witness in favor of the one who was to be baptized, the godparent became "like a guide for his words and actions, teaching him the practices of the spiritual life."[45] This conception is not so very far from what the liturgy and Theodore's commentary on the liturgy attributed symbolically to the guarantor of the one to be baptized: "Your guarantor, standing behind you, will extend a linen stole over your head, will raise you up and will make you stand upright." Helping a person to set himself free and to stand upright—surely the Christian can be given no finer ministry than this?

During the Constantinian era, the institutions of the church were clericalized and made firmer. This resulted in the laity having a much narrower field of action. At the same time, however, as Christianity became the official religion, it also had much more of a free hand and could increase the number of its members. The church undoubtedly took advantage of the opportunities that had been given to it and, in the centuries that followed the conversion of Constantine, extended its mission in all directions. Confronted with this challenge, and despite the great increase in the clergy, it appealed to everyone. Because of the position that they occupied on the frontier between the world and a church based on its clergy, the laity was particularly suited to this missionary work. There were many areas: the mainly cultural mission among the elite classes in the empire, the quasi-diplomatic mission among the royal families of the barbarian tribes and the more modest but equally effective mission abroad carried out by merchants, travelers and captives, the women's apostolate in the home with their husbands and children and, last but not least, the task of proselytizing all believers, each Christian being determined to achieve his own salvation by winning someone for the church.

Finally, as a result of the situation created by the fact that it was almost too easy for the church to spread, Catholic Christians were called to the mission among the Arian Christians and were urged to missionize among brethren. In order to avoid the creation of purely "sociological" converts, who were Christians of mere convenience, because of the excessive number of conversions, the duties of godparents toward their neophytes were redefined. The period of preparation for baptism was shortened, but an attempt was at the same time made to revitalize the faith of the godparents, who had to give an example to their godchildren. Because it was so easy, however, Christianity was, many believers thought, always in great danger of becoming lukewarm. But a new way was opened with the sudden birth of monasticism.

CHAPTER 9

Chaste and Celibate Monks

Paulinus of Nola was a man living in the world who fled from worldliness when he heard the call to leave everything behind, to sell all that he possessed and follow Christ. Rich and powerful men were, however, not the only ones to hear this call. In the fourth century, Christianity was, as we have seen, becoming established as the official religion and the pattern of Christian life was changing. Christians with a strong sense of the absolute value of their faith no longer had the opportunity to win the martyr's crown, and the attempt to live holding all things in common was by this time no more than a splendid idea. But there was a new way of giving oneself totally to God and that was the way of asceticism and flight from the world. In reaction against the institutionalization of the church and to express an ideal, more and more Christians chose this way, becoming ascetics, hermits, anchorites and cenobites.

Anchorites: Laymen in Flight from the World

In the desert of Egypt, which became the cradle of this movement, those who called themselves anchorites (from the Greek verb *anachorein*, to flee) and monks (who lived alone) were not always those on whom the world smiled. The most famous of these men was Antony (251–356). He sold his three hundred acres of land, distributed his wealth among the poor and placed his sister in the care of pious women. Then he withdrew to the desert. According to Athanasius of Alexandria, his three hundred acres of land did not prevent him from remaining illiterate.

Many hermits were originally either rich or poor peasants. Life was not secure in the fourth century and peasants were at the mercy of bad harvests, taxes or plunderers. Others began as humble carpenters, smiths and other tradesmen, slaves or shepherds. There were also those who were so marginal in society—vagabonds, brigands and poor men[1]—that flight from the world was no hardship for them and the desert was often a natural refuge, where, with the help of scripture, they might develop a deeper spiritual life.

The life of these hermits (from the Greek word *eremos*, desert) gave rise to many stories and indeed to a whole form of popular Christianity, in which miracles, marvelous events and above all demons, omnipresent and appearing in many different forms, figured prominently. These fantastic representations must have been favored by the solitude of the desert and the exaltation experienced there.

This popular hermitical movement was above all a lay movement that had come about outside, although not always in opposition to, the clergy. Because it was fundamentally asocial, hermitism was incompatible with the service to the community for which the clergy was destined. The desert called for a deeply committed way of life which was often in great contrast to the mediocre level of life of the local clergy and it was far removed from the successful search for privileges that many members of the clergy undertook in an empire that was beginning to offer this to them. As for the eucharist, this seems not to have been a problem for the hermits. Either they left their desert retreat and went to the nearest Christian community or they received communion with the eucharist reserved in their hermitage. Some hermits were visited periodically by a presbyter.[2]

They did not ask to be ordained for themselves. They did not think of their isolation as an argument for necessarily becoming presbyters themselves. Since ordination was still regarded not as "personal," but as a "service to the community," it was therefore hardly possible for a man living alone to think of being ordained.

Some anchorites practiced such extreme forms of asceticism and mortification that their achievements were almost extravagant. Many of them experienced divine illumination. Their Christianity took such an absolute form that some achieved a remarkable spiritual equilibrium, while others give an impression of madness or folly. Either because of their excesses and or because of their wisdom, their reputation grew, sometimes to the point where crowds of visitors came to disturb their solitude. They had such an influence that the people and the bishops themselves were often tempted to make them their own by ordaining them.

The practice of ordination became so general that John Cassian, writing a century later, made a recommendation to monks that they should at all costs avoid both women and bishops—"quod mona- chus mulieres et episcopos vitare debeat."[3] But however bad many of the aspects of flight from the world may have been, it was essen- tially a question of avoiding wealth, women and, we must add, the clergy.

Life in the Community: A New World Within Christianity

Many true disciples who were ready to embrace the life of a hermit were among those who visited Antony in the desert. At one time, there were so many who were curious to see him that he went even deeper into the desert. From 306 onward, however, he ac- cepted the presence of other disciples living in cells close to his own. After living for about twenty years in solitude, he allowed fellow anchorites to come to see him at regular intervals. This was not, of course, a true community. The hermits simply lived near to each other, without following any communal rule, but grouped, as it were, around Antony as the person at their center.[4]

Pachomius was an ascetic who had originally been a soldier. He was a man with considerable organizational skill, and in 320 he founded the first monastery, a group of cells built adjacent to each other and surrounded by a wall that made contact with the outside world impossible. Those who entered his monastery did not take vows, but they owed total obedience to their superior. Pachomius' solitary monks were bound by a strict organization as far as their activities and their work in the community were concerned, but they had considerable autonomy with regard to fasting and the sup- plementary ascetic exercises that they chose to undertake. They were not required to give up all private initiative. According to the rule, only the hours of prayer and work were fixed.

Pachomius did, however, introduce one element that was new to Christianity—his companions had to wear special clothing. This dress, which was originally a sign of poverty, became the material evidence of the separation of these cenobites from those special laymen who were monks. Pachomius had indisputable authority as the leader of the monastery. He was proud of the fact that he had sent away, within the space of a single year, about a hundred recruits who were, in his opinion, unworthy. On the other hand, however, he allowed his monks to perform excesses in ascetic practice without intervening.

The Pachomian system was very successful, and when the founder died in 346, there were already several houses and thousands of monks. Monasticism quickly spread beyond the confines of Upper Egypt to cover the whole of the east. It also included both sexes, resulting in monasteries being established for women as well as for men.

With so many and such very large communities in existence, we are bound to wonder what had become of "flight from the world" and whether these flourishing monasteries were not in themselves a new world created for a new race of Christians. The success of the monastic movement can certainly be described as popular, even though rich rather than ordinary people were tending at this time to embrace the ascetic way of life.

It is also important to remember that the revolution brought about by Pachomius was not simply spiritual—it was also economic and social. His monks also worked very hard and their work was entirely manual. Like Antony, they too wove mats and baskets for sale to satisfy their modest needs and gave many to the poor. There were, however, thousands of cenobites and they formed an enormous work force in the desert regions that had become very insecure at a time of crisis in the empire. They also produced a valuable surplus that could be distributed to the poor.

Mat and basket weaving and possibly saturating the market with these goods was not the only function of these monks. They were also carpenters, farm workers and even mariners. Members of each trade were grouped within these enormous houses in teams of thirty to forty men living and working under a supervisor. Boats were even built so that the surplus work could be distributed to the poor in Alexandria. Pachomius' soldiers of Christ formed armies of workers—one is almost tempted to call them proletarian armies.

Basil of Caesarea became acquainted with Pachomian cenobitism when he made a journey through Egypt, and he gave it a less rough and more civilized and sociable emphasis when he organized monasticism in Asia Minor.[5] Instead of setting up huge houses of inhuman dimensions, he created small communities of no more than thirty people, each member of which could really know every other member and call him his "brother." The abbot—the "father" or *proestos*— was also really able to guide each member of such a small community.

Basil also set up his monasteries near to small towns and villages with a social and educational aim, and he encouraged as well the creation of monastic hospices and schools. This is a long way from Saint Antony, who, according to the Syriac version of his life, was a solitary figure concerned only with his own person.[6] Basil's form of monasticism was also very different from Pachomius' in that its asceticism was only moderate and the same for all the monks in the community. Unlike Pachomius, he insisted on obedience to the abbot and obedience to the gospel and instituted a kind of novitiate —fundamentally a time of preparation—and the practice of pronouncing monastic vows, often in the presence of the bishop. Finally, and perhaps most importantly, work in Basil's monasteries was not exclusively manual, and those who had other skills could be instructed and devote themselves to intellectual tasks. In this way, monasteries became educational communities and therefore influenced society.

Antony's way of life as an anchorite became widely known throughout the west through the medium of Athanasius, when the latter was in Rome. Jerome became the apostle of asceticism among the aristocratic ladies of the empire. It was, however, the cenobitic form of monasticism that took root in the west rather than the way of life of the solitary hermit. As in the case of Pachomius in Egypt, it was an ex-soldier, Martin of Tours, who gave it a great impetus and initiated its spread in Gaul in the fourth century. Martin's legendary gesture in giving his cloak to a poor man is so widely known that it is hardly necessary to repeat it here. Later, at Lérins, Honoratus founded a monastery which soon began to have a deep intellectual influence. This foundation was followed by others, equally prestigious, in the south of Gaul, for example at Marseilles and Arles. Then, finally, in the sixth century, Saint Benedict wrote, at the monastery of Monte Cassino in Campania, the rule that gradually became generally accepted and used in the west.

The Monasteries' Need for Clergy

Although it originated as a lay movement, the monastic system was also able to attract the clergy. Some presbyters may have become monks with the sole aim of carrying out their priestly ministry

among this special section of the lay people. This was so in the case
of the presbyters Isaac and Dorotheus, both of whom embraced the
monastic way of life and then served their fellow anchorites with
their liturgical ministry.[7]

Monasticism soon became very prestigious, and this made it
both attractive to certain members of the clergy and an object of
jealousy for others. For many Christians, it became fashionable to
take the monk's habit without changing one's way of life in any
sense. There were, however, authentic and deep conversions. One
of these exemplary converts to monasticism was the bishop of
Lyons, Justus, who gave up his episcopal duties and went to Egypt to
follow the monastic way of life in the desert.

Most of the clergy who were converted to monasticism had
reasons of personal holiness in mind rather than service to the
monastic community. The eucharistic needs of such communities
were originally quite limited. It was often only on Sunday that the
eucharist was celebrated. There was no daily eucharist either in
Pachomius' Egyptian monasteries or in the solitary groupings at
Jerusalem (in the *laurae* or "monasteries").

Basil of Caesarea, who made the confession of sins a frequent
practice, seems to have entrusted the task of directing consciences to
lay monks. Even Saint Benedict made a distinction in his rule between a monastic and a clerical hierarchy. The presbyter who made
his monastic profession was subject to the same rules as all other
monks. Nonetheless, as far as the liturgical ministry is concerned, he
could be placed in the second rank, immediately after the abbot.

As for hermits, we have already seen that they managed to get
on quite well without being ordained. In Syria in the fifth century,
we have the example of Zeno, who left his solitude to go on Sundays
to the nearest place where the eucharist was being celebrated.[8]
Then there is the case of Paphnutius in Egypt, who did the same.
Some anchorites were visited each Sunday by a presbyter, while, for
others, the eucharistic celebration was exceptional. There is a moving description in the writings of Theodoret of Cyrrhus of a eucharist
that he celebrated in the cell of a recluse called Maris.[9]

It sometimes happened that a well-intentioned bishop ordained
a lay hermit without being asked. If we are to understand this insistence on ordaining monks, it is important to consider carefully the
position occupied by anchorites and the part that they played. Because of their reputation, they attracted not only disciples who were

looking for examples of and lessons in holiness, but also a great number of people who expected them to bless them, intercede for them, heal them and even work miracles for them. The presence of a hermit near to a village sometimes caused contention among the inhabitants, leading to the hermit being forcibly removed, for example, from one side of a river to the other. Relics also often played a part in this magical conception of holiness. The anchorites' clothes were, for example, believed to have a beneficial effect, and when it became known that the anchorite was dying, there might be struggles between different groups of people to seize hold of his dead body or, if that failed, at least to tear out some of his hair.

This explosive situation, then, with the monk, dead or alive, at the center of it, led bishops to increase the holiness of his presbyters by the addition of monastic holiness. There is the story of Macedonius, a very pious but illiterate hermit who had never read the holy books. He was ordained, unknown to himself and without even understanding what had taken place, by Bishop Flavian.[10] He thanked the bishop for what he had done by chasing him with a stick in his hand! But Flavian at least had a good excuse—he hoped to see Macedonius take part every Sunday in Sunday worship with the whole of his presbyterium, for the edification of its members.

That was, however, not always the case. Anchorites were sometimes ordained simply for their own sakes, to give them additional personal graces or a reward for their exceptional merits. Theodoret describes the curious way in which a recluse who was living in total isolation from the world in a cell without either a door or a window was ordained in the fifth century. A bishop had an opening made in the wall so that he could get inside the cell, laid his hands on the hermit, explained to him the grace that he was conferring on him, and then left without receiving any reply from the newly ordained man and closed the opening behind him.[11] It is difficult to imagine a more personal and less communal ordination that this! The fact that this layman had been made a priest without showing the slightest desire to become one shows that this event took place at a time far removed from that when a man could only be ordained for a particular community.

The case of Paulinus of Nola is, of course, less extreme, but the fact that he was ordained by force on Christmas Day in 394 points to the same development. As the result of a vote by plebiscite, Paulinus only agreed to be ordained in the church of Barcelona on condition that he was not expected to serve only that church, but would be simply a priest in the service of God.[12] But being "simply a priest in the service of God" went completely counter to the decision of the Council of Chalcedon, which had proclaimed in 451 that "no one— neither presbyter, nor deacon, nor any member of the clergy of any rank whatever—might be ordained in an absolute manner, if a town church, a country church, a martyrium or a monastery had not been assigned to him in a precise manner."[13]

In fact, monasticism led to the creation of a third race of Christians. A man was first and foremost a monk, and the distinction between lay and clergy only came after that. The existence of this third race contributed to the ending of the complementary and bipolar relationship existing between lay people and members of the clergy within the Christian community. The presbyter who left his original community in order to become a monk, while still retaining his "presbyteral character," and the monk who was ordained for his own personal merit, without having any particular community to serve, introduced a radical change into the idea of ministry and, at the same time, that of the laity. This change is worth examining more closely.

Before it took place, a man was made a minister of the altar not only because he was regarded as worthy of it, but also because it was useful to the community. The merits of the candidate were valued essentially in their relationship to the common good. The idea of systematically ordaining all those who might be worthy of becoming presbyters would never have occurred to anyone. It was always thought that a man could be quite worthy if he remained a layman. Attitudes toward this question, however, gradually changed, developing until the point was reached where those who were neither members of the clergy nor monks—in other words, those who were called lay or secular—were regarded as less worthy.

This development took place quite naturally as the result of a number of factors. These included the wish of the bishops to ensure that their clergy were of high quality—this led them to look for recruits among the monks. There was also the need felt by the monks themselves to have one of their number ordained to serve the monastery. In the beginning, it was especially when there was a particular need for an ordained member or a lack of local clergy that the bishop looked for a recruit among the monks themselves. Some monasteries, however, like the one at Lérins, soon became seedbeds for clergy or even for bishops.

At the same time, there was also an increasing number of the internal needs in the local Christian communities. The monk-presbyter, who had been ordained essentially to celebrate the eucharist in the monastery itself, could hardly refuse to baptize or bury the inhabitants of the neighboring villages or to take part in the work of evangelization in the district. The numbers of monk-priests and priest-monks therefore increased, and the image of the priesthood and the cenobitic ideal came to overlap.

During the sixth and seventh centuries, the imperial, monastic and papal authorities were all concerned with the problem of regulating relationships between monks and the clergy. In 539 a request was made in a novella that four or five monks who were worthy of ordination should be chosen to serve the monastery church.[14] Toward the middle of the century, Aurelianus stated in his rule that no monk should be ordained as a presbyter or deacon without the consent of the abbot.[15] Finally, Pope Gregory the Great intervened, making it obligatory for bishops to satisfy the request of an abbot who wanted to have a monk ordained for the liturgy in the monastery. He also reminded bishops that they should not take the initiative and ordain monks without the abbot's consent. On the one hand, then, more and more monks were aspiring to become priests, while, on the other, the clergy was increasingly taking over the characteristics of the ascetic way of life.

Virginity—The Christian Ideal

From its earliest times, Christianity had produced men and women who made themselves "eunuchs for the sake of the kingdom of God,"[16] but from the fourth century onward in particular, this ideal of virginity began to develop in a very special way, both in reality and in Christian writing. At least a dozen treatises on virginity were written at this time, and asceticism had become a very successful movement among the most diverse sections of society.

This movement owed a great deal to neo-Platonism. It often strikes the modern reader as totally dualistic and Manichaean, especially in its denial that the body or sexuality had any right to exist. At a deeper level, however, the justification of this fourth century ascetic movement can be found in the situation of great prosperity in which the church had been placed since the Constantinian peace.

Virginity was experienced as a return to the paradisiacal state. This return was, it was believed, made possible by the feeling that the church was going through a period of great expansion in the empire. Christianity was growing and the number of its members was increasing. During this period marriage had a part to play, but now that there were more men and women and peace reigned and Christians were no longer threatened by war, virginity could also spread.

This was the argument put forward by Basil of Ancyra, and it was taken up by Jerome. Within the framework of this idyllic vision of the Roman empire, virginity was seen as a "return to paradise, a transformation into a state of immortality and reconciliation with Christ."[17] It was a restoration to its original integrity of the divine image that had become hidden by the stains of the flesh. It was also becoming what the first man had been in his original state. What, then, was the ultimate goal of this restoration to the paradisaical state? It was deification and the beatific vision. In the words of John Chrysostom, "true virginity and a desire to remain incorrupt achieve this goal so that, through virginity, we can see God."[18] In the west, Ambrose was to present the Virgin Mary as a model for Christians who were attracted by the ascetic ideal.

Virginity was, of course, not enough for Christians. It had to be accompanied by charity. All the same, it is difficult to avoid the impression that virginity was increasingly presented as the only decisive value and as a positive good in itself. The church fathers, who were so anxious to engage in apologetics, often presented it as the only reasonable and right choice and marriage as full of disadvantages. Very gradually, although it was never categorically condemned, marriage came to be discredited and husbands and wives to be ridiculed. Wives especially were vilified. A typical example of this attitude can be found in the work of John Chrysostom, who described woman as "wicked, backbiting, talkative and—the worst vice of all—extravagant, in a word, full of all kinds of faults."[19] The same author also wrote about the sufferings in the daily life of those women who had the misfortune to be married. These included motherhood and household cares. Only virgins were able to have the time and the spiritual freedom to be able to devote themselves entirely to God. Neither John Chrysostom nor Ambrose had a tender attitude toward marriage and Jerome was quite aggressive in his opposition to it. We shall be looking more closely at Jerome's attitude below. In the meantime, however, we should not be surprised to find that the situation led to a critical and even hostile reaction toward the ascetical movement.

The feminine ideal seems also to have been spread rather like a train of gunpowder. Very few women chose to lead the solitary life of a recluse in the desert, whereas, almost since the beginning of the movement, many women lived together in convents, often established alongside the monasteries for men. To begin with, these monasteries or convents for women were very often established by the women who were related to founders of monasteries for men. In the Egyptian desert, for example, Pachomius' sister set up, for reasons of safety, first one and then a second monastery for women, alongside and protected by those of her brother. Many foundations for men were duplicated by foundations for women. Both Ambrose's sister and Basil's embraced the monastic life and attracted other women to join them and form a community. The nearness of their convents to the men's monasteries, however, had disadvantages as well as advantages. There is evidence that there was always a risk of temptation or at least of rumors of scandal. In the centuries that followed, there was strong opposition to establishing monasteries for men and for women in close proximity to each other.

There were also, from very early times, women who lived not in monasteries or convents, but near to their church—in other words, in their parish—taking a vow of virginity and living out their ideal privately in their own homes, choosing to come together when the liturgy was celebrated locally. In Gaul, the bishop received the vows of such women and then took care, as in the case of the widows and orphans, that they had enough to feed and sustain themselves.

Even women belonging to the noblest classes in Roman society practiced the ideal of virginity in this way. What Jerome has to say about the beginnings of this private form of monasticism is interesting: "In those days, no woman of high birth in Rome had a monastic vocation or dared to adopt, because of the novelty of the thing, a name that was regarded by the mass of the people as ignominious and vile. From presbyters in Alexandria, from Bishop Athanasius and from Peter, who, fleeing from the persecution occasioned by the Arian heresy, had sought refuge in Rome as the safest place for members of their communion, Marcella had learned about the life of the blessed Antony, who was then still in this world. She had also learned about Pachomius' monasteries in the Thebaid and the discipline imposed on virgins and widows. She was not ashamed to embrace a profession which she now knew was pleasing to Christ."[20]

Marcella founded the cenacle on the Aventine Hill in Rome, and women from the city's high society met together there, following a happy blend of the ideal of virginity and intellectual activity. Jerome appears to have been very much at his ease in this environment. Marcella gathered around her women who belonged to the highest aristocracy of Rome and who were longing for knowledge. They studied scripture, learned Hebrew and sacrificed everything —their wealth and their fine clothing—to their ideal. In their excessive zeal, some of them even went so far as to sacrifice their children. One of them, Melania, a widow, quite simply abandoned her five year old son to the guardianship of the praetor in order to go to the holy places. In the meantime, however, many Christians were troubled by the increasingly hostile attitude toward marriage and the collapse of family values.

It would, of course, be wrong to think of this growing opposition to the ascetic movement as the work of worldly members of the clergy who were jealous of the success of those who opted for a monastic type of life. It was not just the lax who were shocked by Jerome's scornful descriptions of the foolish state of marriage. There were also many aristocratic Christians who were alarmed by the proselytism of the cenacle on the Aventine Hill, probably because they were afraid that they would have no descendants. Others may have been anxious about their wives and children. Good wives and husbands were undoubtedly troubled and even shocked by the movement's grotesque misrepresentation of family life.

Jerome's first skirmish was with a Roman layman called Helvidius, who had written a treatise against these fashionable new ideas about the superiority of celibacy and virginity. In his attempt to restore the value of the married state, Helvidius had attacked faith in Mary's virginity. Jerome's reply was entitled *De perpetua viginitate Beatae Mariae, adversus Helvidium.*

What is important to remember in this context is that Jerome's religious view—namely that the married woman was inferior to the virgin and the married man to the celibate—had, from this time, that is, 384 or thereabouts, onward, a deep and lasting influence on western Christian thought, certainly at least until Vatican II. In his treatise against Helvidius, Jerome writes, for example: "Do you really think that the woman who gives herself day and night to prayer and fasting can be placed on the same footing as the one who, when her husband arrives, composes her face, adopts a gentler approach and gives him false caresses?"[21] And, in a letter addressed to a young virgin, Eustochium, in 383, he gives the following summary of his conviction: "You should know that you are more valuable than those women."[22]

Jerome did not reply at once to Helvidius. In 393, a monk named Jovinian claimed that to be a virgin or married was less important than to do good works and that the merit of baptized Christians should be measured, not on the basis of the state in which they found themselves, but on that of their good works. This claim evoked a fierce response from Jerome—so violent and unrestrained, in fact, that Pammachius, the Roman who had commissioned the work, tried to have it withdrawn from circulation. Jerome then replied to Pammachius explaining and giving a little more light and shade to his thinking, but without abandoning his principles.

The beginning of Jerome's letter sets the tone for what follows: "The debate between Jovinian and myself is this: He regards marriage as equal to virginity, whereas I regard it as inferior."[23] Jerome was anxious to remain within the bounds of orthodoxy and to avoid encratism, so he wrote a little later: "I agree that marriage is a gift, but there is a difference between one gift and another."[24] He then goes on to put virgins in the first place, widows in the second place and married persons in the third.[25] "The church does not condemn marriage," he says, "but subordinates it. It does not reject it, but puts it in its place, in the knowledge . . . that some are dedicated to honor, while others are handed over to scorn."[26] We may say, then, that the only merit that Jerome ever seems to have conceded to marriage is that of having given birth to virgins!

His zeal for virginity and his indignant attitude toward Jovinian led him to go too far, even in his letter to Pammachius, in which he tried to give a measure of light and shade to his position. The end of that letter gives a good insight into his extreme attitude: "We like to eat a great deal and we are fond of our wives' embraces, but we also want at the same time to reign with Christ in the ranks of the virgins and widows! Should the same reward be given for hunger and for overeating, for dirtiness and for cleanliness, or for a hair shirt and a silken garment?"[27]

It is true that Jerome claims—and rightly—that in many passages he is only repeating opinions expressed by other Christian authors, such as Tertullian, Cyprian and Ambrose. But the denigration of marriage in his writing is not simply an argument ad hominem—it is a systematic argument. He also takes refuge behind the literary genre that he uses and the satirical authors from whom he takes at least some of his cruel portraits of family life. But when it fails to be comic in its intention and is used for the purpose of theological argument, this satirical type of writing takes on quite a different tone. The reader has the indelible impression that Jerome is himself convinced by his own violence.

The Obligatory Chastity of Ministers of the Altar

Not all members of the clergy were as rigorous as Jerome. In 406, when he was approaching sixty and was living as a hermit in Bethlehem, Jerome found a determined opponent in Vigilantius, who was also, like himself, a presbyter and who apparently reflected the views of a group within the clergy who were in favor of marriage and the ordination of married men. Some bishops seem at this time to have regarded celibates with suspicion, thinking that chastity and celibacy exacerbated man's desires, excited his passions and led to an obsession with sex. The married state and fatherhood, on the other hand, was regarded by these men as a guarantee of a balanced way of life.

Jerome deplored this suspicious attitude, although he may have played a part in creating it. "Unfortunately," he wrote in his treatise against his opponent, "it is said that Vigilantius has bishops as accomplices in his crime, so long as he needs to call bishops those men who do not ordain anyone a deacon if he has not previously contracted a marriage. He does not believe in the chastity of any celibate. Even more than this, they show how far their own lives are holy by suspecting that everyone is evil and by only entrusting the sacraments of Christ to members of the clergy whose wives they have seen either pregnant or as mothers with children in their arms."[28]

There can be no doubt that Jerome did not like the sound of

babies crying! He even described the great disadvantages of the married woman's domestic life in his treatise against Helvidius: "Babies begin to cry, the servants make a fuss and the children hang on their mother's neck demanding that she kiss them. The accounts have to be made again and there are more expenses. The cooks are preparing the meals, the women at the loom and the distaff chatter, and then the master of the house comes in with his men friends. Have the beds been made? Has the floor been swept? Have the cups been filled? Has the meal been prepared? Answer me, please: With all these cares and activities, when can you think about God?"[29]

For Jerome, it was not just the cares and ceaseless activities of married life that stood in the way of prayer, but the sexual act itself. However, sexual relationships not only prevented prayer. They also prevented married people from taking part in the eucharist. The layman who wanted to receive communion had to abstain from the sex act with his wife: "It is hard! It is unbearable! What secular person can bear that?" Jerome was quite unsympathetic in rejecting all objections: "Let him who can endure it endure it. If he cannot endure it, that is his problem!"[30] Proud and scornful, yes, but Jerome was quite convinced. For him, complete abstinence from marriage was an obligation for the priest who had above all always to pray.[31]

He therefore replied to Vigilantius that the church of Rome could only accept as members of its clergy men who were chaste virgins or who, if they were already married, abstained from all sexual relationships.[32] This was the discipline that Pope Siricius tried to impose on the clergy. In a letter that he wrote to Bishop Himerius of Tarragona, he wrote, for example: "The one who wants to dedicate himself to the service of the church from childhood onward must be baptized before the age of puberty and accepted in the ministry of the readers or lectors. If he has lived from adolescence until his thirtieth year honorably and satisfied with one wife, whom he married as a virgin with the common blessing of the priest, then he must first become an acolyte and a sub-deacon. After this, he may reach the rank of diaconate, so long as he has previously shown, by his chastity, that he is worthy of it."[33] Siricius had no doubts at all. He was convinced that the man who aspired to join the clergy was called to be converted to a superior state of life. This meant that the layman was thought to have an inferior state.[34]

Jerome was inclined to go even further than this. If it had depended only on him, he would only have admitted virgins to the clergy and not married men who practiced chastity. It was in these terms that he explained the presence of married men among the ministers of the altar: "The reason for this is the need for a greater number of priests than can be found among men who are virgins. Because there is a need to recruit more robust men into the army, are not less vigorous men also accepted, since, after all, it is not possible for every man to be robust?"[35] It is clear that Jerome preferred "clergy who are also monks and whose profession adorns the priesthood as the priesthood adorns the profession."[36] At the same period, Pope Siricius also wrote: "It is our wish and we would like monks to be accepted to perform the functions of the clergy, as the severity of principles and the holy institution of life and faith suggest."[37]

In this way, then, what Tertullian feared at the beginning of the third century gradually came about in the west—there was an increasing reserve of clergy, a reserve, in other words, of laymen who were regarded as worthy to become ministers of the altar because they were following a monastic way of life. The image of the monk gradually became merged with that of the clergy. When Martin became the bishop of Tours, he did not want to abandon the monastic life, and he brought his disciples together in a monastery situated just outside the town. They were either clergy or monks. According to Ambrose, Eusebius of Verceil, on the other hand, was "the first in the west to combine the monastic life with the life of the church."[38] A little later, in Africa, Augustine asked members of his own clergy who wanted to opt for the monastic life to give up their personal belongings and live communally in the episcopal monastery of Hippo.

About 430, Hilary, the bishop of Arles, also established an episcopal monastery in which very young readers or lectors could derive benefit from the example of older men, be initiated into the functions of the clergy, and at the same time remain virgins, so that they might be admitted to the higher orders. This episcopal monastery, however, provided no more than an invitation to the clergy to accept the monastic life. There was no obligation to embrace that way of life. At the end of the fifth century, there were still clergy in Arles living in their personal residences.[39] Whatever the situation may have been, the monastic model played an increasingly important part in the lives of the clergy and, on the other hand, monks more and more frequently aspired to the clerical state. The ascetic way of life, which had been inaugurated by lay people, was increasingly experienced as a clerical attribute.

What Could a Married Layman Do?

Interpreting the Old Testament text in which David and his companions eat the consecrated showbread, Irenaeus, as we have already seen, commented: "Priest—all the Lord's disciples are also priests."[40] Interpreting the same text two centuries later, Jerome gave particular emphasis to the question asked by Ahimelech about the purity of David's men. His conclusion was that "secular" men who wanted to take part in the eucharist had previously to keep themselves from their wives. There is a noticeable distance between the perspective of the two authors and between the path followed by each. What could a married layman do, Jerome is asking, but abstain from his wife? We too should ask that question within a wider perspective: What could a married layman do?

There was no question, at this period, of an individual layman becoming a minister. He could, however, fulfill an important function if he took the role of godparent seriously. He could even, in an emergency, baptize. Like the clergy, he too was invited to share in the missionary work of the church. He was also allowed to carry out this task in a wide variety of forms, and he could, to this end, make use of his own special situation in civil society. He might also be led on occasion to express his own faith to strangers or to pagans.

This expression of personal faith had nothing to do with the official teaching functions within the church. Since the end of the third century, the clergy had developed and made their own the most elaborate forms of Christian knowledge and had taken all authority to teach away from the laity. A collection of canonical texts known as the "Ancient Statutes of the Church," compiled in Gaul in the fifth century, provides confirmation of this development. In it, laymen are explicitly forbidden to teach either in the presence of members of the clergy or without their consent.[41]

As for the attempts made on the frontier between pagan and Christian culture, these, it must be admitted, really concerned no more than one or two generations of the Roman nobility at the beginning of the Constantinian era. It was not long before the barbarians made Christianity look like a bastion of Romanism, with monks and members of the clergy as the custodians of Christian culture.

Laymen with leisure time could, however, still be interested in theological questions. At the time of the Arian controversy, Gregory of Nyssa pointed out that "it is not possible to go to the shoemaker, the butcher or the public baths without someone talking to you about the eternal begetting of the Son."[42] But the laity did not have any authority to make their theological views heard, and the *vox populi* was distrusted. The main preoccupation expressed in several imperial directives concerned with the preparatory work for councils in the fifth century was to eliminate the presence and the intervention of groups of monks or lay people.[43]

In a very general sense, there was also at this time a tendency to distrust interventions made by the Christian people and to reject any claims made by them to a power that had, until then, been traditionally accepted. This was the traditional right of the laity to take part in the appointment of ministers of the altar. Long before this time, Origen had been afraid that this procedure might result in the most political candidates being elected. Jerome, however, made a much more serious accusation, saying that "it sometimes happens that married people, who form the majority of the people, applaud themselves when they applaud the choice of married candidates, believing that they are themselves in no way inferior to the virgins, because they prefer a married to a virgin man."[44] Origen was afraid that the people might be deceived or manipulated, whereas Jerome's fear was that the people, whom he regarded as "inferior," might choose inferior people, in the sense that they were less perfect. The gulf between the clergy and the laity was becoming wider, and from this time onward it became, in principle, impossible for a layman to be elected bishop.

The clerical career, with its time spent preparing for the function, its dignity and its chastity, was in the process of being born in the west. The bishop, promoted, by the grace of the emperor, to the status of being a judge and changing his see according to the needs of the church, was becoming more and more remote from his laity. The clergy, too numerous in some churches thanks to the generosity of the state, could also be moved from one church to another. The link between the church's ministers and the people to whom they were ministering was also becoming looser, even in some places to the

The Church of the Clergy
Sacramentary of the Abbey of Marmoutier. Ninth Century. Library of Autun.
Photo Varlez

point where it became merged with the relationship between the administrators and those to whom they were administering.

This giving of an absolute value to the clergy was, moreover, reinforced by the individual ordinations conferred on those whose monastic life-style was viewed with admiration. Slowly but surely, the idea gained ground that if he belonged to the clergy, a man must necessarily be, in a certain sense, perfect. It was undoubtedly this idea that gave lay people a strange privilege—that of being the only Christians who were admitted to "public" penance, something to which clergy who had erred did not have access. "Canonical" penance was in fact not compatible with the diaconate, the presbyterate or the episcopate. It acted as an obstacle to admission to the church's orders and was therefore exclusively a lay prerogative.

Finally, it is important to mention one further lay "privilege." Lay people could, by means of their gifts, "honor" the ministers of the altar and provide for their needs. This was probably the most constant and the most widely shared lay function, if we bear in mind that they, whom Theodoret of Cyrrhus had identified with the *idiotai* (the "uninitiated" of 1 Corinthians 14:23),[45] no longer had any liturgical activity. At the end of the fifth century, an emperor declared that the contribution made by lay people to the needs of the church was and had to remain voluntary and that extortion, blackmail, threats of excommunication or the withholding of baptism had no part to play in it. He was doing no more than reaffirming Tertullian's principle: "No one is compelled—all contributions are given freely." Making one's contribution had in fact been the real "lay ministry" since the time of Origen.

CONCLUSION

The Laity: A Survey of Five Hundred Years of History

It is not easy to summarize accurately what the lay person represented throughout the first five centuries of Christianity. There was no such thing as a laity in New Testament times. Toward the end of the first century, Clement of Rome used the term "lay" for the first time, but only in the context of the Old Testament. This was followed by silence until the time of Clement of Alexandria, when the laity was really born. It is possible, then, to say that Christianity existed for about two hundred years without a laity.

The laity appeared for the first time in Christian history at the end of the second century or the beginning of the third, but the lay people of that time were not the same as those of today. They can be defined in comparison with the clergy that was evolving at the same time as they were, but, far from representing the totality of the Christian people, they formed an elite. That elite consisted of baptized believers of the male sex, the "husband of only one woman." They were those who, according to Tertullian, were able to baptize and make an offering in the absence of the clergy.

This elitist conception of the layman as a man who had married only once persisted for about fifty years or more. Toward the year 300, however, this tradition was recalled at the Council of Elvira, which prescribed in its Canon 38 that when there was a danger of death or it was impossible to call a member of the clergy, a believer who had "preserved the integrity of his baptism and had not married twice" could baptize. Even when monogamy ceased to be a condition for belonging to the laity, the term "lay" did not automatically become synonymous with the term *fidelis* or "believer." Women were still excluded from the group of lay people and were still forbidden, at that time, to baptize. It was not until the fourth century that the term "lay" was also applied explicitly to women. From then onward, the lay people represented all Christians who were not members of the clergy.

New races of Christians had, however, already appeared in the Constantinian era. In the Roman empire, when the emperor and the public servants who played such an important part in the imperial administration were so impregnated with religion, it took less than seventy-five years for an emperor to describe himself as a layman and only a little longer for monks and religious to be regarded as a third group within the Christian people.

By the fifth century, then, the three great divisions within the Christian people—clergy, monks and laity—had become established, and these were hardly to change at all until our own times. But to return to the subject of this summary of five centuries of Christian history, who were those who described themselves personally as the laity? Justin proudly proclaimed: "I am a Christian. I glory in it." But what about those who said: "I am a lay person?" There was, to my knowledge, only one person who made this claim, that he was a layman, in the first person and that was Emperor Valentinian I, and this claim to the name "layman" was not a claim to responsibility in the church, but rather a pretext to avoid being committed.

Two Different Ecclesiologies

Summarized and oversimplified in this way, the history of the laity—understood in the strict sense of the word, that is, as those Christians who were described as such in the course of the first five centuries of Christianity or who claimed this name for themselves —makes a disappointing impression.

There is, however, another way of approaching the problem. We can take a wider and more modern definition of the term "lay" as our point of departure. In other words, we can regard every Christian who is not a minister of the altar as a lay man or woman. In these conditions, we have to be careful not to present a false view of history and therefore must make a distinction between two periods.

The first of these periods goes to the end of the second century. There is no theological argument at that time justifying a dichotomy between the ministers of the altar and the people. The question of the laity is only introduced if we create an artificial anachronism. The ecclesiology of the second period, which begins in the third century, is, however, quite different. The distinction between the minister of the altar and the people is justified theologically from several points of view. The first justification is ordination for liturgical service. The second argument used is that of the levitical typology of the Old Testament, which implies a special economic relationship between the minister of the altar and the believing people. The distinction between these two groups of Christians is, in the third argument, justified by the part played in the Old Testament by the high priest, who could purify and remit sins. In this way, the idea of "clergy" was, in this second period of Christian history, confined to a clearly defined group of ministers.

In their broad outline, the church's structures in the third century more or less correspond to those of the twentieth century ecclesiology which reflects the rebirth and resurgence of the laity. From the third century onward, it is possible, by analogy, to raise the question of the part played by the laity in the church by applying it to the whole non-clerical body of Christian believers. The situation was quite different in the first two hundred years. In those centuries, all Christians represented God's *kleros*, and there were many other features that characterized those early years of the church's life. The various functions that existed in the church could not be called "lay" rather than "clerical" or "clerical" rather than "lay." All Christians were regarded as holy and as chosen. The unity of the race of Christians took precedence over the diversity of their attributes. Even though the ministers of the altar were already beginning in the second century to form a group that was distinct because of the function exercised by its members, there was at this time still no frontier, justified by theological argument, between one group of baptized Christians and the other. During the whole of this early period, the idea of a ministerial priesthood was not in competition with that of the universal priesthood of all Christians. Even for Irenaeus, who thought of the church's presbyters as "masters" possessing the charism of truth, all the disciples of Christ were priests and no special subject could, in his opinion, make an exclusive claim to have the right to make an offering.

True Lay Ministers

In the writings of Irenaeus, presbyters and their spiritual disciples lived in a state of peaceful co-existence, but from the time of Clement of Alexandria until that of Origen, all the masters of Christian thought put the spiritual and the institutional hierarchy in the scales and weighed one against the other. It cannot be denied that they tried to give a relative value to the importance and the power of the institutional hierarchy, but they never went so far as to dispute the positive value of the existence of a Christian clergy. From the third century onward, the need for the people of God to be split into two groups—clergy and faithful believers—was postulated in all ecclesiological teaching.

Not all the functions that were useful to the Christian community were as yet carried out by the clergy, that is, ministers exclusively dedicated by their ordination to the service of the altar. There were also lay ministers, that is, individuals who were not ordained and who performed in a lasting and continuous way a service that was useful to the community. The earliest and the most prestigious of these were certainly those of the *didaskaloi* and the doctors. There were lay teachers or *didaskaloi*, but it cannot be claimed that this teaching function was a specifically lay ministry because it could be carried out by a member either of the laity or of the clergy. It tended to disappear, however, as an independent ministry, and from the second half of the third century onward there were hardly any more real lay *didaskaloi* to be found. The same applies to the function of the catechist. This came increasingly to be exercised by presbyters, who were known as "catechist-presbyters" or "doctor-catechists."

As for the lector, by the beginning of the third century he had already lost his interpreting function and had simply become a reader, a lay function performed alongside that of the liturgical ministers. From the middle of the third century onward this reader was sometimes regarded as a member of the clergy, but his precise status seems to have been disputed by Augustine. He was sometimes ranked among the "church readers." At the time of Cyprian he could exercise, apart from his function of lector or reader in the strict sense, the functions of archivist, secretary and messenger. The loss of his original prestige continued until he was regarded as having a position lower than that of the sub-deacons.

For the author of the *Apostolic Tradition*, these sub-deacons were laymen. They were servants of the deacons whom they were able to assist in their liturgical, charitable or administrative functions. Following the model of the readers, they could also be employed as messengers. They were admitted to the clergy and regarded as superior to the readers from the second half of the fourth century onward.

The exorcists were not members of the clergy, but were regarded as charismatic ministers possessing the gift of healing. Their situation developed differently, depending on which part of the Christian world they lived in and which church they belonged to. They too soon lost their true function and became integrated into the clerical hierarchy as a step in on the promotion ladder to higher functions. In certain cases, however, they disappeared completely. Those who performed secondary liturgical or paraliturgical functions or who exercised the charism of healing could, by analogy with the situation today, be regarded as lay ministers.

There was, however, one charism that continued, from the beginning of the third century onward, to transcend the dichotomy between clergy and laity, and that was the charism of bearing witness. In the case of the church's martyrs, the frontier between ordained and not ordained ceased to exist. By virtue of their confession of faith, they had the honor of the presbyterate. This exception did not, however, last very long. From the time of Decius' persecution, Cyprian cautiously questioned the privilege that allowed the martyrs to situate themselves above the frontier dividing the clergy from the laity.

Women Outside the Theology of the Laity

So far I have not spoken about female lay ministries, and with good reason—in the third century women were placed outside the clergy/laity dichotomy. Widows and virgins were states of life. They were in a similar position to the clergy as far as their economic situation in the Christian community was concerned—a situation that enabled them to live from the gifts made by Christians. They could be honored and they could perform good works. They were, however, never ordained and could never be regarded as forming part of the clergy.

Widows had a separate place in the assembly and a special function, that of prayer. Penitents often came to a widow and bowed down before her as they did before a presbyter. They were in the same position as all women, however, in that they were not allowed to baptize. Widows were, in other words, regarded neither as lay women nor as clergy.

"Women—Apostles Without Status"

Ivory, ca. 400   Bavarian National Museum, Munich

This ambiguous situation cannot be seen simply as a kind of historical digression from the norm. Women had charitable functions in New Testament times. They performed good works. They made their homes places in which Christians could meet and the apostles could stay. They shared in the work of evangelization, worked with Paul and accompanied him on his mission. They even taught, although they did not lay claim to any special title or any particular ministry. In the first letter to Timothy, the women who have a place similar to that of the "deacons" are not given any distinctive name and, unlike the men who were in a similar position, they were not able to "gain a good standing for themselves."

We may therefore conclude that in spite of the services that they undoubtedly rendered to the Christian community during the apostolic period, they remained on the periphery of the process of hierarchization, just as they also remained on the periphery of the clergy/laity structure until the end of the third century. Even today, when women are regarded as members of the laity, it is possible for them to carry out the same functions as laymen. They still cannot, however, claim the same status as men within the framework of the "lay ministries" that the Catholic Church is trying to restore to an honorable position of "good standing."

The Collective and the Occasional Functions of the Christian People

Lay ministers performed individual functions, but there were also, in the life of the church, functions that were carried out collectively by the whole of the Christian people. They were, for example, called on to intervene in the choice of clergy and especially in the election of the bishop. In the fourth century the people played a decisive part in the choice of the bishop. They also had a disciplinary part to play when penitents were to be readmitted to the community. Finally, the assembled laity or at least representatives of the laity could be consulted when either delicate or particularly important theological matters were being debated. In all these cases, the "Christian people" were, of course, the people or the assembly of the local church.

Both the strengthening of the clerical structures and the development of supra-local organizations and decisions, however, combined to make these assemblies first purely consultative assemblies and then, very rapidly, assemblies where decisions were merely registered or recorded. All the same, even though the collective function of the people ended by being no longer operative, its existence was less ephemeral than that of the individual lay ministers. It has continued, even until today, to be possible for the people to intervene in the ritual of ordination, at least in a symbolic form.

Apart from the functions exercised by the assembled people, there were also various functions that could be carried out by any Christian, as the occasion arose or the need was felt. The apostolate was one of these. As we have seen, this apostolate was, for example, carried out among the ordinary people such as humble craftsmen or among slaves or prisoners. There was also an apostolate among the intellectually more developed people and the more favored classes in society. Another form of this apostolate was practiced in the private or domestic sphere, and there was also a "political" apostolate. There was a need to spread Christian faith on foreign territory and to work for the orthodoxy of faith within the empire.

Lay men and women were engaged in all these different forms of the apostolate. Perhaps the most important lay apostolate, however, was that of the godparent, for this sponsorship was really an extension of the apostolate, and both men and women members of the laity performed it, often in the form of pre-baptismal catechesis.

All these "occasional" functions performed by the laity formed part of the ministry exercised by the people of God with regard to the world. They were there in all weathers, to such an extent that the apostolate can even be seen as the characteristically lay ministry. In this paradoxical situation, the apostolic succession was the attribute of the bishops, while the ministry of the apostolate was the characteristic of the laity.

Is the Theology of the Laity a Dead End?

There is a tendency today simply to identify the laity with the people of God. That did not happen originally. The laity only represented one part of the people—that part that was distinct from the clergy. It is therefore legitimate to ask whether the theology of the laity has not remained, since its origin, to some extent ambivalent. In theory, the theology of the laity does not exclude any believer from its subject matter. In practice, however, there is always a risk that this will result in new divisions between the militants who are commissioned by the hierarchy, the lay ministers who are officially recognized by the institutional church, and the rest of Christian believers. On the one hand, there are these believers in considerable numbers who often simply want to be "administered" to. On the other, there are the "true lay people," far fewer in numbers, who are quite close to entering the ranks of the clergy. Caught between these two groups, it is quite difficult for those engaged in the theology of the laity to make decisions that enable them to single out, in a really positive way, the specific part played by the laity.

It may be this difficulty that led to the emergence of a theology of the people of God. It is obviously easier to point to the missions to which all Christians are called than to try to define an original mission granted exclusively to non-clerical Christians. The theology of the laity should not, however, be confused with this theology of the people of God, since it necessarily postulates a dichotomy within that people. It excludes the clergy from its subject matter and does not include all Christians within its perspective. A theology of the laity certainly has one outstanding merit—it makes it clear to ordinary baptized Christians that they are also called on to act as the salt of the earth. To make believers once again conscious of their Christian identity, it constructs a personality for them—that of the lay person—and urges them to develop that personality. At the same time, however, it also defines the limits of their way of being and acting as Christians. This is undoubtedly why it has such a fragile existence as a theology that has positive values to offer.

Is the theology of the laity, then, a dead end? Its emergence at the beginning of the third century pointed to a change in the study of ecclesiology. It enabled some Christians to feel that they were still members of the people of God, despite the place that the clergy was increasingly occupying in the life of the Christian community. The laity emerged as such in the palaeochristian period, at a time when the church had the feeling that it was taking part in a race against a great growth in the number of communities and did not know which course to follow. What was the most urgent need? Would it be better to increase the number of clergy capable of guiding these many new Christians or should their own dynamism be harnessed and motivated?

The rebirth of the laity in the twentieth century has taken place in a race against the dechristianization of our society, and the dilemma confronting the church is very similar. What is the most urgent need today? Should those who still believe be mobilized or should helpers be found for the decreasing number of clergy? In the third century, individual lay ministries only survived for about fifty years. This does not necessarily mean that the theology of the laity —in the positive sense—is a dead end. Appearing and reappearing at times of change, it makes it possible for believers themselves to change from one type of ecclesiology to another. It is not, in other words, a dead end, but a temporary diversion making movement forward still possible, even though the old road, which is being repaired or even completely remade, can no longer be used. The theology of the laity is, in other words, a theology of public road works and at the same time a theology of public health, especially when the rhythm of society and the world makes it necessary for Christians to continue their journey despite the bad condition of the older roads. It is also operating while waiting for a new ecclesiological road to be built.

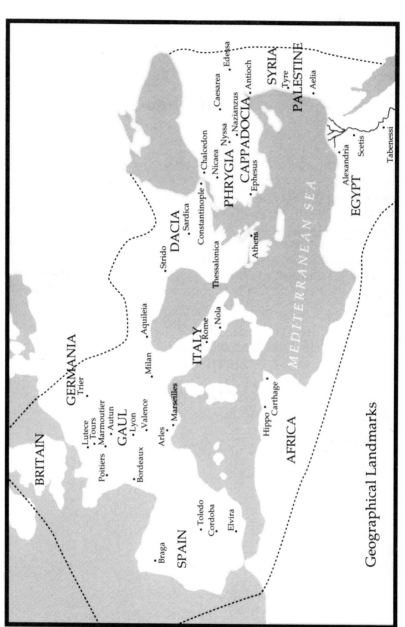

BRITAIN

GERMANIA
Trier

GAUL
Lutece
Tours
Poitiers Marmoutier
Autun
Bordeaux
Lyon
Valence
Milan
Arles
Marseilles
Aquileia

SPAIN
Braga
Toledo
Cordoba
Elvira

ITALY
Rome
Nola

AFRICA
Hippo
Carthage

Strido

DACIA
Sardica
Constantinople
Thessalonica
Athens

Chalcedon
Nicaea

PHRYGIA
Nyssa
Ephesus

CAPPADOCIA
Nazianzus

Caesarea
Edessa

SYRIA
Antioch
Tyre
PALESTINE
Aelia

EGYPT
Alexandria
Scetis
Tabenessi

MEDITERRANEAN SEA

Geographical Landmarks

NOTES

Introduction

1. The most important pontifical texts will be found in *Le laicat*, Tournai 1956, and *Consignes aux militants*, Tournai 1958, both volumes edited by the monks of Solesme. A study of the idea of the laity in Pius XII should begin with a reading of his two addresses to the World Congresses for the Lay Apostolate. The first of these was given at the First Congress on October 14, 1951 and the second at the Second Congress on October 5, 1957.
2. Pius XII, Address to those taking part in the Second World Congress for the Lay Apostolate (October 5, 1957), AAS 49, 1957, p. 922.

PART I
THE FIRST AND SECOND CENTURIES:
THE BIRTH OF A LAITY

Chapter 1: The Wonderful Time When There Was Neither Clergy Nor Laity

1. Heb 8:4.
2. Heb 7:14.
3. Mt 4:23 par.
4. Lk 11:37.
5. Lk 11:5.
6. Mt 21:12–13.
7. Mt 21:23.
8. Mk 12:38–40.
9. Mk 12:28–34; Lk 10:25ff; Mt 13:52.
10. Mk 1:22.
11. Acts 4:32.
12. Acts 2:42.
13. Acts 2:44–45.

14. Acts 11:26.
15. Acts 6:1; 7:7; 9:1; 10:9.
16. Acts 10:45; Eph 1:2; Col 1:2.
17. Rom 1:7; 16:15.
18. 1 Cor 1:1.
19. 1 Cor 7:14.
20. Eph 2:19.
21. 1 Cor 1:2.
22. Gal 3:28–29.
23. Col 1:12.
24. Acts 20:32; 26:18.
25. 1 Pet 1:5.
26. Gal 3:29.
27. Eph 1:11.
28. Col 3:12.
29. For the evidence to the contrary, see Jas 2:5.
30. See Eph 1:4.
31. 1 Pet 5:1–3.
32. Rev 1:5b–6; 5:9–10.
33. 1 Pet 2:9; 2:5.
34. Eph 2:20–22.
35. Rom 12:1.
36. Heb 10:20.
37. 1 Cor 12:7–11.
38. 1 Cor 14:18.
39. 1 Cor 14:19.
40. The *idiotai* (the "uninitiated") are, it is true, associated in 1 Corinthians 14:23–24 with the "unbelievers," but this noun, like the word "lay," seems to be used in two senses.
41. 1 Cor 12:29–30.
42. 1 Cor 12:28.
43. 1 Cor 13.
44. Rom 12.
45. 1 Pet 4:10.
46. 1 Tim 3:1.
47. See Rom 12.
48. 1 Thess 5:12.
49. 1 Tim 1:2; 2 Tim 1:2.
50. 1 Tim 4:6.

51. 1 Tim 4:14.

52. 1 Tim 5.

53. 1 Tim 6.

54. 2 Tim 4:5.

55. 1 Thess 3:2.

56. 1 Tim 3:1.

57. 1 Tim 5:3–5.

58. 1 Tim 5:10.

59. Acts 9:36–39.

60. Acts 12:12.

61. Acts 16:14, 40. See also R. Gryson, *Le ministère des femmes dans l'Eglise ancienne* (Recherche et synthèses 4), Gembloux 1972, 22.

62. Rom 16:12.

63. Rom 16:3.

64. Acts 18:18–19.

65. Acts 18:24–19:1. See also R. Gryson, *op. cit.*, 21–25.

66. 1 Tim 3:11.

67. See Rom 16:1–2.

68. 1 Tim 3:13.

69. See Canon 230, *Codex iuris canonici*, 1983.

70. 1 Tim 2:12.

71. 1 Cor 11:5.

72. Acts 21:9.

Chapter 2: The Appearance of the Laity

1. See I. de la Potterie, "L'origine et le sens du mot 'laic,' " *La vie selon l'Esprit* (Unam Sanctam 55), Paris 1965, 13–29.

2. 1 Clem 54:2.

3. 1 Cor 1:10–16.

4. 1 Clem 57:2.

5. 1 Clem 37:3; 41:1.

6. 1 Clem 40:5.

7. Num 16.

8. 1 Clem 4:12.

9. Num 17.

10. 1 Clem 41:1.

11. 1 Clem 8:5.

Chapter 3: The Period of Christ's Disciples

1. Justin's literary work can be dated between the years 135 and 165. His *Apologia* (cited in these notes as *Apol* I and *Apol* II) can be dated at 150. Even if it was conceived when Justin was still in Ephesus (about 135), his *Dialogue with Trypho* (cited here as *Dial*) was written after the *Apologia*. A translation of these works can be found in *La philosophie' passe au Christ* (Ichtus, Les Pères dans la foi), Paris 1982. Here I quote *Apol* I,1.
2. *Apol* II,12.
3. *Apol* II,13.
4. *Dial* 17:3.
5. *Dial* 92:2.
6. *Apol* I,4.
7. See *Dial* 35.
8. *Dial* 63:5.
9. *Dial* 64:1.
10. See *Dial* 80.
11. *Dial* 17:1.
12. *Dial* 35.
13. *Dial* 2–8.
14. *Dial* 35.
15. *Dial* 7.
16. *Dial* 11.
17. *Dial* 39.
18. *Apol* I,61.
19. *Dial* 80:10.
20. *Dial* 9.
21. See, for example, M. Jourion, *L'eucharistie des premiers chrétiens* (Le point théologique 17), Paris 1976, 75.
22. *Dial* 42.
23. *Dial* 63.
24. *Dial* 58.
25. See, about thirty years later, Irenaeus, *Adv haer* II, 32.4.
26. Tatian, *Oratio* 32.
27. Athenagoras, *Legatio* 11.
28. *Dial* 41.
29. *Ibid.*
30. *Dial* 116.

31. *Apol* I,65.
32. *Apol* I,67.
33. Pliny the Younger, *Letter to Trajan,* Letter 96.
34. 1 Tim 5:17. See also Hermas, *Visions* 2.4,3.
35. See A. Faivre, "Clergé et propriété dans l'église ancienne," *Lumière et vie* 129–130 (August–September 1976), 51–64.
36. *Apol* I,61.
37. *Apol* I,6.
38. *Dial* 14 and 19.
39. See *Dial* 43:2.
40. *Dial* 130:3.
41. *Dial* 135:3.
42. *Dial* 135:6.
43. *Dial* 138. See also *Dial* 84.
44. *Dial* 42:3.
45. *Dial* 63.
46. *Dial* 134:3.
47. See *Apol* I,61.
48. *Epistle to Diognetus* 6:7.
49. *Dial* 39.
50. We now have a complete edition in a single volume, with introductions, notes and a translation of the whole of Irenaeus' *Adversus haereses* (cited below as *Adv haer*) in the series *Sources chrétiens*, Paris 1984. Here I quote *Adv haer* I,24.6; III, 12.7; IV,26.1.
51. See, for example, *Adv haer* III,11.1.
52. *Adv haer* IV,21.3.
53. *Adv haer* V,6.1.
54. *Adv haer* II,32.1–2.
55. *Adv haer* IV,32.1–2.
56. 1 Sam 21:4–7.
57. See Mt 12:3–4.
58. *Adv haer* IV,8.3.
59. *Adv haer* V,34.4.
60. See *Adv haer* IV,12–18.
61. *Adv haer* IV,17.5.
62. *Adv haer* IV,18.6.
63. *Adv haer* IV,18.1 and 4.
64. *Adv haer* IV,17.5.
65. See *Adv haer* I,6.4 and III,15.2.
66. *Adv haer* III,15.2.

67. Adv haer IV,32.1–2.
68. Eusebius, *Ecclesiastical History* (cited below as *Eccl Hist*) V,4.2.
69. Adv haer IV,26.3, quoting Dan 13:20.
70. Adv haer IV,26.5.
71. Ibid.
72. Adv haer IV,26.1.
73. Adv haer IV,26.2.

PART II
THE THIRD CENTURY:
THE PEOPLE OF GOD SPLIT IN TWO

Chapter 4: Lay People, Disciples and Spiritual Masters

1. Tertullian, On Modesty 21:7–17.
2. Origen, Homilies on Jeremiah 4:3.
3. Origen, Homilies on Leviticus 6:6.
4. Jerome, On Illustrious Men 53.
5. J. Quasten, *Initiation aux Pères de l'Eglise* I,2, Paris 1958, 393. The translations in this book are by J. Laporte.
6. For the chronology of Tertullian's work, see R. Braun, *Deus christianorum. Recherches sur le vocabulaire doctrinal de Tertullien* (Etudes augustiniennes) Paris 2nd. ed. 1977, 563–577. The French translation of the titles of Tertullian's works is taken from J. Laporte's work in J. Quasten, op. cit., 298–379.
7. See, for example, On Monogamy 12.2.
8. On the Exhortation to Chastity 7.
9. On Baptism 17:2; De Praescriptione haereticorum ("A Demurrer to the Heretics' Plea," cited below as De Praescr haer) 41:8; On Flight in Persecution 11:1.
10. On Monogamy 11–12.
11. On Flight in Persecution 11.
12. On Monogamy 11–12.
13. Rev 1:6.
14. On the Exhortation to Chastity 7.
15. See C. Vogel, "La chirotonie presbytérale du liturge comme condition de la célébration eucharistique?" *L'Assemblée liturgique et les differents rôles dans l'assemblée*, Rome 1977, 316–319.
16. De Praescr haer 41.
17. Ibid. 41:8.

18. *Ibid.*
19. *Apologeticus* ("A Defense of Christianity," cited below as *Apol*) 39:5.
20. *On Fasting* 17.
21. *Apol* 39:5.
22. *On the Veiling of Virgins* 9:22–23.
23. *On the Exhortation to Chastity* 13:4.
24. *Ibid.* 7.
25. See *Le Monde,* 27 January 1983, 9.
26. *On the Veiling of Virgins* 9:1.
27. *On Baptism* 17:4.
28. Clement of Alexandria, *Stromateis* ("The Patchwork Quilt" or "Miscellanies," cited below as *Strom*) I,1.11,2.
29. *Paedagogus* ("The Tutor," cited below as *Paed*) III,10.83,2.
30. *Ibid.*
31. See 1 Tim 5:14.
32. *Strom* III,12.90.
33. See 1 Tim 3:2 and 12.
34. *Tit* 1:6.
35. *Strom* III,18.108,2.
36. Tertullian, *On Monogamy* 11:12.
37. Clement of Alexandria, *Quis dives salvetur?* ("Who is the rich man who is saved?" cited below as *Quis dives*) 36.
38. *Paed* II,77.1.
39. *Ibid.* II,9.80,1.
40. *Ibid.* II,1.7,4.
41. *Ibid.* II,1.15,1 and ff.
42. *Quis dives* 11.12.
43. *Ibid.* 41.
44. *Paed* II,120.3–4.
45. *Strom* VI,13.106.
46. *Ibid.*
47. Origen, *Homilies on Leviticus* 6:6.
48. *Homilies on Numbers* 10:3.
49. *Homilies on Jeremiah* 11:3.
50. *Ibid.*
51. *Homilies on Ezekiel* 5:4.
52. See Rom 15:1.
53. *Homilies on Numbers* 10:1.
54. *Homilies on Leviticus* 5:7.

55. *Ibid.* 5.3.
56. See also *Homilies on Exodus* 11:5.
57. *Commentary on Saint John* 6:59(38).
58. 1 Cor 1:2.
59. *Fragments on the First Epistle to the Corinthians* 1.
60. *Homilies on Saint Luke* 17.
61. See *Homilies on Joshua* 17:3.
62. *Discourse with Heraclides* 4:22–5:7.
63. 1 Clem 41:1.
64. Eusebius, *Eccl Hist* VI,19.17–18.
65. See *Apostolic Tradition* 19.
66. The technical argument of this collection of texts known as the *Pseudo-Clementine Literature* will be found in A. Faivre, *Naissance d'une hiérarchie* (Théologie historique 40), Paris 1977, 153–170.
67. *Clementine Homilies, Letter of Clement to James* 13.
68. *Ibid.* 14.
69. *Ibid.* 15.
70. *Homily* III,71.
71. Cyprian, *Letter* 29.
72. Origen, *Homilies on Joshua* 9:9.
73. *Apostolic Church Order* 16:1–2.
74. *Solemn Commitment* 5.
75. Hippolytus, *Philosophoumena* ("A Refutation of All Heresies," cited below as *Philos*) IX,12.

Chapter 5: Clergy and Laity: An Institutional Barrier

1. For a detailed presentation of these documents and their different editions, see A. Faivre, "La documentation canonico-liturgique de l'Eglise ancienne," *Revue des sciences religieuses* 3 (1980), 204–219, and 4 (1980), 273–297.
2. The author of the *Apostolic Tradition* was undoubtedly Hippolytus of Rome, that conservative presbyter whose pamphlet criticizing Callistus, who was the bishop of Rome at the time and in competition with Hippolytus, we shall encounter later in the section on Callistus ("A Portrait of the Troubled Life of a Slave Who Became the Bishop of Rome").
3. See B. Botte, *Le mouvement liturgique* (Témoignage et souvenirs), Paris 1973. See especially the author's chapter on the rites of ordination, 165–177.

4. *Apostolic Tradition* 10.
5. See the *Canons of Hippolytus.*
6. *Apostolic Tradition* 19.
7. Hermas, *Similitude* IX,25.6; *Vision* III,5.1 and IV,2–3.
8. Tertullian, *De Praescr haer* 3.5 and 14.1.
9. *Letter of Clement to James* 13 and 14.
10. *Apostolic Church Order* 19.
11. For the history of the functions of the reader or lector and the catechist, see, for example, A. Faivre, *Naissance d'une hiérarchie, op. cit.,* 145–170.
12. *Apostolic Tradition* 11.
13. *Ibid.* 12.
14. *Ibid.* 13.
15. *Ibid.* 14.
16. *Ibid.* 9.
17. *Ibid.* 16.
18. *Apostolic Church Order* 10.
19. Cyprian, *Letter* 25.
20. Hippolytus, *Philos* IX,11–12.
21. *Homily* III,61–62.
22. *Didascalia* (cited below as *Did*) II,20.2.
23. Mt 20:25, cited in *Did* II,20.11.
24. *Did* II,24.4.
25. *Ibid.* II,21.
26. See *Did* II,22.6–8.
27. Lk 10:16, cited in *Did* II,20.1.
28. *Did* II,26.
29. *Ibid.* See 1 Pet 2:9 and Rev 21:2.
30. Both in Greek and in Syriac, the first letter of the name "Jesus" points to the figure 10.
31. *Did* II,26.2–3.
32. *Ibid.* II,26.4–8.
33. *Ibid.* II,24.4.
34. *Ibid.* II,34.5–6.
35. *Ibid.* II,35.3.
36. *Ibid.* II,28.5–7.
37. *Ibid.* II,35.4.
38. *Ibid.* II,35.3.
39. *Ibid.* II,35.4.

40. Jer 18:6 or Is 45:9–10, cited in *Did* II,36.1.
41. *Did* II,36.3.
42. *Ibid.* II,36.3–4.
43. Ex 23:15, cited in *Did* II,36.5.
44. Mt 6:20, cited in *Did* II,36.6.
45. Lk 6:37.
46. *Did* II,36.7–9, citing 1 Pet 4:10 or 1 Cor 4:2.
47. *Did* II,59.
48. *Did* II,57.5.
49. *Did* II,57.9–10.
50. *Did* II,27.1–3.
51. *Apostolic Constitutions* II,27.3–4.
52. 1 Clem 40.5. See also the section on "The Layman and His Place in Worship."
53. *Apostolic Constitutions* II,27.5–6.
54. *Did* IV,11.4–5.
55. *Ibid.* IV,11.6.
56. *Ibid.* IV,1.
57. *Ibid.* IV,2.1–2.
58. *Ibid.* IV,3.1.
59. See, for example, *Did* II,4.1; II,25.1–3; IV,3.1.
60. *Did* II,26.8.
61. *Ibid.* III,6.3.
62. *Ibid.* IV,5.2.
63. *Ibid.* IV,6.1–7. See also IV,7 to 8.
64. *Ibid.* III,5 to 12.
65. *Ibid.* III,5.1.
66. *Ibid.* III,6.4.
67. *Ibid.* III,6.6 to 7.5.
68. *Ibid.* III,7.3, citing Phil 3:19 and Mt 6:21.
69. R. Gryson's *Le ministère des femmes dans l'Eglise ancienne*, *op. cit.*, and G. A. Martimort's *Les diaconesses. Essai historique* (*Bibliotheca Ephemerides liturgicae*, Subsidia 24), Rome 1982 are still the best works on the women's ministries in the palaeochristian period.
70. *Did* III,9.1–3. I have tried, in my book *Naissance d'une hiérarchie*, *op. cit.*, 131–138, to outline the development of the women's ministries from the position of widows as presented in the *Didascalia* (ca. 230) to that of the deaconess as shown in the *Apostolic Constitutions* (ca. 380).

71. *Apostolic Constitutions* III,9.1–3.
72. *Did* III,5.4, citing Mt 7:6.
73. Ibid. III,8.3–4.
74. Ibid. II,26.6.
75. Ibid. III,12–13. See also G.A. Martimort, *op. cit.*, 34–35.
76. *Did* III,12.1.
77. Ibid. III,12.2–3.
78. See, for example, *Did* I,8, which makes use of Eph 5:22–23, 1 Cor 11:2 and Prov 8:20. This text can be compared with Clement of Alexandria, *Strom* IV,20 or with the same author's *Paed* III, 63–67.
79. *Did* II,57.
80. Ibid. III,12.4.
81. Ibid. II,34.4.
82. Ibid. II,35.3–4.
83. Ibid. II,36 and 37.
84. Ibid. II,25.6.
85. Ibid. II,25.8.
86. Ibid. II,25.6.

Chapter 6: The Life of a Church in the Middle of the Third Century

1. Cyprian, Letter 1.1. My quotations from Cyprian's letters are taken from L. Bayard's edition in two volumes: *Saint Cyprien. Correspondance* (*Les Belles Lettres*), Paris 1925.
2. Cyprian, Letter 1,1.
3. Origen, *Homilies on Joshua* 17:3 (*Sources chrétiennes* 71, 381).
4. Cyprian, Letter 1,2.1.
5. Ibid. 34,4.2.
6. Ibid. 40.
7. Ibid. 29:39.
8. Ibid. 2.
9. Ibid. 12,1.1.
10. Ibid. 5 and 7.
11. Ibid. 13,7 and 14,2.
12. Ibid. 12,2 and 14,2.2.
13. Ibid. 14,2.3, citing 2 Thess 3:8.
14. Ibid. 41,1.2.
15. Eusebius, *Eccl Hist* VI,43.11.

16. Cyprian, Letter 14,4.
17. V. Saxer, Vie liturgique et quotidienne à Carthage vers le milieu du troisième siècle. Le témoignage de saint Cyprien et de ses contemporains d'Afrique (Studi di Antichità Cristiana 29), Vatican City 1969, 73.
18. Cyprian, Letter 16,4.
19. Ibid. 17.
20. Ibid. 30,5.3.
21. Ibid. 31,6.2.
22. Ibid. 55,5.1.
23. Ibid., for example, 34,4.1.
24. Eusebius, Eccl Hist IV,43.6.
25. Cyprian, Letter 50,2.5.
26. Eusebius, Eccl Hist VI,43.17.
27. Cyprian, Letter 55,11.1.
28. Ibid. 67,6.2.
29. Ibid. 52,1.2.
30. Ibid. 32,2.1.
31. Ibid. 65,3.3 and 81,1.3.
32. Ibid. 39,1.1.
33. See A. Faivre, Naissance d'une hiérarchie, op. cit., 253.
34. Augustine, Letter 64 (Christmas 398).
35. Cyprian, Letter 23.
36. Ibid. 29.
37. Augustine, Letter 64.
38. Council of Carthage sub Grato (345–348), Canon 5.
39. Cyprian, Letter 39,5.2.
40. Ibid. 39,4.1 and 2.
41. Ibid. 38,2.2.
42. Ibid. 29.
43. Ibid. 22,1.2.
44. Ibid. 29,2.2.
45. Ibid. 45.
46. Ibid. 69,1–6.
47. Ibid. 69,7.
48. Ibid. 69,12.1.
49. Ibid. 69,14.2.
50. Ibid. 70,3.
51. Apostolic Tradition 21.
52. Ibid. 5.

53. Cyprian, Letter 72,4.1.
54. *Ibid.* 75,7.5.
55. *Ibid.* 71,2.
56. *Ibid.* 72,1.1.
57. *Ibid.* 73,2.
58. *Apostolic Tradition* 9.
59. Cyprian, Letter 49,5.2.
60. *Ibid.* 39.
61. *Ibid.* 12,1.1.
62. *Ibid.* 13,2.1.
63. *Ibid.* 13,4.
64. *Ibid.* 14,2.2, citing 11:28.
65. *Ibid.* 18,1.1 and 3.2.
66. *Ibid.* 41,1.2.
67. *Ibid.* 14.
68. *Ibid.* 17,2.1: 16,2.3.
69. *Ibid.* 20,3.3.
70. *Ibid.* 36,2.3.
71. *Ibid.* 34,3.2.
72. *Ibid.* 49,13.5.
73. *Ibid.* 48,4.2.
74. *Ibid.* 17,3.2.
75. *Ibid.* 64,1.1.
76. *Ibid.* 35,4.1.
77. *Ibid.* 30,5.3.
78. *Ibid.* 31,6.2.
79. *Ibid.* 49.
80. *Ibid.* 67,5.1.
81. *Ibid.* 59,6.1.
82. *Ibid.* 43,4.1.
83. *Ibid.* 45,3.2.
84. *Ibid.* 55,8.4.
85. *Ibid.* 67,3.2.
86. Eusebius, *Eccl Hist* VI,29.
87. Cyprian, Letter 14,4.
88. Lampridius, *Severus Alexander* 45,6–7.
89. See, for example, Cyprian, Letter 25.
90. *Ibid.* 27.
91. *Ibid.* 30,31.
92. *Ibid.* 43,3.

PART III:
FROM THE FOURTH TO THE SIXTH CENTURY:
THE NEW RACES OF CHRISTIANS

Chapter 7: When the Civil Authorities Went Over to Christ

1. See, for example, M. Carrouges, *Le laïcat, mythe ou réalité*, Paris 1964, 63.
2. Tertullian, *Apol* 30.1–3.
3. Eutropius, 9.27–28.
4. Ammianus Marcellinus, 21.10,8.
5. At the end of the fourth century, the term "priest" (*sacerdos*) still pointed essentially to the bishop.
6. Sozomen, *Ecclesiastical History* VI,7. A presentation and a translation of the texts cited here can easily be found in H. Rahner, *L'Eglise et l'Etat dans le christianisme primitif* (*Chrétiens de tous les temps 2*), Paris 1964.
7. Ambrose, *Letter to the Emperor Valentinian* II (March 386).
8. *Ibid.*
9. Theodoret of Cyrrhus, *Ecclesiastical History* V,17–18.
10. *Vita Constantini* II,55.
11. Lactantius, *On the Death of the Persecutors* I,2–3.
12. *Vita Constantini* II,28.
13. *Ibid.* III,15.
14. *Ibid.* II,7.
15. *Ibid.* IV,24.
16. *Ibid.* I,44.
17. I have made use here of the work of my late colleague C. Vogel, "Circonscriptions ecclésiastiques et ressorts administratifs civils durant le première moitié du quatrième siècle," *La géographie administrative et politique d'Alexandre à Mahomet* (*Travaux du Centre de recherche sur le Proche-Orient et la Grèce antiques*), Strasbourg 1981.
18. Sardica, Canon 7.
19. *Decretal to the Bishops of Gaul* II,13.
20. See P.-H. Lafontaine, *Les conditions positives de l'accession aux ordres dans le première législation ecclésiastique (300–492)*, Ottawa 1963, 309.
21. *Apostolic Tradition* 8. See also 1 Tim 3:13.
22. Nicaea, Canon 2.

23.   Sardica, Canon 10.

24.   For the documentation of this part, see A. Faivre, *Naissance d'une hiérarchie, op. cit.,* 309–370.

25.   Council of 595, Canon 2: "Laymen should no longer be employed in the personal service of the pope as they have been for some time in the past. These offices must be filled by members of the clergy or monks." This theme is taken up by Gregory the Great in his Letter 5.57a.

26.   Council of Antioch, Canon 25.

27.   In Cyprian's work, Letter 50 (Bayard 2, 122–123).

28.   Cyprian, Letter 52 (Bayard 2, 125–126).

29.   Chalcedon, Canon 26.

30.   Theophilus of Alexandria, Canon 10.

31.   Gregory the Great, Letter 1 (September 590). See also A. Faivre, *op. cit.,* 356–357.

32.   J. Gaudemet, *L'Eglise dans l'Empire romain (1Ve-Ve siècles),* Paris 1958, 190–191.

33.   Elvira, Canon 19.

34.   Theodosian Code XVI,2.1 and XVI,2.2. The probable date of both texts is 313.

35.   *Ibid.* XVI,2.14.

36.   Basil of Caesarea, *Canonical Letters,* Canon 89.

37.   Theodosian Code XVI,2.3.

38.   Chalcedon, Canon 3, forbade this practice.

39.   Code of Justinian I,13.1 and 2.

40.   *Ibid.* III,12.2 and Theodosian Code II,8.1.

41.   See Theodosian Code I,27.1.

42.   *Canons of the Apostles* 15.

43.   Sardica, Canon 19.

44.   Basil of Caesarea, Canonical Letter I,3 (to Amphilochius on the canons). The essential documentation on the return to the lay state will be found in C. Vogel, *"Laica communione contentus." Ordinations inconsistantes et caractère inadmissible (Etudes d'histoire du culte et des institutions chrétiennes* 1), Turin 1978, 1–67.

Chapter 8: Christianity Confronted with Pagan and Barbarian Cultures

1.   Jerome, *On Illustrious Men* 80.

2.   Lactantius, *Divine Institutions* V,1.10–11 (Sources chrétiennes 204, 129–131).

3. *Ibid.* V,1,25–26 (*Sources chrétiennes* 204, 133).
4. *Ibid.* V,4.8 (*Sources chrétiennes* 204, 151).
5. *Ibid.* V,14.13 (*Sources chrétiennes* 204, 203).
6. *Ibid.* V,2.17 (*Sources chrétiennes* 204, 139).
7. *Ibid.* V,14.17 and 15.2 (*Sources chrétiennes* 204, 205 and 207).
8. See M. Perrin's important work, *L'homme antique et chrétien. L'anthropologie de Lactance* (Théologie historique 59), Paris 1981, 250–325.
9. Lactantius, *The Work of God the Creator* 20:9 (*Sources chrétiennes* 213, 217).
10. *Ibid.*, *Divine Institutions* V,1.12 (*Sources chrétiennes* 204, 131).
11. *Ibid.*, *The Work of God the Creator* 20:5 (*Sources chrétiennes* 204, 217).
12. See, for example, Nicaea, Canon 19, and Egeria, *Pilgimage* 24:1 (*Sources chrétiennes* 296, 235) and the comment on p. 24: Egeria "made use of the word *laicus* in contrast with the word *monachus*. This was not usual in Christian Latin, in which the contrast between *laicus* and *clericus* was more common." Egeria does, however, make a clear distinction between *viri* and *mulieres*.
13. Ausonius, *Carmen* X, vv. 103–118 (written ca. 393).
14. *Ibid.*, *Edyll.* III,21.
15. Prudentius, Preface, vv. 22–34, translated by M. Lavarenne, in the series *Les Belles Lettres*, Paris 1943, I,1,2.
16. Ausonius, Letter 27, vv. 51–66, and Letter 29, v. 60.
17. *Ibid.*, *Carmen* X, vv. 19–46, translated by P. de Labriolle, *La correspondance d'Ausone et de Paulin de Nole* (*Chefs-d'oeuvre de la littérature religieuse*), Paris 1910, 29.
18. Basil of Caesarea, *To the Young* IV, translated by F. Boulenger, *Aux jeunes gens sur la manière de tirer profit des lettres helléniques* (*Les Belles Lettres*), Paris 1965, 45.
19. *Ibid.* III, translated by F. Boulenger, *op. cit.*, 43.
20. *Ibid.* IX, translated by F. Boulenger, *op. cit.*, 58.
21. *Ibid.* VII, translated by F. Boulenger, *op. cit.*, 51, citing Mt 5:39.
22. E. Trocmé, "Paul-la-Colère: éloge d'un schismatique," *Revue d'histoire et de philosophie religieuses* (1981), 345.
23. Origen, *Against Celsus* III,55.
24. *Ibid.*, III,9.
25. John Chrysostom, Homily 46 on Matthew and Homily 6 on 1 Corinthians.
26. *Ibid.*, Homily 33 on 1 Corinthians.

27. Augustine, *Commentary on Psalm* 96:10.
28. Sidonius Apollinaris, Letter 2,9.4.
29. Gregory of Tours, *History of the Franks* I,28–31.
30. Bede, *Ecclesiastical History* I,25 and 62.
31. Rufinus, *Ecclesiastical History* (cited below as *Eccl Hist*) I,9–10. See also F. Thélamon, *Paiens et chrétiens au IVe siècle. L'apport de l'"Histoire ecclésiastique' de Rufin d'Aquilée (Etudes augustiniennes)*, Paris 1981.
32. Origen, Homilies on Numbers 11,4 (*Sources chrétiennes* 29, 215).
33. Rufinus, *Eccl Hist* I,11.
34. *Did* III,6.1–2.
35. Gregory of Tours, *History of the Franks* II,31.
36. Avitus, Letter 46.
37. John Chrysostom, Homily 8 on Genesis 1.
38. *Did* II,56.4.
39. *Apostolic Tradition* 30.
40. Egeria, *Pilgrimage* 46 (*Sources chrétiennes* 296, 311).
41. John Chrysostom, *Baptismal Homily* 1.16.
42. *Testament of Our Lord Jesus Christ* II,1–2.
43. Tertullian, *On Baptism* 18.3.
44. Theodore of Mopsuesta, *Homily* 12.14–16.
45. Narsai, *Homily* 22.

Chapter 9: Chaste and Celibate Monks

1. For this subject, see A. Martin, "L'Eglise et la Khora égyptienne au quatrième siècle," *Revue des études augustiniennes* 25, 1–2 (1979), 3–26, and "Aux origines de l'Eglise copte: implantation et développement du christianisme en Egypte," *Revue des études anciennes* 83, 1–2 (1983), 35–56.
2. For this practice of keeping the eucharist with one (in one's home), see Basil of Caesarea, *Extracts from a Letter to the Patrician Lady Cesaria*, in P.-P. Joannou, *Discipline générale antique* 2, Rome 1963, 192: ". . . all the hermits living in the desert without any priest present keep communion with them and give it to themselves. Christians in Alexandria and in Egypt go even further than this. Each one, even if he is a layman, keeps communion most of the time in his home and receives it whenever he wants. . . ."
3. Cassian, *Institutes*, Title of Book 11.

4. See R. Draguet, *La vie primitive de S. Antoine conservée en syriaque. Discussion et traduction* (Corpus Scriptorum Christianorum Orientalium 184), Louvain 1980.

5. E. Amand de Mendieta, in his article "Le système cénobitique basilien comparé au système cénobitique pacomien," *Revue de l'histoire des religions* 151 (1957), 31–80, provides a helpful comparison between Pachomius' work and that of Basil.

6. *The Early Life of Saint Antony* 3 (R. Draguet, *op. cit.*, 7).

7. See C. Vogel, "La règle de S. Benoît et le culte chrétien. Prêtre-moine et moine-prêtre," *Atti del 7o Congresso internazionale di studi sul alto medioevo*, Spoleto 1982, 415.

8. Theodoret of Cyrrhus, *Eccl Hist* V,12.

9. See A.J. Festugière, *Antioche paienne et chrétienne. Libanius, Chrysostome et les moines de Syrie* (Bibliothèque des écoles françaises d'Athènes et de Rome 194), Paris 1959, 298.

10. *Ibid.*, 286 and 288.

11. *Ibid.*, 298.

12. Paulinus of Nola, Letter 1 (to Sulpicius), 10.11.

13. Chalcedon, Canon 6.

14. Justinian, Novella 133.2.

15. Aurelianus, *Regula ad monachos*, c. 46.

16. Mt 19:12.

17. Methodius of Olympus, *The Symposium* IV,2.

18. John Chrysostom, *On Virginity* 11.

19. *Ibid.* 40.

20. Jerome, Letter 127. Jerome was born at Strido, ca. 347. He studied in Rome, returning there between 382 and 385 after making several journeys and staying in the desert of Chalcis. He became Pope Damasus' secretary, but did not succeed him on his death in 384. He then withdrew to Bethlehem, but continued to intervene even from there in most of the conflicts that took place during the rest of his life, often engaging in violent polemics. He died in Bethlehem in 419. Seven volumes of his Letters have been presented and translated by J. Labourt in the series *Les Belles Lettres*, Paris 1949–1963.

21. Jerome, *Against Helvidius* 20.

22. *Ibid.*, Letter 22.16.

23. *Ibid.*, Letter 46 (to Pammachius), 2 (J. Labourt, *op. cit.*, II, 119).

24. *Ibid.*, Letter 49,4 (J. Labourt, *op. cit.*, II, 123).

25. *Ibid.*, Letter 49,10 (J. Labourt, *op. cit.*, II, 131).

26.   *Ibid.*, Letter 49,11 (J. Labourt, *op. cit.*, II, 132).

27.   *Ibid.*, Letter 49,21 (J. Labourt, *op. cit.*, II, 150).

28.   Jerome, *Against Vigilantius* 2. For this question of chastity imposed on the clergy, see R. Gryson, *Les origines du célibat ecclésiastique du premier au septième siècle* (*Recherches et synthèses, Section d'histoire* 2), Gembloux 1970. The same author has also published a very valuable review of work on the same subject entitled "Dix ans de recherche sur les origines du célibat ecclésiastique. Réflection sur les publications des années 1970–1979," *Revue Théologique de Louvain* 11 (1980), 157–185.

29.   Jerome, *Against Helvidius* 20.

30.   *Ibid.*, Letter 49,15 (J. Labourt, *op. cit.*, II, 141).

31.   See R. Gryson, *op. cit.*, 153–154.

32.   Jerome, *Against Vigilantius* 2. See also R. Gryson, *op. cit.*, 156.

33.   Siricius, Letter 1 (to Himerius of Tarragona), 9.13. See also A. Faivre, *op. cit.*, 314.

34.   Siricius, Letter 1,10.14. See also A. Faivre, *op. cit.*, 314–315.

35.   Jerome, *Against Jovinian* 1.34.

36.   *Ibid.*, Letter 52 (to the priest Nepotianus), 5.

37.   Siricius, Letter 1,113.1. See also A. Faivre, *op. cit.*, 315.

38.   Ambrose, Letter 63.

39.   See E. Griffe, *La Gaule chrétienne à l'époque romaine* III, Paris 1965, 105.

40.   See above, the section on Irenaeus.

41.   *Statuta ecclesiae antiqua* ("The Ancient Statutes of the Church"), Canon 38.

42.   Gregory of Nyssa, *Dogmatic Sermon on the Divinity of the Son and the Holy Spirit* (*Patrologia graeca* 46,557).

43.   These texts can easily be found in Volume I of P.R. Coleman-Norton's three volume work, *Roman State and Christian Church. A Collection of Legal Documents to A.D. 535 II*, London 1966, 545, 633, 774. They refer (respectively) to the Edict of Marcellinus on the procedure to be followed during the Council of Carthage in 411, the Letters of Theodosius II and Valentinian III on the procedure to be followed during the Council of Ephesus in 431, and the Letters of Valentinian III and Marcian concerning the procedure to be followed during the Council of Chalcedon in 451.

44.   Jerome, *Against Jovinian* 1.34.

45.   Theodoret of Cyrrhus, *Commentary on 1 Corinthians* 14 (*Patrologia latina* 23,341–342).

Bibliographical Orientations

I have limited the bibliographical details in the notes to a strict minimum, for the most part citing only primary sources so that the reader can, if he wishes, carry out his own work on the texts. (Wherever possible, I have also referred to French translations of these original texts if they are easily obtainable.) The books and articles listed below are those which will enable the reader to find a more complete bibliography or which may, in my opinion, help him to understand the hypotheses considered.

1. BOOKS OR ARTICLES OF SYNTHESIS

There are very few books or articles of synthesis on the laity during the palaeochristian period, and they are for the most part not very satisfactory. They are often anachronical and make little distinction between precise shades of meaning in the vocabulary—that is, between lay and laity, faithful, believer, Christian, etc.

Caron, G., *I poteri giuridici del laicato nella chiesa primitiva*, Milan 1948.

Frend, W.H.C., "The Church of the Roman Empire, 313–600," *The Layman and Christian History. A Project of the Department on the Laity of the World Council of Churches*, London 1963, 28–56. This work provides the most complete synthesis on the history of the laity.

Lanne, E., "Le laicat dans l'Eglise ancienne," *Verbum Caro* 18, 71–72 (1964), 105–126. The whole of this number of *Verbum Caro* is interesting because it shows how far research into ministries and the laity had reached by 1964, at the time of Vatican II.

Schenk, A.W., "Le laïcat dans l'histoire de l'Eglise," *Zestyty Naukonwe Katolickiego Universytetu Lubelskiego* 11,1, Lublin (1968), 9–19. This article is in Polish, with a summary in French.

Seumois, V., "L'apostolat laic de l'antiquité selon les témoignages patristiques," *Euntes docete* 1 (1952), 126–133.

Williams, G.H., "The Role of the Layman in the Ancient Church," *Greek, Roman and Byzantine Studies* 1 (1958), 9–42. This article was republished in *The Layman in Christian History*, London 1963, 28–56.

Articles in Dictionaries

Dictionnaire de théologie catholique: It is interesting to note that the term "lay" is not used until Vol. VII, which is dated 1925 and goes up to letter L. "Lay" and "laity" are, however, found in the tables (Vol. XVI,2, col. 2862–2870, which is dated 1960). This is proof, if any is required, of the newness of the idea of the laity and its problems in the twentieth century.

Dictionnaire de spiritualité: The article "Laic et laïcat" in Vol. IX (1976), col. 79–108, written by Yves Congar, is by far the best synthesis in French. The author's excellent bibliography will enable the reader to continue research into the subject. Congar made a study of the renewal of the theology of the laity in the twentieth century, and the development of his thinking on this subject can be measured by comparing his basic work, *Jalons pour une théologie du laïcat* (*Unam Sanctam* 23), Paris 1953, English translation: *Lay People in the Church*, London and New York 1957, with his articles collected in the volume, *Sacerdoce et Laïcat devant leurs tâches d'évangélisation* (*Cogitatio Fidei* 4), Paris 1962, English translation in three volumes: *Priest and Layman* and *A Gospel Priesthood*, both London and New York 1967, and *Faith and Spiritual Life*, London and New York 1969.

2. THE VOCABULARY USED

The state of the questions and the earlier bibliography will be found in:

De la Potterie, I., "L'origine et le sans primitif du mot 'laic,' " *Nouvelle Revue Théologique* 80 (1959), 840–853. This article was also republished in *La vie selon l'Esprit* (*Unam Sanctam* 53), Paris 1965, 13–29.

Jourjon, M., "Les premiers emplois du mot laic dans la littérature patristique," *Lumière et Vie* 65 (1963), 37–42.

Mohrmann, C., *Etudes sur le latin des chrétiens* (*Storia e letteratura* 65), Rome 1961. See especially Vol. I, 117: II, 238: III, 102,104,130–131.

Nervada, J., *Tres estudios sobre el uso del termino laico* (*Coleccion canonica de la Universidad de Nevara*), Pamplona 1973. See especially the bibliography, 23, n. 13.

Wingren, G., "Der Begriff 'Laie,' " *Vom Amt des Laien in Kirche und Theologie. Festschrift für Gerhard Krause zum 70. Geburtstag*, ed. Henning Schröder and Gerhard Müller, Berlin and New York 1982, 3–16. This work also contains several articles on the period studied in the present book.

3. THE SITUATION OF THE LAITY IN THE HISTORY OF THE PALAEOCHRISTIAN INSTITUTIONS

Sources and a fundamental bibliography will be found in:

Faivre, A., "Clerc/laic. Histoire d'une frontière," *Revue des sciences religieuses* 57,3 (1983), 195–220.

Idem, "Société, Eglises, ministères: les questions des communautés paléochrétiennes," *Lumière et Vie* 167 (1984), 5–25. This article contains the minutes of the meeting held at l'Arbresle on 4–9 July 1983.

Idem, *Naissance d'une hiérarchie* (*Théologie historique* 40), Paris 1977.

Gryson, R., *Les origines du célibat ecclésiastique du premier au septième siècle* (Recherches et Synthèses. Section d'histoire 11), Gembloux 1970.

Idem, *Le ministère des femmes dans l'Eglise ancienne* (Recherches et Synthèses. Section d'histoire 4), Gembloux 1972.

Vogel, C., *Ordinations inconsistantes et caractère inadmissible* (*Etudes d'Histoire du culte et des Institutions Chrétiennes* 1), Turin 1978.

Idem, *Institutions cultuelles aux IIe et IIIe siècles.* This volume is to be published in the series *Histoire du Droit et des Institutions de l'Eglise,* under the direction of J. Gaudemet.

4. RESEARCH INTO THE SOCIAL AND POLITICAL CONTEXT

Gomez, Manuel Guerra, "La 'Plebs' y los 'Ordines' de la sociedad romana y su traspaso al pueblo cristiano," *Teologia del Sacerdocio* 4 (*Teologia del Sacerdocio en los primeros siglos*), Burgos 1972, 252–293.

Noethlichs, K.L., "Zur Einflussnahme des Staates auf die Entwicklung eines christlichen Klerikerstandes," *Jahrbuch für Antike und Christentum* 15 (1972), 136–153.

Richard, J.C., *Les origines de la plèbe romaine,* Rome 1978.

Rouland, N., *Pouvoir politique et dépendance personelle dans l'Antiquité romaine. Genèse et rôle des rapports de clientèle* (Latomus 166), Brussels 1979.